SHIP'S HUSBAND

Ship's Husband

by

ROBIN S. SALVESEN

The Memoir Club

© Robin S. Salvesen 2003

First published in 2003 by
The Memoir Club
Whitworth Hall
Spennymoor
County Durham

British Library Cataloguing in
Publication Data.
A catalogue record for this book
is available from the
British Library.

ISBN: 1 84104 053 3

Typeset by George Wishart & Associates, Whitley Bay.
Printed by Bookcraft (Bath) Ltd.

Contents

Illustrations

Preface

SHIP'S HUSBAND explores and describes a variety of experiences which were opportunities to travel in groups with people who shared joys and pleasures as well as risks. Many of these companions have helped and encouraged me and although often unnamed in the text are sincerely thanked for the shared experience.

It is a fact that the teamwork of many people creates the story and the simple jobs done well are fundamental to major achievements. Readers who enjoy the stories here honour and thank the soldiers or sailors, shipowners and clerks, family and friends from wide and different backgrounds who have contributed often unknowingly in the events portrayed.

In the endeavours to manage change and create perhaps a better world, one needs to set priorities and allocate time to essential and urgent tasks. This can leave a heavier load on colleagues. There are so many people who helped and did more than a fair share. I recognise their contribution.

I would like to dedicate this book to Sari, who has been a wise friend, wife and mother, keeping a calm home and base, without which my energy could not have concentrated on daily problems.

Sari and my children all have my most grateful thanks for their support in this life.

Sights and Sounds of Home

A bit of land called a garden
Where the grass is patchy, but green;
A length of line tied from here to there
Where the washing hangs nice and clean;
The sounds of my children's voices
From below, where all day they roam;
There are the things I remember,
The sights and sounds of home.

The bustle of the traffic
As it passes my front door –
The milkman rattling bottles,
Letters landing on the floor;
The whistle of the kettle,
Someone murmuring on the phone;
These are the things I remember,
The sights and sounds of home.

A cup of tea by the fireside
When the lights are all turned low;
Contented, at peace, the kids safe in bed,
I sit in the firelight's glow.
Alas, too soon it is over,
Once again I am all alone;
But these are the things I remember,
The sights and sounds of home.

For just a short while they are with me,
Then are stored in memory's lane.
Another leave has ended
And it's time to sail again.
Wherever my ship may take me,
Wherever I may roam
The things I shall always remember
Are the sights and sounds of home.

CHAPTER 1

Early Life

ROBIN SALVESEN was born on 4 May 1935 in a tall house, No 6 Rothesay Terrace, in Edinburgh. Edinburgh is of course an historic city with a large castle, Princes Street opposite with its gardens and shops and the old town running down the hill from the Castle to Holyrood. In the New Town, on the north side of Princes Street, there are Georgian terraces, line upon line set out in squares and rows and further out of town in curves round a garden. The two families that joined together, the Salvesens and the McClures, both lived in the New Town.

Iver Ronald Stuart Salvesen was the youngest son of quite a large family of girls, his two older brothers having both been killed during the First World War. Iver grew up in Edinburgh, going to Fettes College where he excelled in fencing and eventually represented Scotland. He then trained as a chartered accountant, still in Edinburgh, and went to join his cousins in the family shipping company, eventually becoming one of the partners, with his three cousins, Harold, Norman and Noel Salvesen. The McClure family was steeped in the law. Marion McClure's father was a Sheriff and very proud of being a member and a commissioner of the Northern Lighthouse Commission. He enjoyed visiting the lighthouses and having responsibility for the safety of the shipping lanes around the country, and Iver was very much involved with running small ships between Norway, Denmark and Scotland. So there was a good family link in this way.

As soon as electricity was available, the city fathers made use of it, and Edinburgh became a city of trams. For a mere penny or two, passengers could travel from one end of the town to the other. The trams ran on fixed rails right along Princes Street, down Leith Walk and away out as far as Musselburgh. To the west, the trams ran as far as Murrayfield, which was almost the edge of town in those days. The streets outside Rothesay Terrace were lit by gas manufactured at Granton; the street lights were lit every night by the gas lighters and Robin was able to look out and see them in the evenings before he went to bed.

Rothesay Terrace was an extraordinarily tall house with one or two rooms on each level. On the ground floor Iver had his library in a separate

1

extension to the building, with many books. Up one floor was the big drawing room, and two or three rooms could be joined together to form a huge reception room on this level; the family had quite frequent dinner parties. There were about twelve servants; the nursery floor had two nurses, and downstairs there were housemaids and cooks, so the family lived in quite some style.

Iver Salvesen and his bride went to St George's church in Charlotte Square, now the Public Record Office and the Registry Office, but it was then a magnificent church. Charles Warr was the minister, and he had very recently travelled to the Holy Land so when Robin's christening was to take place at the family house, he used water he had brought back from the Jordan river to baptise him. The Rev. Dr Charles Warr and Iver Salvesen must have been fairly close friends. Charles Warr eventually became the minister of St Giles', the High Kirk of Scotland.

John, the older brother, was fair-haired like his younger brother Robin. They were very much in the care of the nannies who would take them daily for a walk with the two prams to Inverleith where they fed the ducks and swans. They actually walked quite far with the nannies, down to the shops at Haymarket for newspapers and past Donaldson's Hospital to Roseburn and Murrayfield. On other days, especially at the weekends, Iver and Marion would take the children in the car for picnics, sometimes up to the Pentland Hills, through Balerno and out to Threipmuir Reservoir, where they would stop the car and make a little bonfire to cook their tea and have their sandwiches. The children could run around the woods and play hide and seek amongst the trees before being driven back home again, to climb the staircases, be put in the hands of the nannies, given their baths and off to bed.

Their parents meanwhile would be changing to go out to a theatre, or to a dinner party with their many Edinburgh friends. There was a lot of social life in Edinburgh between the wars and the recession, from time to time, seemed far away. The shipping industry, exporting coal from Scotland and importing timber to Scotland from Norway, became quite a big enterprise and freight rates kept a very good income coming through to the family.

In 1938 Iver and Marion were looking forward to having their next child, and did as many Edinburgh families did at that time: they hired Penicuik House from Sir John Clerk, and moved their family, the nannies and some of their servants out to the country, where they lived for two months during the summer. The main house at Penicuik had been burnt down, and the family of the Clerks lived in what had been the stable block, so the house was built round a courtyard, where the children could play in a garden with flagstones, and they could run around and even start using tricycles, the two boys really being old enough to romp around quite hard at this stage.

Iver travelled in from Penicuik House to the office in Leith most days or even stayed in town overnight from time to time during the week, but he spent several days in the country with his wife and family. Hilary was born at Penicuik, so the two boys now had a young sister.

Penicuik House is really quite a distance south from Edinburgh, with the Pentland Hills to the north, lying on flat ground surrounded by trees and, in the spring, a large number of daffodils, but of course in the summer holidays it meant the garden with the rosebuds, the peonies and the herbaceous border. There were walks with the nannies around the park, because Penicuik has drives going in all directions from the main house. Out towards the west is low-lying ground with heather and peat and a flat grouse moor in August, and during the summer holidays, the men would gather at 9 a.m. and start shooting grouse. The grouse butts were very often in the stream bed and the grouse would fly from one side of the valley to the other, over the heads of the guns. There were also tennis parties, because the young folk, young married couples, would meet for tea and tennis, as a regular part of their lives.

It was when Iver was called up for full time service and Rothesay Terrace was requisitioned that the young boys and their mother went to Curriehill House to stay with Violet Wye, Iver's eldest sister. Curriehill House is at Balerno, to the west of Edinburgh, quite a long way out of town. In those days it was a great big house, sitting in its quite wide acres, and the boys remember a walkway through the woods and round all the fields which had been set up for the ladies of the house to walk round and look at the wild flowers, as an afternoon exercise after their lunch. Curriehill House was full of young people in those days, because Violet Wye had two daughters, Lilias and Barbara, both of whom married young officers, brothers Henry and Pat Turcan, in 1940 after the war started. Whilst the boys were staying there, the wedding presents were delivered in great boxes and piles, and there was great joy, as they were opened and discussed and stored in one of the rooms. The dining room was set aside so that all the beautiful presents could be put out on display. Curriehill House, at that time, was full of gaiety and joy and happiness with Aunt Violet entertaining to tea and tennis the friends of Lilias and Barbara and their husbands.

Curriehill had long and rambling stone flagged corridors, down to the kitchens which were ruled by a very diminutive lady, Agnes, who had a red scarred face, a birth mark, but who was a most magnificent cook. The boys however had a very strict regime. They had their own lunch in the nursery and as the war was getting closer, they would sit at the dining room table with their plates in front of them and have to be quiet because the nannies wanted to hear the one o'clock news from the radio on the table. So there was gaiety and also the worry of potential war at the same time.

In 1939, much of the family went up to Kinloch House at Amulree for the summer holiday. This again was a grouse shooting estate, and still is. But the great excitement for young Robin and his brother John, was that the family gathered together at Curriehill House at Balerno, and were all uplifted by bus – the whole family with their servants, twenty people or more piling into a bus with their luggage – and then took off on the long, long journey to Perthshire – down to the ferry at Queensferry, across the river, and on through Fife, through Crieff until they were surrounded by the heather hills.

Kinloch House was a huge great pile, actually rather like Curriehill House, in that it had many guest bedrooms upstairs and a large rambling kitchen area on the ground floor. It had woods and gardens, and the garden at the front of the house had a six-foot high bank of grass which was mown every week by the gardeners, a great joy to the young boys who could roll over and over on a sunny day, down the bank. At the river they could dangle a worm on a hook and hope to catch a little brown trout. The adults would have their friends to play tennis or for picnics in the countryside, and of course they were a big house party themselves.

In the early days, the war seemed to be quite far away, although many of the family, including Iver, served in the Territorial Army. Iver was a Major and about to take over from his brother-in-law, Tom Grainger Stewart, as Lt. Col. of the 7/9th Battalion, the Leith Battalion of the Royal Scots, which was the only kilted Lowland Battalion. Iver had a chauffeur, who took him in to town to the office from time to time and did the repairs and maintenance of the family car, but was also his batman in the TA. On drill nights, therefore, it was not unusual for Iver's chauffeur to come to the door of the house with two horses and pick up the Colonel, and they would solemnly ride their horses, down from Rothesay Terrace to East Claremont Street, through the New Town and down the hill. On weekends, the Territorial Army seemed to go on very long route marches, the senior officers on horseback and their men marching really quite a long way, stopping for their meal and then marching home again; this was exercising the discipline and the strength that they would need eventually for fighting.

Iver Salvesen and his Battalion didn't go across to France in the very earliest part of the war, but the family was moved down to quarters in Yeovil. The whole of the summer until June 1940 was spent there in training ready for war. The young boys and their sister went with their nanny for walks, and Marion as Colonel's wife would, from time to time, dress up for reviews and inspections of the Regiment. Eventually the 7/9th Royal Scots went abroad and were the second expeditionary force into France, where they faced battle and then were taken back home again, by sea, having left much of their equipment behind in France, but at least they did come home again.

Once Iver was back from France and the battalion was relocated in its position between Inverkeithing and Kirkcaldy, the family lived in a small house in Aberdour with one nursemaid and Marion really had to learn to cook and care for her own children herself, a thing that she had never before had to do. Their father came home at night exhausted, having been running the affairs of the battalion in the daytime, and of course hardly saw the children at all. They were still there when the Forth Bridge raids and the bombing were taking place; Donibristle aerodrome had its one balloon and there was one night when it brought down a German aeroplane, only about half a mile away from the house. As the German aeroplanes were chased by Hurricanes or Spitfires, in the air overhead at night, little boys could lie in bed and listen to the aeroplanes and they learnt very quickly to recognise the distinctive noises of the British and German planes, and could hear from time to time bombs falling and bursting, because many of the German aeroplanes, when they were being chased, dropped their bombs in order to fly faster and escape. So there were bombs on the hills not that far from Aberdour as the Forth Bridge and Rosyth dockyards were targets for the German bombers.

Aberdour was a quiet village with its own little baker's shop and butcher's shop, and as rationing came on, country folk were probably a bit better off than those in town because, somehow or other, rabbits and other game appeared in the shops and the local butcher made his own meat patties out of scraps. Marion had been very sensible at the beginning of the war and stocked up a larder by buying up a lot of flour and sugar, so she was able to make jam in the summer when the fruit was ripe in the garden.

Later in the war, Iver Salvesen was sent abroad to Africa to look after the convoys that were crossing the Atlantic and going down the west coast of Africa round the Cape to the Middle and Far East. During this time the boys had a governess to teach them how to read and write at home; then

John went first to Cargilfield in Perthshire, by train from Aberdour and up to Comrie.

Iver Salvesen had managed to settle his wife and children into Aberdour House before he went off to Africa so Marion and her small family moved from the village centre. He had leased the house from the Earl of Morton. Aberdour House sits right beside the railway station, and is a yellow sandstone building with a short drive and about an acre of garden. The garden had formal rose beds with lavender hedges and there was a walk from the garden running towards Aberdour Castle. Going through the castle grounds one got towards the western part of Silver Sands, where the church lay, so the boys and their mother used to go by this walk to church regularly every Sunday. The church itself was said to have been used by Robert the Bruce at the time when he was a leper, and in the church wall there is a little hole through which it is said that the King used to listen to the service.

The garden at Aberdour House had large lavender hedges, and each year as the lavender ripened, and the smell grew greater and the seeds formed, the boys would go out with scissors and clip the hedges and take the stalks of the lavender and spread them out on newspaper in the house. As the seeds dried, they would collect up all the dried seeds and save them. This was all done as part of the war effort, because Marion Salvesen taught the boys not only how to sew and mend their own socks, but also how to sew little bags, and the lavender was put into the little bags which were sold at Church sales and in aid of the war effort. The same sales happened in the spring, when the daffodils in the garden flowered and the boys bunched them with rubber rings and wandered round the village with a can selling them and gathering money which then also went off to help the war effort. Marion also showed her sons how to cook in the kitchen where there was a big Aga cooker. You were able to get extra sugar if you made jam. The family kept their own hens and had their own eggs. All the scraps from the table went to feed the hens each day, so in the morning and evening the boys and their mother would go out to collect the eggs and feed the hens and then they would help their mother to set the table and cook. John became very good at baking scones and Robin took to jam making.

The castle at Aberdour was opened with a key which they had in the house, so the family would take visitors to walk round the castle. Some parts of it were breaking down and a bit dangerous, but of course the boys would clamber up the stairs without worrying about that too much. The big hall was quite sound and had an enormous fireplace. The knights had very big dinners in Aberdour Castle in days gone by.

Early in the war some of the officers in the Navy at Rosyth would come ashore and occasionally three or four of them would be asked if they would like to come to tea, so a good relationship slowly developed with the young officers of HMS *Nelson*, which was stationed in Rosyth dockyard, almost certainly undergoing repairs but awaiting the German deep sea fleet going to sea. The boys were therefore occasionally asked to go and visit the ship. John and Robin were riding on their bicycles and with very little traffic on the roads it was perfectly safe for them to go off together as a pair, and they cycled along all the small roads round that part of Fife, and certainly up to Rosyth dockyard. The guards at the gate would show them the way to HMS *Nelson*, where the Captain took them to his cabin and the officers showed them the bridge and the engine room and gave them tea in the stateroom in the warship. They were taken up into the major guns because HMS *Nelson* had a series of three gun turrets with 6 inch guns. The boys would be shown how the ammunition could be lifted up in a hoist and put into the breech of the gun and they wondered at the size and the weight of these enormous shells which could be fired by a battleship.

Trains went from Aberdour to Waverley and Haymarket stations in Edinburgh. The boys and their mother went very frequently and they would leave the train at Haymarket and walk the short distance either to their Granny's house, 20 Eglington Crescent, or to Aunt Veronica's (Auntie Ron's) house in Magdala Crescent. Auntie Ron was Iver Salvesen's sister and she lived on her own. She had been at Edinburgh University reading Architecture at the beginning of the first world war and had joined the VAD and been an ambulance driver. After the war she'd gone all the way out to Japan, one of the first British ladies to go there on her own, to visit Niko and the temples. So she was a very adventurous lady. She and her brother Iver had owned one of the first privately owned cars in Edinburgh and had taken the roads up into the Highlands together. They had a pretty good look around Scotland in the days when there weren't that many cars on the road.

However in those days, Auntie Ron's main interest appeared to be her collection of stamps. She gathered stamps from letters from her sister in Australia and relations in Canada and she had books of them. She also enjoyed playing bridge with her friends and playing golf – eventually she taught both John and Robin how to play golf at Aberdour. The professional showed the rudiments of how to swing a club and hit the golf ball and

Auntie Ron would go round the course with the boys to teach them golfing etiquette and stop them arguing with each other when they were having a bad time. Golf is a very frustrating game and often a ball doesn't go into the hole although you carefully aim.

Granny McClure lived in Eglington Crescent in the ground floor and basement and she used to invite the boys in for lunch or tea. It was very generous hospitality always, and it was very nice for the boys to go in and visit either their Granny or their Aunt and to go for walks or to the shops with them and then get the train back to Aberdour. Granny started having regular pantomime parties at Christmas time and she used to collect her grandchildren and usually a party of about ten would go to the King's Theatre.

Iver Salvesen eventually came back from Africa. He brought with him a great basket full of fruit and Robin and John helped cut the string and open up the basket. Oranges were something they had seen before, but bananas were completely new and the boys had no idea of what to do with them. Iver and Marion watched as the boys opened the parcels and saw grapefruit and oranges, bananas and paw-paws spilling out onto the floor. These were things which had not been available in the shops, so they were shown how to peel the skin from a banana. They were allowed half a banana each as a treat because it was a very rare surprise to get that sort of fruit in war-time.

Iver's arrival home again coincided with the time when Robin was going for his first term on the train to Cargilfield School. His brother had been there for a year already. Robin was going at quite a young age, at the beginning of the summer term at eight years old and one of the youngest boys at the school.

CHAPTER 2

Education

AFTER THE ESCAPE of the 7/9th The Royal Scots from France, Iver Salvesen's battalion was posted to Fife and really had an enormous area to look after. The beaches along the coast were defended with various obstacles such as timber posts which were put in to stop aeroplanes landing on the beaches. Donibristle Airport was one of the features which had to be guarded but also Methil and Kirkcaldy and the coast the whole length of Fife from the Forth railway bridge.

Many of the Territorial Officers had very valuable detailed skills from their civilian life. Iver Salvesen had been a Chartered Accountant and then a shipowner and so the government took him out from Regular Army service and made him into a Civil Servant with a view to looking after ships and war transport and the convoys. The story goes that when he was put into a Scottish Office room in Edinburgh he felt he couldn't abide the furniture, so during the weekend he moved into his office his own desk and chair from his office in Leith, put a carpet on the floor and made himself comfortable with his own filing cabinet so that he could work in the way in which he was accustomed. This absolutely shattered the Civil Service who had rules and regulations about the amount of carpet that each man of each grade should be allowed, and Iver was not allowed his innovations.

Having learned the Civil Service tricks, Iver Salvesen was sent to West Africa and for a long time was based at Takoradi in charge of the convoys which went from the United Kingdom down the coast to West Africa and right round the Cape to bring the troops round to the Suez Canal or to Australia. Quite a lot of the convoys that were going to North America, instead of going the northern circle route up around Greenland, went to West Africa before they crossed the Atlantic in an attempt to avoid the U boats working violently on the North Atlantic approach. The convoys congregated at Takoradi and other ports under the control of Iver Salvesen and his team.

In 1941 when Hilary was three, their brother Alastair was born. Robin remembers learning the joy of reading at Curriehill House at the age of four or five, when he discovered a library full of books which his first cousin Eric Wye had read when he was a child. After lunch he always had to go and lie on his bed and have a rest, so that was when he had time to read. Enid Blyton was a great favourite and there was a series of books about twins, starting with the Indian twins, and these were fascinating stories of what little boys might do in different cultures round the world. Later on came the Biggles books with stories of adventure by airmen in the First World War.

In the Summer Term of 1943 when he was eight, Robin joined his brother at Cargilfield School at Lawers in Perthshire, a big country house sitting between Comrie and Crieff. Quite a lot of the boys lived in the big house but some of them overflowed into dormitories in a farmhouse which was two or three hundred yards away. Parents only managed to visit boys at Cargilfield in those days about twice a term and Robin and John's mother was unable to go there at all because she had the two younger children to look after, and the car was laid up for the duration of the war.

The first impression when everyone arrived from the train and went into the Hall at Cargilfield was a babble of noise as boys greeted each other and met their friends again – Robin felt a shy little boy as all these others knew each other. He was given a senior boy to look after him for the first week or two who told him what the rules were, and little boys didn't get punished for misdemeanours during the first two weeks. The main feature, however, of Robin's first term at school was that he developed whooping cough and any running caused him to cough and sometimes to be sick, so Robin and several other boys were put in the San and kept remote from others so that the infection wouldn't be passed round. He was allowed to go out into the garden and climb the hill nearby while the other boys were in their classes at school. He made dams in the stream and sat in the sunlight watching the gardener on the mowing machine preparing the Cricket Ground. When they got up in the morning the boys had to make their beds and keep their room tidy but shoes were done for them and they had to wear tidy and smart shoes when they went to Church on Sundays.

Discipline at Cargilfield was very severe. Talking after lights out meant that all the little boys in the dormitory had to get up and be beaten by the Headmaster. The major punishment for noisy boys was to stand with their nose against the wall – they called it 'nose it' – which felt rather ridiculous.

In the second term the bewildering experience of learning to play rugby took place and it really was an extraordinary game. The ball was thrown in and all the boys would scrum round it and fight for the ball. There didn't seem to be any particular rules and it was very difficult to understand what

Peter Henderson (the England Hooker) coaching Fettes 1st XV. Robin is at the back of the line-out. Ken Mackinnon has a scrum cap. Peter Ellis has a hand on his head. Giles le Maitre (wing three quarters) stands beside Peter Henderson.

you were meant to be doing at all. In the second year in the summertime, Robin was taught cricket. He was for some reason appointed wicket keeper. It wasn't very long before he missed the sight of the ball and it hit him on the nose causing his collapse and he had two jolly good black eyes. But once he had recovered and stopped crying, he was removed from the cricket field and the master in charge suggested that in order to calm himself down he should walk home by himself. When he got to the main school he was greeted by the Matron with a 'Well done, brave little boy walking home all on his own.'

In the first winter, Robin fell on the ice and blood was everywhere. He got three stitches in his knee and the whole thing was then dowsed in iodine which nipped.

In the morning everyone had to run along the corridor, take off their pyjamas and dive into a freezing cold bath which had been filled overnight. Students and parents never quite understood why this was considered a particularly good thing for little boys to do but that was the custom at Cargilfield School. In the bitter cold weather, all the windows were always opened in the dormitories at night. All the boys seemed to develop chaps on their knees, whether from the rugby or just the cold for which the doctor provided a sort of greasy ointment and at night time the boys would put this on their chapped knees. Many people also got chilblains on their fingers and the best cure for that apparently was a spoonful of malt – so many of the boys queued up at Matron's and were given a spoonful of malt to suck before they went to bed at night.

At night the boys went to bed and then dormitory by dormitory they read the Bible, verse by verse, each round the room. At the end of each year the whole school did the same test about the Bible readings from that year and very often one of the young children in the school got better marks than the Sixth Formers. Robin came fairly near the top of the class with sums. He did not, however, enjoy Latin or French, and the learning by heart of vocabulary, spelling and poetry were things which he found particularly difficult. History was the learning of dates by heart and geography was drawing maps by memory. Little boys with a visual memory who could remember what Africa looked like got good marks for geography.

The school went for walks after lunch on a Sunday. A master would take a group of forty to fifty boys into the hills and round the roads so they all got their exercise. During the middle of the week they either played rugby or went for runs, or played cricket in the summer.

After the Normandy invasion of Europe, Iver returned from Africa and saw his family but was soon sent away again.

Iver's final job in the Ministry of War Transport was in Antwerp as one of the first civilians from Britain. Many ships had been sunk in Antwerp's harbour and the Army in Europe required to be provisioned by ships from America coming across with equipment, ammunition and food, and so it was necessary to open the port of Antwerp as soon as possible. The civilians in Europe were very short of foodstuffs at that stage too and so there was an enormous supply requirement for all the people of Europe which had to come through the ports of France, Holland and Belgium as soon as they were relieved from German occupation. Iver Salvesen got various medals after the war for his service.

At the end of the war there was VE Day and then VJ Day. There were great celebrations at Cargilfield for the Victory Day in Europe, but Robin was in the San with a high temperature and didn't join in the party at all.

At the end of the war Cargilfield moved from Lawers back to their purpose-built building near Cramond in Edinburgh and Robin went into a dormitory there with fifteen or twenty boys. The regime of bed making and cold baths continued. There was a big swimming pool so Robin and John were taught how to swim and for the first time Robin was shown how to play hockey which later in life he enjoyed very much – he played in the Army and at Fettes.

Some of the masters were very effective and efficient people. Mr Kittermaster was the Headmaster. There was a Mr Maine who also ran the Scouts and many of the boys enjoyed camping and getting badges. Robin joined them when he got to Cramond and he learnt a little bit about camping and how to tie knots and various other Scout activities. One of the things he really did learn in the Scouts was a value for trees and the names of trees and how they grew – which has stayed with him since then. Mr Randolph taught French and he was also one of the leaders of music in the school. The choir at Cargilfield was very good and the boys sang anthems on Sunday evenings in the chapel. The school put on a performance of *Iolanthe*. The boys all learnt by heart the songs to sing and learnt to walk onto the stage and do a little bit of acting. There was a real character called Mr Cranmer who came back from the war reputed to have a war wound and a metal patch on his head, on his skull. Many of the teachers were people who were left at home unfit for war service.

One summer, after the war was over, Iver Salvesen took his whole family up to Eriska House Hotel, north of Oban on the west coast of Scotland, together with their first cousins, the Younger family. Marion's elder sister was Lady Younger and their children – George and Bobby, Sandy and Rosalind – were the same sort of age as the Salvesen boys. They had picnics together and were taught how to catch mackerel and other fish in the sea, and many times had their own camp fires. Aunt Veronica Salvesen was at this holiday as well and she would relieve the fond parents by taking the boys for a walk up the hills.

John did rather better at school than Robin and he reached the top form at Cargilfield before he moved on to Fettes. Here he learnt not only Latin but also Greek so at Fettes he got into the scholarship boys' form and continued with Classics. Robin reached only the second top form so he never did Greek. He was still doing quite well at mathematics but found Latin and French really quite difficult.

At Fettes, Robin went into 3A, in the Autumn Term when he was thirteen. He was immediately in the under thirteen and a half rugby side because he was quite big for his age – nearly five foot ten at the age of thirteen, though John was well over six foot. Mr Timms coached the team and that year they won every match they played against other schools. It was an extraordinary record for no score was gained against the Fettes team, neither a try nor a penalty, while the Fettes side often scored 30 points in a game. It was a very good year group for Fettes at that time and this continued through Robin's school career. John had been in the choir at Cargilfield and continued to sing at Fettes but he was rather uncoordinated because of his height and was either teased or bullied by the other boys. Robin seemed to be more able to look after himself and of course was in a games team when he got to Fettes.

In Robin's second year at Fettes he was going to play in the under fourteen and a half team but before Christmas he got scarlet fever and was moved into the fever hospital at Edinburgh. There was quite an epidemic of scarlet fever running round the schools at that time and Robin was laid out in the hospital with fever and felt very shaky. Every day he was given an injection of penicillin into the backside. Robin had an impressive rash and various students came to be shown the little boys – Robin was shown off as being a good specimen of what a scarlet fever rash should look like. It took quite a long time to recuperate and the doctors were quite worried about side effects on eyes and ears so after a month in hospital the boys were allowed to go home – but not back to school.

In the weeks before Christmas Robin was taken out by his father in the car to get a bit of fresh air and went rabbit ferreting with the 4.10 shotgun, then a 20 bore gun. When John returned from school they all spent one or two days standing near the burrows and putting the ferrets down the holes and when the rabbits came running out they tried to shoot them.

In the following August, Robin and John both started shooting grouse in the Pentlands, walking in line with the gamekeeper who had a wonderful spaniel. When the grouse got up the boys would try to shoot and by and by they got quite proficient and occasionally achieved a right and left.

The next year Robin was in the under fifteen and a half rugby team and for the first time was seriously coached. Instead of being a second row forward, because of his speed he was taught to play as one of the wing forwards. This team had some good players in the three-quarters as well as in the forwards and once again it won every match against the other schools. Robin joined the school corps and then worked for the School Certificate examinations where he took eight subjects; the only one he failed was Latin but he succeeded at the second attempt – the next year.

Then he was moved into the Sixth Form and studied double maths and physics with a view to getting his School A Level Certificates and perhaps going to University. Here he was taught by Bill Aitken and Mr Brewer, and physics was taught by Mr Naife. Bill Aitken was the school chaplain, a member of the Iona community and a follower of George Macleod, besides being a very good teacher of mathematics.

In the Sixth Form Robin joined 'big side' and played for the second fifteen. After Christmas 1951, at the age of sixteen, he was playing in the first fifteen for Fettes against Merchiston and this very hard game was drawn. Indeed the first three games Robin played against Merchiston were drawn matches each time. In the two years Robin was in the first fifteen at Fettes, the team was never beaten by another school. He became a House Prefect and a Games Captain of Moredun House, which meant he had to take the parade of all the boys in the House after lunch and to allocate some kind of exercise for the boys who weren't playing in matches or practices.

For Robin, it was quite a relief in the Summer Term when he was sixteen that he no longer had to play cricket. He still played for Moredun against the other Houses in the Inter-House Competition because he was an all-round games player but he didn't enjoy standing on the boundary – especially in Edinburgh where there's always a wind and very rarely a hot and sunny day. He did, however, become the CQMS, the second highest appointment in the school Army Cadet Force at Fettes, and he taught the younger boys how to do their drill and use their weapons. He was in charge of boys at Camp.

Robin became a School Prefect in his last year at Fettes and was given specific jobs to do by Donald Crichton-Miller, the Headmaster, when visiting parents came. He would be allocated to take them round the school and show them what it looked like and answer many questions.

In the holidays at this age, Robin was shown by his father how to drive the car and he took his driving test as soon as it was possible – and passed it in Edinburgh. Then he and John were allowed to use Aunty Ron's second-hand car which was a Wolseley. Iver Salvesen bought her car for his two sons to drive and this enabled them to go to dances and parties under their own steam.

John went to Oxford the year before Robin left school, to University College to study PPE. He found economics and logic really quite difficult to get his mind round but he also got very much involved with amateur dramatics during his first year and perhaps just didn't work hard enough. After his first year the College said he hadn't done well enough in his exams there and perhaps Oxford wasn't for him. After recuperating from an operation on his toes, John went out to Australia, where he enjoyed plenty of meat to eat, riding horses and working as a student on the farms with his relations out there. He came back a very big man of fifteen stone. He really put on strength and weight by getting fed and watered in Australia.

Robin passed his exams to go into Oxford, but was going to do his National Service in the Army first while John went to Agricultural College in Edinburgh. So John and he didn't see each other so much from that time onward.

In the meantime, Iver Salvesen had come back from his war service and rejoined Christian Salvesen running the shipping company. He also became Consul General for Norway and Master of the Merchant Company in the City of Edinburgh. He and his wife went to all the early performances of the Edinburgh Festival, including the Tattoo. The whole idea of the Festival was to extend the summer holiday season for the hotels and the tourist industry in Scotland to August and September, one of the nicest times of the year in the Highlands.

Iver Salvesen bought a part of the Pentland Hills up from Flotterstone with the Black Hill and Carnethy. Year upon year while he was alive there were always grouse to shoot there and the family enjoyed many happy days. The family always gathered at Bonnington for the first fortnight of the grouse shooting season from 12 August to the end of the month. Sometimes they would walk up grouse together as a family and sometimes there would be guests for grouse driving, when John and Robin would either take the end butt of the line or else walk with the beaters and help their father and his friends to enjoy their day.

In September Iver Salvesen would want the boys and his daughters Hilary and Evelyn (born in 1947) to see different parts of Scotland so he took them each year to a different part of the North of Scotland. One of the holidays was at Dornoch where John and Robin played a lot of golf but also leased a day or two rough shooting. Robin shot his first partridge on one of those days. Hilary at this time (as her mother had before her) went to Priorsfield School, together with Rosalind Younger. They used to have tennis parties at Bonnington House after the war and Robin and John invited a lot of friends there on Sunday afternoons after Church to play tennis on the grass court.

Going to Oxford in October after two years in the Army was great fun and Robin joined the Rugby Club at University College Oxford and started playing in the trials for University Teams as well. He started off by reading Maths and Physics. He joined the Iona Society which is the Church of Scotland organisation and met a lot of the Scottish students in that way.

First year students also made a lot of friends right across the various disciplines. Robin's best friends were people like David Morris who was a scholar reading PPE, and John Wolstenholme.

In the second year Robin started his Engineering course, with surveying and engineering drawings and mechanical engineering, structural theory and electrical engineering as well. Students got a basic knowledge of all branches of engineering. It was quite a small school with its own building on the Banbury Road and it had only about thirty or so students in each year group. This course did quite a lot of extra work at weekends and in the evenings and afternoons doing engineering drawing. It was a very structured course and everyone had to attend a certain number of lectures every day. Students reading the Arts were much freer in their choice of which lectures to go to. In Engineering the timetable had a full programme of lectures in the mornings and practical work in the afternoons – which didn't fit in all that well with games. However, Oxford was a lovely place to work in, with all the College buildings with their ancient history and the number of young intelligent people that one met and worked with and enjoyed – and boys and girls made very special relationships.

CHAPTER 3

Home and Family

DURING WARTIME school holidays Marion Salvesen tried hard to find toys and projects to entertain her sons. John and Robin were full of energy but the roads and the beaches at Aberdour were empty of visitors and so walks up to the dairy farm to see the milking of the cows or round the park at Donibristle soon gave way to longer bicycle runs as the two boys went off together. They used to cycle as far as Rosyth but also back into the hills to one of the little reservoirs. Near Donibristle there was a loch where there were hens and ducks and sometimes even geese to feed.

Marion used to take John and Robin to buy their clothes with their carefully saved coupons so that they had new and bigger clothes for school. The main shop for buying school clothes was Forsyth's in Princes Street. The wartime rations were very tight and, for instance, each had a small pat of about one-third or a quarter of the half-pound butter packs that you get now, that would have to last for a week – so both at school and at home each person had a little dish with their own butter ration so that all had their fair share.

Robin and John were brought up to write letters home from school every week and it was a Sunday job. This habit lasted well through their lives and indeed Robin, when he had his own children, used to make a big effort to write to them when they were away from home and at school. Aunt Veronica Salvesen wrote to her sister in Australia on a very regular basis and Granny McClure wrote to her relations in Newfoundland and received the occasional parcel of special foods, like maple syrup from Canada, right through the war.

Iver Salvesen came home from Africa once the warfare in North Africa had ceased and Italy had been invaded and the war was beginning to swing in the British favour, and the boys used to listen to the news and move the flags up on their map of Italy which they kept in one of the rooms at Aberdour House.

It was about that time that Iver took Robin and John with Hilary to Nethy Bridge for a holiday with the bicycles. The car was laid up so they had to travel by train, as did everybody in those days. They took bicycles with them and one of the little exercises at Nethy Bridge was to put the boys onto the train and they would travel for two or three stations, get out at a stop and then cycle on the road back up the River Spey to the hotel again. There were picnics in the woods and it was probably at this time that Robin first got his liking for seeing the great trees, for trees in the Nethy Bridge/Spey Valley area have wide trunks and underneath them there is lots of open space with not much undergrowth. Robin saw big ant hills for the first time under these trees and the colonies of ants taking food back home and carrying weights that looked heavier than themselves as they struggled on the little ant paths through the woods. At Nethy Bridge Iver Salvesen had a little seat at the back of his bicycle and Hilary sat on this pillion behind her father when they went off on a bicycle run and for a picnic. Quite different from the legislation of nowadays where everyone riding a bike has to wear a hard bonnet to keep safe – there were no restrictions at that time for people on bicycles at all and taking a child on the back seat behind you on a bicycle was a common picture.

Marion Salvesen was very careful to look after her complexion and one of Robin's very vivid memories is of his mother doing up her long hair into curlers, putting on a hairnet and putting various skin creams on her face which always seemed a bit greasy but when she was eighty she still had a wonderful complexion. This was almost certainly because she had looked after herself earlier. The boys used to help make the beds, and were expected to pull the sheets so straight that there weren't any wrinkles in them.

One holiday was at St Fillans and the family stayed in the hotel there for about a week. Robin and John were taken by their father to one of the smaller lochs nearby where there were brown trout in fair quantity and John and Robin were shown how to throw the line out and feel the tug of the trout; they came home to the hotel with eight or ten trout which were laid out on a plate in the front hall of the hotel for the other visitors to see. They had also been shown how to fish with a worm by the keeper at Kinloch House. Robin caught trout on a worm – throwing it upstream and letting it drift with the current, hoping for the line to stop and the little tug of the fish eating the worm. When he got to Fettes he started learning from a book how to make his own flies to the colour-coding of flies that you could buy in the shops – so he copied the patterns. One or two of the other boys there were into making bigger salmon flies, but Robin never had the opportunity of fishing for salmon, so he learned how to make the smaller flies and to discover the thrill when he caught a fish on a fly he had made himself.

Iver Salvesen negotiated the purchase of Bonnington House with some acres of fields and woods when he recommenced work in Leith and the Ministry of War Transport released him from his Antwerp post.

Iver and Marion made sure that their sons and daughters pulled their weight to some degree during the holidays. One family job at Bonnington House at the end of the war was keeping hens in enclosures near the garage. Scraps were put into a big pan and kept in the oven overnight so they were cooked slowly and all the old potato skins and things like that would be made into a mash to feed the hens – so the family got fresh eggs and occasionally the meat from a hen as well. The children also learned to chop the wood for the fires, to cut the grass and use the mowing machines, to drive the small tractor into the woods to collect wood and to take the grass-cuttings away. Robin read up one or two books at this stage and thought that he would be able to prune the roses or the plum trees and he prides himself on it – it is very nice to see the plums or roses that you have pruned producing better and better blooms or coming into flower and producing the plums later in the year.

The Salvesen family ties were really strong and because of their Scandi-navian origins the Salvesens always gathered as a family on Christmas Eve rather than Christmas Day. The first Christmas Eve party Robin remembers was Great Uncle Fred and Aunt Robin's party. He went back in the taxi up to their home via Haymarket Station; the stars were shining in the sky. It was a nice clear night and the moon came out and it was very pretty after getting Christmas presents at the Christmas Tree party. After the war the Christmas Tree party was held alternately within the bigger houses owned by the family. Harold Salvesen had his house at Inveralmond at the mouth of the river Almond near Cramond where visitors went through a glasshouse with flowers in it into the main part of the house. It was a tea party and the family had their cup of tea, cakes and sandwiches, and then went out to sing 'The First Noel' round the Christmas tree; and it was only after all that had been done that any of the children were allowed to open a parcel. First of all children went to the tree and found a parcel and then looked at the name on it and tried to deliver it to the right member of the family. This was one way of introducing the family to each other. One of the other big houses they went to was Clifton Hall, the boys' school when the owner of the school, who was also Headmaster, was Mr Killick, who had married a daughter of Lord Salvesen (a Judge). In the Christmas holidays the whole main hall of the prep school was available for the use for the Christmas Tree party.

Robin recollects his first dance at Curriehill House which was the house owned by Iver Salvesen's elder sister Violet Wye. Her second husband had died, around the time the Second World War started. She was a very generous hostess and she arranged dances for the young people in her house. Robin vividly remembers dancing Eightsome reels and other dances with a girl called Jill Pearson and once he had had two dances with her, he was separated from her and told that he really must dance with other people and not the same girl all night. It was a little bit hard for a boy who was probably only twelve or thirteen at the time.

There were always holiday jobs to be done on the bicycles. Marion would think of things she wanted from the grocer or the baker or the butcher and the boys would be sent off to East Calder or Mid Calder to go and get these items of shopping. John and Robin also had golf lessons – not only at Aberdour during the war but at Dalmahoy Golf Course when they were living at Bonnington. John became quite proficient. Robin remembers well that John could always use a 7 or 9 and the ball would go really high in the air and land on the green. Robin was a bit frustrated that he couldn't compete with him at golf.

In the Christmas holidays there was a Badminton Club near Roseburn. Here they met quite a lot of the boys and girls who went to Public Schools and they would pick partners. There would be some competitions from time to time but really it was a very good way of letting the boys and girls whose fathers and mothers knew each other quite well, meet each other. Marion became Secretary and organiser of the Badminton Club Ball. She took John and Robin with her to the shop which was going to do the catering for the party and help to choose menus etc. The boys learned the ins and outs of how to organise a party – and they were very much consulted as to which dances they would like on the programme; the regular dances like Petronella and Hamilton House and the Duke and Duchess of Edinburgh, and of course the Eightsome and Foursome reels were all in the programme, and to allow a cooling off period between the vigorous Scottish country dances, some waltzes, foxtrots and quicksteps would be added to the programme. Nearly everyone who went to the Ball had had dinner before 8 pm when it started so although there was a meal laid on at the dance the boys very rarely stopped dancing to go and eat – but it was good to have some good long soft drinks in between the vigorous country dances.

John and Robin had their rooms up in the attic at Bonnington, right under the roof, and as John grew taller he had to remember that he could knock his head quite easily. They enjoyed being up in the attic; there was a certain of freedom that the boys had – away from the rest of the family. Hilary was now growing older and she had a room of her own, just next door to the bedroom that Iver and Marion shared, so she was always on the main floor of the house near her parents. Alastair and Evelyn were in a room on the attic floor too, which they shared with a nanny.

Both John and Robin while they were at Fettes College would have a day out on Sundays about three times each term; they would be picked up at 8 o'clock in the morning, either by Iver or the chauffeur, and driven home for their breakfast at Bonnington. They would often have a day playing tennis with their friends or going for a walk with their father, or perhaps gardening together because Iver Salvesen usually had some plan of cutting down some bushes or trees in some part of the estate which he wanted to be cleaned up. At the back of the garage at Bonnington House there was quite a large acreage of woodland called Gala Hill and the boys immediately called it Gallows Hill and wondered why it had been called by that name. They were reading books like *Ivanhoe* and *Robin Hood* at that time and it seemed quite appropriate for John to be Little John and Robin to be Robin Hood so they made their own bows from branches and strung them with a bit of string; and then they used canes from the garden or the straight shoots from an elder tree as their arrows. They became proficient in shooting arrows at targets. Hilary, of course, became Maid Marion.

On one of the summer holidays the Younger and Salvesen boys were shown how to play bridge by Aunt Veronica Salvesen and quite enjoyed it although they don't play it often now. Iver Salvesen took the family out, hiring a fishing boat to go to the sea with a ghillie to show them where to fish. They put mussels onto hooks and lowered the bait to the bottom of the sea. They came back sometimes with a great big pile of fish – rock cod, haddock and whiting. On other occasions they would tow the line with just a bit of feather or a bit of red or yellow rubber over the hook and this would be sufficient bait for the mackerel to come and tug the line and then they would have the fun of pulling the fish onto the launch. Sea-fishing was great fun because they nearly always came back with some fish, whereas if they went out onto the loch to catch trout they very often didn't get tugs on the line.

By the time of the Dornoch holiday John and Robin were reasonably proficient at golf and they would go as a foursome with Iver and Marion, playing a two-ball foursome round the lovely links course. It was a very encouraging course because it was a sandy links course and a ball hit from the tee would sometimes bounce on over the grass, almost as far as it flew the air. In fact the Dornoch course seemed to get very much less rain than other parts of the surrounding countryside. The younger children went to the beach and adults having played a round of a golf went from the 18th hole to the shore and found the rest of the family and the picnic ready. They all could have a swim in the afternoon.

When John and Robin were at Fettes and were fifteen or sixteen years of age it became a habit for Aunt Veronica Salvesen to bring Granny McClure out to Bonnington for Sunday lunch. After the boys had gone with their parents to Church at Ratho, they came back home and found lunch ready and Aunty Ron and Granny McClure would join Iver for a glass of sherry before the roast beef or roast lamb was served in the dining room. It was Iver's habit to offer cider as the main drink at Sunday lunch so they had a glass of sherry and then a glass of cider, and then coffee was served in the drawing room after lunch. But each Sunday at 2.30 prompt Aunt Veronica Salvesen would say, 'It's time for a walk', and Iver and his sister would take the children out for a walk round the fields or round the wood or down the drive – a circular trip round the roads for three miles or so before coming back for a cup of tea. There was always a superb tea at Bonnington. Marion had the silvery tray with the teacups on it and there would always be either bought or home-cooked cakes and very often home-made scones and fresh jam and butter to go with them. Marion liked pancakes and they always had to be bought in Edinburgh so she used to buy shortbread biscuits and pancakes for Sunday tea at McVities. Aunty Ron would take Granny home, back into Edinburgh, round about 6 o'clock on a Sunday evening, and the boys would either be going back to school or else it would be holiday time and they would sit down and read a book or listen to gramophone records.

Iver and Marion thought that the boys would do better at their French exams if they took a holiday in France so one year they took John and Robin to St Jean-de-Luz. This entailed a train journey to Paris and a night sleeper from Paris right down to the Basque country in the south-west of France. There they stayed in a hotel and took some day trips almost to the border of France and Spain and to St Jean Pied-de-Port in the hills. As they were staying together as a family the boys didn't speak a lot of French, although they were encouraged to do so; but it was a great opportunity after the war to see another country and to bring back some food from France, the like of which was never seen in Britain at all at that time. Rationing in France seemed to be far more liberal than rationing in the United Kingdom. They brought back a huge great ham and the Customs people

A winter day in the countryside. Robin Salvesen in the centre, happily talking to 'guns'.

said, 'Oh there's nothing in our rule book to say you can't take that home.' Certainly no shop in Britain at that time was selling a full sized ham.

When Hilary was bigger and Alastair came too, Iver and Marion took the family to Mandal on the south coast of Norway. This entailed a journey in the Rolls-Royce down from Edinburgh to Newcastle to catch the ferry across to Oslo. That was an exciting trip, going to sea for the first time and staying in a cabin for the journey overnight across to Norway.

The Salvesen family historic home was at Mandal, a little bit west of Kristiansand, and Iver took that opportunity of visiting the old family house which was then a museum. There was no chance of seeing the family sawmill because it had already fallen into disrepair and become part of a field running down from the family house to the edge of the sea. Harold Salvesen and the other relations owned a house across the bay from Mandal museum which they had had for quite a number of years. Harold also had a house up in the hills which they called a hut, but in fact it lodged about twelve people and was really a shooting lodge. Harold's family had to walk most of the way to get there because there were no roads though they could take their foodstuffs and equipment on horses in panniers. They used to be able to go out and shoot the willow grouse on the heather and had the opportunity to try fishing in the loch as well. Iver Salvesen and his family didn't do this but the holiday was really quite superb because the summer sunshine in Norway was nice and warm and the beaches were very pleasant. The family all squeezed into the Rolls and went for picnics and to look at the lovely trees and woodland and small farms up the different glens into the hills in the south part of Norway.

There was a memorable holiday from Eaton Hall when Robin was doing Officer training. The Christmas holidays started with really snowy weather for the train journey from Eaton Hall. The trains went from Chester Station to Crewe where the cadets changed trains and joined the slow train going north from Crewe, which split at Carstairs, with part of the train going to Glasgow and the other half meant to go towards Edinburgh. However, because of the snow the train from Crewe was delayed and arrived into Carstairs about 11 o'clock at night when the last engine driver had already been signed off for the night. So there were about twenty soldiers coming home for Christmas holidays who were on this platform at Carstairs with no shelter at all because the various buildings on the station had been closed for the night. The station master, having announced that there would be no more trains for Edinburgh, really had to eat his words because one of the drivers volunteered to take a train and a couple of carriages from Carstairs to the Caledonian Station in Edinburgh 'because the soldiers had to get home', so Robin was very lucky. It was a busy holiday for Robin because he had so many dancing engagements and almost every night, except Christmas day, there was a party of one kind or another, and he was able to meet his friends in Edinburgh before he went back to finish his training at Eaton Hall.

Hilary, of course, being quite a bit younger, was taken by Iver as he went into the office each morning to a school in Edinburgh. When she was fourteen years old she went down to Priorsfield to join her cousins. Until that time Iver had to try to get Hilary ready so that he could get her to school for nine o'clock. It was quite difficult to get Hilary up and give her breakfast, and make her clean her bedroom and brush her teeth because Iver wanted to leave Bonnington at about 8.15 to get her into school on time.

When Robin came back from Nigeria, having had his year out there as an Officer, he found that the family were on Mull. He had to come back up from London and report in to Glencorse Barracks on his arrival, but was told that he could go on leave before reporting back to Glencorse for his demob, so he journeyed up to Oban and across on the ferry to Mull. One day they went across on the ferry to Iona. This was Robin's first visit to the

Community where George McLeod was beginning to do a re-build of the old Abbey with his volunteer youth workers from Glasgow and Govan. It was a very exciting project, though the Church of Scotland viewed it with some concern, but it was certainly interesting for Iver and his family to go to Iona and see this historic Abbey and the restoration which was beginning to take place there. It was a lovely sunny day and Iona was looking at its best and the sandy beaches beyond the cathedral were very attractive. On another day John and Robin went off together with the fishing rods and found a loch near the roadside, where the hotel had said they could go and fish. It was very good for them both to see each other after they had been separated and been abroad in different parts of the world.

CHAPTER 4

Army Training

At THE AGE OF FOURTEEN everybody at Fettes had their first year in the cadets dressed up as military in battledress and boots and learning first, foot drill, and then how to drill with weapons. In the second summer the whole lot went to camp, and the first camp was Barry Buddon which is up near Dundee. The cadet corps marched from Fettes to Waverley station and formed up on the platform waiting for the train to come. First the luggage came and groups were taken away to load the kit bags onto the train. Then the boys entered the carriages, eight or more to each carriage, for the journey. Now the extraordinary thing: nowadays a car from Edinburgh up to Dundee takes about an hour and a half. A troop-train loaded about eight p.m. and took all night, going from siding to siding, often stopping, and the boys in their carriages either had books, or played cards, perhaps just generally slept. But it was past dawn and the sun was getting up, by the time the train shuddered into the station beyond Dundee.

The boys then were marched into the camp where they were allocated their tents and given breakfast which was a great joy. Everybody took out of their pack their mug and their knife, fork and spoon and were given jolly good bacon and eggs and some tea or coffee. They were given a huge bag which they had to fill with bracken to sleep on. The young lads were all put into tents, eight in each, in sections with an NCO and this was the first lesson of joining the Army.

Each day there were exercises, some days at the shooting ranges, splendid in the sunshine. There was a watchman up in the tower who would signal if a ship was going to pass by and shooting had to stop. Then there were other exercises, doing section attacks mostly, learning how sections did 'fire and movement'; one group would be lying on the ground firing their guns while the other ran round the corner to attack the enemy. Later on the corps had a full dress parade and inspection from a brigadier who came to visit the camp so everyone had to dress up smartly, polish their boots, march to and fro and do a general salute then march past. All this was marked as the schools were in competition against each other.

The second year camp was near Helensburgh, and the journey didn't seem so bad. On the third night the rain started falling and because the tents were on a slope on the hillside, round about the time when everyone was beginning to get to sleep the rain came flooding down the hill and through the bottom of the tent and the boys were all standing up trying to keep their clothes dry. There were no duck-boards and so the water went through everything.

National Service came at the end of school. Some people could put it back and serve when they were qualified as a doctor or specialist but the perceived wisdom at the time was that it was better to go to university when you were a bit older. So Robin was called up and sent for a medical examination which he took at Dean Park House, off Queensferry Road in Edinburgh.

The doctor said, 'Sit down,' and then said, 'Oh, you are in the first fifteen, playing rugby for Fettes against Edinburgh Academy. I think I saw you playing, my son was playing on the other side, do you remember who won that match?' and then he went on, 'Well, do you want to go into National Service?'

The answer of course was 'Yes'.

'Medically I can't fail you so we'd better just sign you up. You are obviously fit enough to play rugby for Fettes so you'll be fit enough to go into the Army.'

His stethoscope never came out and there were no figures put on a bit of paper to say what Robin's blood pressure was or any other physical inspection at that time. Later in the Army, however, it was very clear that the doctors were quite concerned with the height of the instep in Robin's feet and thought that marching for long distances might cause problems, though none in fact materialised.

Three weeks after the medical Robin Salvesen was called up to Glencorse Barracks to report at 11 a.m. and again there were long queues and a full medical inspection. There was also a test in which all recruits had to write an essay and were asked certain things to spell and to do a certain amount of simple arithmetic, and then they marched to the barrack room where all civilian clothing was put away. The only clothes from then on that recruits were allowed to wear were what had been issued to them so everybody was dressed in service kit from top to toe, from inside to out. Most of the work was done in denims with a shirt, the issue drawers underneath. The boots which were issued were very oily and immediately had to be blackened and polished, day by day. A corporal showed one or two of the thirty in the room how to make up their beds, and inspections took place every morning. All the kit had to be very tidily put on top of the bed or in the locker in a specific order and folded neatly for inspection. A senior sergeant came round and eventually an officer would inspect each place *and it had to be spotless*. The floors had to be polished and then rubbed and rubbed and the kit had to be clean and the boots had to be clean and the brasses had to be brassed and polished and rubbed, especially the cap badge. Many of the soldiers in the room would be working and cleaning long into the night.

Having been at Fettes in the cadet force, boys such as Robin were not starting from scratch because they had done Certificate A at Dreghorn Barracks and had therefore reached a competence of sorts in both drill and fieldcraft.

Robin's next door neighbour was a coal miner and the son of a coal miner. When they were issued with kit, the man next door thought that Robin's denims kit looked rather better than his and did a filch. Now this caused a rather immediate fracas between the coal miner and the public schoolboy, and the next thing that Robin knew was that the boy was doing a rather practised head butt, trying to use his forehead to hit the nose of the other. However, at Fettes a bit of boxing had been done and a quick, short jab stopped the head butt fairly rapidly. It paid off very quickly just to show the people round about that a soldier was prepared to look after his own kit and just wouldn't be put down by a bully.

Glencorse Barracks had been built as a guard for the river and its factories, during the war between Britain and Napoleon, in the area of Penicuik and Edinburgh. Later in the war when prisoners came back from France, it was used as a prison for the French soldiers and sailors who had been captured. The old guardroom at the gates of Glencorse Barracks dated from that period, and the bunks round the room were in fact sloped wooden boards, the feet towards the centre of the room and the heads out towards the outside. On guard overnight at Glencorse Barracks, a sergeant and eight men would take duty two by two throughout the night, with a regular patrol around the whole camp site. The NCO would leave the guard room and take two men who were armed with pick-axe handles as their only weapons and would go round the boundary of the camp to see if there had been any intrusion.

Most of the instruction was done in small groups of eight to ten, and if the weather was at all good even the lectures were outside. Everyone had to learn how to use a rifle, a Sten gun – a very noisy weapon which wasn't terribly accurate – and a Bren gun and then towards the end of the first six weeks they were taken out to throw grenades on the range. First of all recruits had to clean and check the grenade and then throw it, knowing that they had three seconds to see where it landed and get down on the ground so that the shrapnel didn't come back and hit them. If a grenade did not blow up, the soldiers and the officer had to go forward and lay a demolition charge beside it, knowing that if the ground was shaken too hard the spring might just loosen at any time which would give an immediate explosion.

The first ceremonial parade in which Robin took part was while he was still at Glencorse Barracks as a lance corporal. The Royal Scots were offered the freedom of Peebles, and a guard of young Royal Scots who were passing out from Glencorse Barracks were a feature of the freedom parade. They regarded themselves as pretty smart in the guard of honour when they received the freedom of Peebles.

At the end of the initial training there was a passing out parade before a weekend's leave, and after twelve weeks Robin (a potential officer) was made a Lance-Corporal and given some leadership training before he went off to Eaton Hall. Eaton Hall was beside Chester, a huge palace-like building with large lecture theatres and bedrooms and ground floor rooms which had obviously been decorated with polished floors and plaster work round the ceilings. Of course, as a barracks, the rooms, equipped with blackboards and chairs, were scraped as people ran in and out in tackety boots. The majority of the students however lived in hutted buildings in section and company strength, so platoons would live together, about thirty people in one hut, and three huts together would form a company.

Eaton Hall had entered a rugby team into the Army Cup competition and were looking for players who had experience to form the team. Robin was found to have been playing rugby for his school and was very quickly selected to play in the team for Eaton Hall. This was a great honour and privilege because at that time, there were also two if not three potential international rugby players available as staff or students. There was a large second row forward and a centre three-quarter who had already played in trials for their country. Much of the practice rugby was played against Welsh teams who knew all the tricks of the trade, but the Eaton Hall boys were on the whole very fit indeed and however strong and rough the play was, in the scrum with the Welsh forwards, the Army team got possession of the ball and passed it back to their three-quarters and ran with it. The Army strategy was to run the Welsh teams ragged and to keep the ball flying rapidly from hand to hand, passing it and running fast – so this team beat most opposition.

In the Army Cup the team drew one match and then lost the replay against the Royal Signals at Catterick and Catterick went on to win the Army Cup that year so Eaton Hall felt that they'd acquitted themselves quite well.

One part of the training at Eaton Hall was learning qualifications in the use of signals, and the cadets did quite a lot of small signals exercises. The phonetic alphabet had to come into play and there were various methods of passing questions and giving orders over the radio in a logical sequence. These skills could save lives at a later time so it was important to learn them very clearly.

It was deep in the winter time when the company of young cadets from Eaton Hall were sent to their camp for field firing and live ammunition training, in the snowy mountains of Wales. The snow wasn't so bad but as they moved through the hills, they found that in fact there was a covering of frost over the top of bogs that they could not see, and heavy men with equipment broke through this crust and got absolutely soaked in the bog underneath. One or two of the young cadets found the going hard, and in the inter-company competitions and platoon competitions it was necessary for other members of the platoon to assist them. It was very much an object lesson that the platoon had to work together and bring each other through, whether it was in drill or in the outdoors. The snowy mountains in Wales were a very beautiful sight, but the cadets came back with absolutely numb fingers. They had to get out of bed in the morning and hurry to shave and be dressed in time for breakfast and parade with no hot water at all.

They were able to go for a night out or for a Sunday leave and a group of young chaps from Scotland used to go to Chester to the Church of Scotland. They had a tremendous welcome, and were invited to go on Thursday evenings to join the Scottish dancing parties and meet some of the local people. Chester was a very interesting town: there were two levels to the shops and visitors could go up the stairs to the higher level and walk round another row of shops, in a covered way. Then from the shops on top they walked onto the old walls of the town and round virtually the whole of the centre of Chester, on top of the walls. It was a very pretty place to visit with good hotels and good meals.

During the Christmas holiday from Eaton Hall, Robin Salvesen discovered, in conversation, that the Royal Scots were going to be coming back from Egypt and his likely job for the rest of his National Service would be as a training officer at Glencorse Barracks, so when he returned he took the plunge and volunteered to serve in West Africa. His father Iver had spent quite a considerable time there in the war, running the convoys from Takoradi. Robin was ordered to join the Royal West African Frontier Force, and his posting came through as he passed out from Eaton Hall. In the meantime he was sent home for embarkation leave. At Glencorse Barracks the adjutant said that his tickets and posting hadn't come through yet, but he should keep in touch; and would he play hockey for the minor units. They had got through the first two rounds of an inter-unit hockey competition; Robin Salvesen had played in some of the initial matches. It was a mixed bunch, some officers, some NCOs and some ordinary ranks, all playing together, hockey for the unit. Robin, being faster and fitter than most, was put to play at one of the most difficult positions on a hockey team, left wing forward. He turned up to play in his first match, and the team won, and the final in fact took place about three days before embarkation to Africa. The field was at Redford Barracks, which is one of the flattest, most wonderful hockey pitches that Robin had ever played on. Players could flick the ball from place to place without it really bouncing very much. It was a good match which Glencorse won; the brigadier general presented little prize badges to each of the players in the team. It was a good send-off to West Africa.

The beginning of the journey to Nigeria was quite interesting. Orders came through that Robin was to get a ticket to London and to report into Goodge Street underground railway station. Underneath Goodge Street was an Army run area which had been used as a shelter during the war, when London was being bombed by the Germans. It was still equipped with bunk beds and a kitchen. So Robin was given a bunk bed there, and was told he would be called at 7 o'clock in the morning and be taken off in transport to an aeroplane. The aeroplane was effectively a converted bomber which had seats in it. It flew to Lagos in three stages: south of England to Tunis, landing on the edge of the desert; Tunis across to Kano; and down to Lagos. At Tunis soldiers were able to walk out of the airport building and have a look at the sand and the small mud brick built houses with flat roofs and get a smell and feel of desert sand and completely different country from anything that had been experienced before. The heat was something that one doesn't feel in Scotland. Travelling down to Kano and across the desert was a very exciting flight, because once up at the cruising height, the pilot said, 'Keep your seatbelts fastened, we are going to go through turbulent climate,' and a few moments later there was a huge sheet of lightning across the sky and the plane was going through an electric storm. Robin experienced an electric storm in his first time in an aeroplane.

On arrival at Lagos airport, Robin was taken in a jeep with an escort to Ikoye island where the Army unit was established. His initial reaction was that this country had an extraordinary new smell caused by the heat and the smell of tropical spices in the air. After reporting to the adjutant and the command office he was told that he would be taken north to Ibadan the next morning, but in the meantime 'he had better get himself ready for dinner in the mess and no doubt he would need some sleep before the next journey'. The journey from Lagos to Ibadan is about 100 miles, on bumpy laterite roads, like going over an asbestos roof, with undulations of ups and downs all the way.

The first week with a new unit is a mixed memory, but in West Africa it is normal for almost every new white man to get a fever within the first week. The temperature gets quite high and men feel alternately sweaty or cold; Robin found that the clothing he had been issued with at Glencorse Barracks was not the smart clothing that 5NR was going to wear. In Africa two officers would share a chalet with a bedroom each and a sitting room and bathroom between the pair of them and each of them was allocated a man to look after his gear. While officers were having a siesta in the afternoon, visiting tradesmen would come round and offer a haircut or there would be tailors to offer clothes or else traders would be selling various goods from parts of Nigeria, perhaps little models of animals and ladies' clothing. The tailors were in fact very good indeed and certain of them were recognised by the military as tailors. They knew the pattern of the clothes and they would measure men up and actually deliver the clothes within three days so the young officers were equipped and ready for parade within a very short period of arriving. The dress for officers was a wide rimmed hat, khaki short sleeved top, short trousers, very smartly pressed and washed every day, green stockings, fawn putties and black boots. All this was worn with a Sam Browne belt. At breakfast every morning every officer was given a Paladrin anti-malaria tablet to swallow.

The adjutant said, 'Oh Salvesen, yes, looking forward to seeing you, you'll be going to headquarters company and to the signals platoon, the officer there is going to go on leave shortly and you'll just run the show, the company commander of headquarters company will see you all right. See the quartermaster tomorrow, get yourself kitted up and we'll see you in the mess from time to time.' So quick dismiss and off Robin went.

Ibadan had a population of well over a million people, in houses clustered together in a very big bowl of a valley, the rivers virtually being dried up most of the year. On top of one of the hills nearby was government house which was set in wooded countryside, with grass lawns and sprinklers on virtually all of the time to keep the place looking green and tidy: a lovely country house for the governor's residence. Across the valley on the other side was the Army barracks, which was remote from the town and consisted of married quarters for British officers, running along the roadside, the mess building just off to the right, and further up the hill, the smaller, unmarried officers' chalets, on either side of the road. On the top of the hill was the flat parade ground and the headquarters buildings, the quartermaster's buildings away down to the right and the company barracks laid out in rows further up the hill. These were mostly very small dwellings, not really more than one room in each, where the soldiers lived, very often with two or three wives and their children. From time to time, the officers had to inspect these and they used to turn out the Army property on the front lawn outside to count the number of chairs and tables. The wives with their children would very often stay inside during the inspection. There was a strong pervading smell throughout the barracks which was the same throughout the whole town. It was mostly the smell of cooking with quite high seasoning of herbs and spices. The ladies of the house worked outside preparing the food using a pestle and mortar to bash either cassava or yam into a paste, which they would then make into little fried pancakes to eat with their meat sauce. The soldiers' family would dip a pancake or roll rice into the sauce before putting it into their mouth. The soldiers also had a fair liking to their own kind of beer and a spirit which they made from palm trees, which was highly alcoholic.

The daily routine in the barracks, started in the dark when officers rose and showered and shaved with cold water in the chalet, and then marched up the hill. On the first day the young officer sharing the room with Robin took him up and showed him the headquarters company. After the sergeant major had taken the roll call, he would march forward to the company commander and report the company on parade and how many were present. The CO would detail each of the young officers to go and inspect his own platoon and then they marched back and saluted the company commander who would then probably bring the parade to attention, and address some remarks to them before he dismissed them for their day's duty.

Robin Salvesen would then go to the signals platoon headquarters and check the stores and look at the 62 sets and the 88 sets, which were the main signals at that time. 62 sets had a pretty good long range especially with morse, and signallers could often speak, over the 100 miles from

Ibadan to Lagos, when they erected the right aerials and masts for the purpose. The problem in Nigeria was that at certain times of the day there were atmospheric electric storms of some kind and there was a lot of distortion. Very often it was better in the evening. The 88 sets were short range sets, easy to carry in the small pouches on web equipment; they were used on company exercises so that platoon commanders could speak to the company commander.

This morning work would continue right through until a fairly late lunch. The men would go off for some kind of a coffee break during the course of the long morning, but after lunch, there would be siesta time and games in the late afternoon. The officers had a swimming pool down by the mess, and quite often, having had a siesta and read for a bit, there would either be some basketball or some football. Officers trained their particular platoon or company for an inter-company games competition.

Every day by 7 p.m. on the dot it was dark. After dusk, there was a huge number of mosquitoes which bit like fury, so it was the rule that between 6 and 7 o'clock everybody would go to their chalets and change into evening clothing: long trousers, mosquito boots, and long sleeved jackets so that really only faces and hands were exposed to the mosquitoes. At night, officers slipped into bed and carefully tucked round the mosquito net, because otherwise the insects got a bite. Mosquitoes carried not only malaria but also yellow fever, and there was a kind of seven-day fever that people caught from time to time. On the whole, there was not a problem, if the cooks put a tablet in the drinking water.

The signals officer duly went on leave within a day or two and Robin Salvesen was left to run his platoon: quite a lot of ordinary administration work with people wanting to go on leave to their families and some defaulters who had misbehaved. Then there was the continuous checking of the stores making sure the equipment was in good order and issuing equipment to various companies who were going off on exercise. Each officer also had a turn as duty officer for a complete day. The duty officer had to report to the adjutant first thing in the morning and receive orders for the day. Sometimes that would be an instruction to inspect B company lines and report, and see the cook houses, and sometimes there was a need to look after a visiting officer from another unit. The adjutant would then have a pack of cards; if the orderly officer chose card number 10 he would be inspecting the guard at 10 o'clock; if 3 then it would be 3 o'clock in the middle of the night, so he knew his fate quite early in the day.

Each day there was a parade of the duty guard and at 6 o'clock bugle call, the flag would come down at that hour precisely and the officer in charge drew his men to attention and saluted as the flag was lowered each day. Then the young officer would go down to the mess to join the others for dinner and would be the only one there who continued to wear his Sam Browne belt so that anyone looking for the officer in charge could identify him sitting at the dinner table. Inspecting the guards meant taking the Land Rover and going to Government House where there was a permanent overnight guard from the battalion. Then the officer would look at the camp guard, have a look round and inspect some of the camp and then get to bed, hoping not to be called by some emergency during the night.

The ceremonial guard at Government House wore small red pill-box hats, carried their rifles, had dark green stockings, fawn puttees and black polished boots and wore their overnight kit which was long-sleeved jackets and long trousers, all highly starched.

The evening dress for the officer was black tie, a short white waistcoat style jacket, a red cummerbund round the waist and long white trousers with black mosquito boots. It was really quite colourful and smart.

Robin's period as signals officer didn't last terribly long. The officer who'd gone on leave was an African officer and an incident took place during his leave. Rumour had it that there was a fracas in his village and some kind of assault took place, so he didn't come back to the battalion again, and a more experienced officer was put in charge of the signals platoon. Robin was given the job of resident Quartermaster for all the stores at Ikoye barracks at Lagos, doing the stores and provisions supply for effectively half the battalion. He had an inspection of all the buildings and stores at Ikoye barracks and signed for it all and it became his responsibility on his signature: quite a severe responsibility for a person who'd only been an officer in the Army for few months.

One of his routines was a twice a week trip from Ikoye to the other side of Lagos up to the quartermaster's issuing stores area with a corporal in a small vehicle. When they got to the food rationing place, dry stores were issued for 5th Nigerian Regiment Units and very often a voucher or cash to pick up fruit and vegetables from the market. The corporal would suggest which vegetables the men would eat; there were paw-paws and plantains and ordinary bananas and lots of oranges. Some of the oranges looked a yellow colour but they had a very good taste.

The Quartermaster had to make sure that all equipment (all the issued tables and chairs and light-bulbs etc.) were in order because when hand-over time would come he had to present everything to the incoming unit and they would not accept deficiencies or any breakages. He could exchange broken light-bulbs for a good ones without payment from the battalion's funds because he had an allowance but he had to keep up to date before the time of the inspection and hand-over. The day came when the Lagos barracks had to be handed over to the 3rd battalion of the Nigeria Regiment and on that day all the equipment was lined up in front of the barracks and it was a full day's job inspecting everything. Naturally there were some deficiencies found and some surpluses too (things like blankets and light-bulbs would go walkabout) but within reason it was quite a good hand-over and some credit fell on both the Quartermaster 5NR and his staff for this.

During the time that Robin Salvesen was in Lagos, the Queen's birthday parade took place so the whole company guard of honour had to be turned out in dress uniform to march from Ikoye barracks down to the racecourse in Lagos where they formed up for inspection by the Governor General. This was undertaken just before the wet season started and the weather was beginning to get fairly hot and thundery although no rains had appeared at that time, so although the soldiers were very smart when they were ready for the first inspection, by the time the companies had marched to Lagos and back again from the Lagos racecourse, the uniforms were all suffering from perspiration and the starch was no longer stiff. But Robin felt very good being a young officer with a platoon of soldiers marching through Lagos for inspection by the Governor General.

There were other good events in Lagos. On a Thursday night there was a Scottish country dancing club at the British club in Ikoye Island. Robin and his friends were able to meet up with some of the nurses from the local hospital. The Glasgow Highlanders and Scottish Reform and some very popular dances took place and quite often the young men would take the girls back in a taxi to their homes but because they were all working the next day they didn't linger terribly long, usually. There were however one or two romances and the officers concerned were teased.

There was going to be an inter-company basketball competition and Robin decided to see if he could build up a little team to compete. He got volunteers from the soldiers, some of whom had a tremendous amount of natural skill; they could throw the ball from really quite a long range and plonk it into the net, scoring goals without a lot of practice. It was however quite difficult to train them to understand that it was a team game and that they ought to pass to each other and not try and do it all themselves, but this was all a question of practice.

Then the Nigeria Regiment started to look for rugby players for a match against the Gold Coast. There seemed to be quite a lot of big men who were prepared to do a scrum, but not so many fast and fit people so Robin, instead of playing as a wing forward, was asked to play as a full back. Eventually the match took place, probably the first time there had been an international match of rugby between these two countries.

The Army reserved an area of the beach that officers could reach by boat where huge rollers from across the Atlantic made surf bathing in the very hot sunshine a tremendous joy. There was an Army hutted camp which offered billets for the weekend recreation, taking own supplies and making own food as required. The sand was so hot that feet almost burnt getting across to the sea, and there were men up the watchtower to make sure that the sharks were not in the fenced off area. Visitors would walk out with the surf board as far as they could go and these big waves would come and they would soon learn to be able to run the wave on the surf board, right up to the beach. The other joy in Lagos was that the Army had a yacht, which was occasionally available for young officers to get out into Lagos bay and sail for a day in the sun. One of the great things was that although it could be terribly hot and humid, there was a cooling breeze that came off the water almost every evening, and officers could sit at the mess and have a glass of gin, and enjoy the very much cooler air. Officers had a siesta after lunch; there was no air-conditioning but all rooms did have fans.

The final act from the Lagos experience was getting the company in convoy back to Ibadan, straight north on these long bumpy roads through the jungle. The transport was taking not only the soldiers but also their wives and children and cockerels and livestock, all in a convoy of 3-ton trucks. The 5th Nigerian Regiment detachment had two companies which is something well over two hundred soldiers, so there was a convoy of trucks, and three or four Land Rovers. Both the wireless sets and motor bike escorts controlled the journey. They had to halt once or twice on the route for rest and recreation.

On arrival north Robin was detailed to serve in B company, who were to go on a jungle trek, following the route of an earlier explorer, right up the border between French Dahomey and Nigeria, but the company first had to be taken down by train to Lagos. The train journey took a complete day and was disrupted because at one of the stations, a man threw himself under the wheels of the train which had to stop while the police made enquiries. This man was the first dead man Robin Salvesen had seen in his life and he was in quite a mess. There wasn't much time in Lagos before the company had to join the boat which took them west along the coast to land on the beach at the edge of the jungle, with French West Africa not very many miles further west. They set up camp for the night in the jungle where there was a tremendous number of mosquitoes, and bigger flies which were said to carry yellow fever.

The concept of the trek was that the soldiers would carry everything that they required and when the company arrived at certain villages a signaller could radio home and get a simulated air drop with wagons coming with top-up supplies. The whole exercise was to practise a jungle march and supply by air in case of a war emergency. Because of the intense heat, they started in the dark in the morning and marched until midday when all ranks stopped and rested for the afternoon, cooked an evening meal and went to bed early. It got even hotter as they went north leaving sea breezes behind. This southern part of the jungle was rough, no tracks at all. They just went by compass, with Jack Hart, the company commander, leading them northwards all the time. The jungle has huge teak trees and many creepers – eliminating the sunshine – and has standing water and deep ponds.

The water was not at all safe. Pills were used for drinking water and for cooking. Going through the water as the troops had to do from time to time, there was not only the danger of snakes but also the water was said to be contaminated so that men could get elephantiasis, a very nasty disease requiring hospitalisation. So everyone was a bit careful about getting across the streams and getting wet in the jungle water. There were ticks which filled with blood and had to be released with care.

There was quite a lot of cleaning and dressing, changing clothes after a long and sweaty walk with very high humidity. And of course all of the weapons had to be cleaned and inspected, because in these damp conditions, they could get rusty very quickly. The company of 100 men was separated into platoons and sections; a section would have 10 people with its own radio which one man would carry, the Bren gun would be carried by one of the people in the Bren section, the rest of the section would carry rifles and the 3 sections together would form a platoon, each with an officer, a sergeant, the batmen and a signaller. So the three young officers each had their own groups to inspect and make comfortable. They had a foot inspection after the first real day's march, to see if any of the men had developed blisters or sores which were quickly treated with little bits of plaster and iodine.

On the second night they stopped quite near a little village and the evening meal was compo rations from great tins, supplemented by a young goat given by the village chief. But as the evening drew on a rainstorm broke and camp was no longer satisfactory, so the whole company moved into the church building and spent the night under cover which was very much more comfortable

As they travelled north there were jungle tracks, because the villages were linked. Each of the men was carrying a load of not less than 80 lbs. Each had his own clothing in his big pack and on top of that many of them would have a box of compo rations, or a wireless set or just the stores that they needed to keep themselves going for several days. They had spare shirts, underclothes and socks and there was time during the rest and refreshment period each afternoon to do a quick wash every two or three days, and dry the clothing.

On either the third or fourth day of this march Jack Hart went to a village where there was to be a drop of food. The drop had already occurred and they spent the night near a district officer's guest house and the senior officers were actually staying within the hut, while the rest of the company camped round about. This was a more established village area, with fields with pineapples and cassava growing, and really quite a big community of people. In this part of Nigeria, a whole village would move when the land got worked out and the crops didn't grow and they would clear another bit of jungle and replant their fields. The maps weren't at all accurate, and troops would follow a path expecting to find a village and sometimes find they had to walk for another three to five miles. The bits that were accurate were the rivers and valleys, and in the jungle of course you couldn't really see any hills because of the thick cover.

At this camp, one of the young officers became ill. The heat or the exhaustion of the march must have really got to him because while the company were camping and getting ready for their evening meal his batman found that Dick had disappeared. One of the soldiers went to talk to the villagers who were of the Yorroba tribe. The company only had one or two soldiers who could speak Yorroba well. Major Hart sent out a patrol or two following the ideas of where he might have gone and they picked him up almost delirious. The company commander phoned through that evening to headquarters and the company stayed an extra night in this particular location while a vehicle came down and took Dick back for medical attention. He left Nigeria and went home again. It was a salutary lesson to all, that heat and exhaustion is something which has different effects on human bodies and their minds.

Another two days journey further north and the trek entered the area where the rift valley between Dahomey and Nigeria was very clear. The soldiers stayed in a village on the British speaking side and during the rest hour some of them went across to French speaking Africa. They walked down a very steep cliff, for about 30 to 50 feet, then there was a long flat stretch, half a mile or so at this lower level. On the French side, again there was a change in altitude of rather less than 50 feet, but it was quite apparent that a whole chunk, about half a mile wide, just sank – or the two sides of the rift lifted. This goes north and south and forms the boundary between French speaking territory and English speaking territory. The officers traded some beer for wine, and had wine with their dinner that evening. Very extraordinary: two parts of West Africa cheek by jowl; French influence on one side and English influence on the other and in each case the African people had adopted their mother tongue and tribal language, as well as some of the culture.

Nigeria is divided into three parts by the river Niger and to generalise enormously, the western part of the Y is Yorroba speaking tribes and the northern part of the Y, which is by far the biggest part and stretches right up to the desert and north, is Hausa speaking and there were quite a lot of different tribes with very different facial marks there. To the east are the Ibo speaking tribes. Most of the Ibo people had been indoctrinated either by the Catholic Church or the Presbyterian Church and there were missionary schools from Lagos all the way to the Cameroons who encouraged bright students into Universities so becoming really very well educated Nigerians. There was a period much later, and after independence, when the Ibo people from Biafra wanted to break away from the rest of Nigeria. They of course had oil revenues round about Port Harcourt and felt themselves able to be self governing, but the breakaway was not in the national interest. In the end the civil unrest quietened down but still it is the majority Hausa speaking people who have many of the positions of power in Nigeria. There were, in the Army units, quite a lot of Ibo speaking people who became very good sergeants and colour sergeants. The Army also included a large number of Hausa speaking soldiers who had the tribal discipline and were the core of the Army really. A lot of the sergeant majors and senior NCOs were Hausa speaking. They were superb people, very loyal, and it was good to be with them.

Back at Ibadan Robin Salvesen was immediately involved with the routine of camp life and as the company that had been in Lagos was due annual leave, many of the soldiers were sent to their home villages for a month. So Robin was appointed to A company. The senior officer commanding A company had gone home and his replacement wasn't yet in post, so Robin was acting company commander at this stage and had to 'take company orders'. When a man had been charged with some disciplinary offence the company commander had to 'take orders' and the man charged was marched in by a corporal, the charge would be read out, the company commander would ask some questions, the man would reply, sometimes this reply had to be translated into English, and then a sentence was passed. At company level a very limited punishment was able to be awarded: two days confined to barracks perhaps. Defaulters would have to parade on both these days after normal working hours in full kit and were inspected very thoroughly and then they would be given a course of drill and really given quite a hard time by the sergeant on duty that day, doing some quick marching and drill and running on the spot, and of course if the kit did not pass inspection properly the chap could be put on another charge and his time extended.

Robin's main task however was the company stores and checking all the records within the office. All the company stores and equipment was on his signature, and it was necessary for him to compare the paper records with the actual stores on the ground and see if they were in good order and condition. From time to time he had the men standing outside their houses, checking their furniture and equipment with the company records to make sure that the record was sound.

There was one particular instance when a man reported to the company commander saying that his father had died. He was asked, 'How did you know? – what happened?' The man could give no details, but he wanted to go home to a very remote village in the very far north near the desert. He said his family were grieving, but he hadn't got a letter to that effect, he just seemed to know. So Robin sent letters to the district officer in command of this area of Nigeria to make enquiries about this particular incident. The message took nearly two days to get there but eventually the story came back that the man's father had indeed died, at the village, on the day when the man had started his request for leave. Somehow or other the man had known of his family tragedy in his own mind and he was quite right. Robin had heard of this kind of intuition taking place in the north of Scotland and in the islands because Dr Charles Warr, the minister who had baptised him in Edinburgh, had written books after the first world war relating incidents in the trenches where the soldiers knew that something had gone wrong at home on the islands, or their families had known about their being wounded or killed.

There was polo to be played at the English club in Lagos and Ibadan where there were also bars and dances from time to time; one could also play tennis or squash. One or two of the officers kept their own polo ponies. Two of the officers entered their horses and themselves as jockeys in the local races in Ibadan which encouraged others to watch the horse racing to place their bets and enjoy a day out. The race track in Ibadan was only about a mile down the hill from the military camp.

Ibadan university was set in its own campus at the other end of the town. It had a good reputation with quite a lot of British and European lecturers and senior officials at the university. The playing fields were in very good shape and there were games to be played. Robin joined in hockey on several occasions, playing in scratch teams there. This all happened in the evening as the day got slightly cooler before the sun went down.

During the rest period after lunch men would come to the door on bicycles and offer a hair cut. The officer would sit in a chair outside in the garden and the man would wrap a sheet round him and start cutting his hair just as in a barber's shop in Britain. There were also visiting traders and when Robin came home he brought with him a set of ivory animals which had been carved out in Nigeria and also some really very lovely ebony walking sticks and ebony carvings of West African faces.

Some of the senior officers who had married quarters would ask the young officers to go to Sunday lunch or dinner in their houses, with their wives and other friends from the local area, because there were quite a lot of Europeans trading in the town; and some of the senior officers also met the Cypriots who had settled and were also trading with the Africans. There was one native African officer in the 5th battalion of the Nigeria regiment who had a house further up the hill and he invited Robin Salvesen and some of the others to Sunday lunch after they had been to the church in camp. The church was an all ranks service; the chaplain was Church of England and many of the soldiers, especially the Ibos from the south and east of Nigeria, had been to mission schools, either Roman Catholic or Presbyterian. But Robin found that the service was not very much different from the one he had attended in Fettes college chapel.

Around this time there were riots in the Gold Coast and the 5th Battalion of the Nigerian Regiment were put on three days notice to fly into the Gold Coast to help quell them. In fact they were never asked to go, but the fact they were on notice and prepared for a very sudden move really brought the whole training to a very high pitch. On several days, the platoons were out practising riot drill, where a platoon of soldiers with their officers would be blocking a road off with a barrier and facing down the rioting civilians on the other side; and in the end, of course, threatening to fire shots and even charge the civilians. Some of these practices got quite realistic as the wives and families of the soldiers who lived in the barracks would enter into the spirit of the thing and act as the rioting crowd, facing the men-folk formed up there with their rifles and pick handles practising their Army drill.

The next major incident in Nigeria was a visit by Her Majesty the Queen to West Africa. This required much rehearsal of parades for the event. All the Subaltern Officers had to parade at 7 o'clock in the morning, in full smart uniform, and start learning how to do their sword drill. The whole of the battalion was involved in the parades. The battalion 5NR was to provide two guards of honour, one of them at Parliament House when the Queen was to arrive, in Ibadan at lunch-time. Robin Salvesen was chosen to be one of the officers carrying the battalion's colour, at this one. The colour party had also several morning rehearsals, how to salute and parade and recover the colours.

It was a very hot day when Her Majesty came to Ibadan, and the men were in their full uniform at an early hour in the morning, inspected by the regimental sergeant major and marched to their parade duties. The Queen arrived at about 11 o'clock, at Parliament House and inspected her guard of honour; after the general salute when she arrived she went into Parliament House. The guard of honour stood there until she came out of the building again and so Robin and the guard of honour were standing on parade in the public eye for probably about three hours, in the midday heat in Nigeria. On another day, Robin was involved in the route lining, where Her Majesty was going to be driven down one of the main roads in the town and many people were gathering at the side of the road to watch her pass. The men were lined out at about eight yard intervals down the whole of the long road to the town and each young officer was involved with his group of thirty men, which covered a long stretch of the road – men smartly dressed, facing the main driveway and a rope behind them hoping to keep the crowd back from rushing onto the road when the cavalcade of cars came by.

Probably the nicest part of the Queen's visit was the Governor General's garden party. All the senior people from the whole of that part of Nigeria were asked and the young officers were set to stand at certain parts of the garden, two by two. Robin and one of his companions were placed at one of the staircases in the garden where there was a group of about ten steps from one level to another. When the Queen was at the top level there was a rush of people wanting to climb up, so the task was really trying to control the traffic.

The Nigeria, Gold Coast and Sierra Leone troops together formed the West African Frontier Force but after Her Majesty had left Nigeria the Regiment had a name change and Robin's battalion became the 5th battalion of The Queens Own Nigerian Regiment instead of 5 Nigeria Regiment.

The final major episode of Robin Salvesen's time in West Africa was a bush camp when the battalion went for field training in a rough and wild part of the country. Each day, the soldiers would march out of camp to train in the countryside nearby. There was one long route march which Robin undertook with his men, carrying all the kit that they required for a day or two away from the camp – marching out through grassland like a high plateau area, well away from the major forests. Robin remembers particularly leading on a small path through the grass county, and suddenly seeing in front of him, a snake in the middle of the path. He hesitated but one of the soldiers pulled out his knife (part of the West African Frontier Forces equipment), and put it in front of the snake; the snake struck at the knife blade, and in no time at all, the blade was lifted and the snake's head had been separated from its body. On one of the days 'A' Company were practising tactics and section attacks and platoon attacks, and four days later they were doing the same exercise but firing live ammunition as they went. They first worked out the safety angles and cleared the area so that there weren't any visitors or animals watching.

Then Robin had to pack for his journey home via Lagos. A particular incident had taken place there and one of the soldiers had died. So Robin's final duty for the 5th battalion of the Nigeria Regiment was to take command of a firing party and organise the burial after a soldier had died. He had to go to the police station and the morgue, making sure that the photograph on the Army papers was the same as the dead man's face. The next day there was a small guard of honour, half a dozen men and a corporal, and Robin in charge, and they marched to the graveside and lined up and as the padre said his words and gave his blessing, a short military salute was fired to Robin's orders.

Eventually at Glencorse Barracks Robin was told that he was now a reserve officer and not required for further National Service.

Within a day or two, Robin Salvesen had signed on as a Territorial officer with the 7/9th Royal Scots. Robin's family had a long tradition of service with both the 7th and the 9th Royal Scots: the Leith battalions who merged to be the only kilted battalion in the Royal Scots, the pipers and the band wearing the red Dress Stewart tartan, and the soldiers and the officers wearing the green Hunting Stewart. Robin's father had been a Territorial officer after the first world war and his uncles Chris and Eric had been killed in it, one of them in the Gretna disaster. Grandfather Thomas Salvesen had been a colonel in the 7th Volunteers Royal Scots and wore a volunteer decoration; Iver Salvesen had the Territorial Decoration, this medal being re-named after the first world war. Iver had taken over as colonel of the 7th/9th Royal Scots before the second world war started, from Uncle Tom Grainger Stewart who married Pansy Salvesen, Iver's sister. So Robin was following quite a tradition in the 7th/9th Royal Scots.

At this time all National Service people had to serve for two years in Territorial Forces, continuing training after they left their two years of regular service. They were training to keep their skills up to date during an annual camp. They also had a commitment to do about twelve evenings of drill nights. There were drill halls at East Claremont Street in Edinburgh and in the surrounding towns such as Peebles, Penicuik, Dalkeith and Tranent, run by 7th/9th Royal Scots and the 8th Royal battalions respectively. Robin was signed up to go to Oxford in the autumn, so although he made his very best effort to do camp each year, with the battalion, he didn't exactly carry out his full commitment in the drill nights and had exemption.

The first camp that Robin went to was again up at Barry Buddon, which marches with Carnoustie golf course, where the ranges face out toward the sea over the estuary of the Tay. Troops had to stop shooting from time to time when ships were going by, but there is a very big area of sand dunes forming a flat training ground there. Much of the work at camp involved getting qualifications annually for shooting a .303 rifle, the Bren gun and the Sten gun.

There was always a mess night in full uniform with a certain number of guests invited to attend and a rehearsal dinner night when the waiters were taught how to do the thing properly and the young officers were taught the tradition of the various toasts which this particular battalion would propose. At the cocktail party the young officers were told to hand round drinks and savouries and Robin found that this was in fact the best way of circulating round a party.

After the first camp Her Majesty the Queen was going to visit Edinburgh for the first time as Queen, and the Royal Yacht was to come into the port of Leith. The 7th/9th Royal Scots being the Leith battalion was to provide a guard of honour, and Robin was ordered to be one of the colour party and carry the colour on this parade. The colour party went through the exercise of dipping the colour and raising it again and then being steady for inspection and of course there was the final royal salute before the Queen went away in her limousine. On the day of the parade, the typical Edinburgh gale of wind caused the colour drill to become a slightly more tricky manoeuvre than at rehearsal.

Each year at Armistice day the battalion would do parades in various churches and also have their own service in East Claremont Street because there is a memorial there commemorating those who had died during the first and second world wars. Many of the people serving were related to the people who had died so there was quite a gathering of the friends of the battalion. After this service the officers would have a tea party with the extended family in the officers mess and the sergeants would have a similar party upstairs in their mess and the men would also have high tea and beer! There was also a ball each year, and Robin and the other young officers would invite a party of friends and a lot of Scottish country dancing would take place.

In the summer time some of the drill nights were carried out on the ranges, one of which, Hunters Bog, was actually on Arthur's Seat. The first duty was to get the flags out and to clear the area of any hikers and boys and girls who were out courting. Later on as more and more people went out on the hills and Arthur's Seat, the Army had to go to Dreghorn and shoot there instead. When Robin was promoted to captain, the Battalion went to camp at Millom in Cumbria, and had specific civil defence training i.e. what that battalion might have to do if there were nuclear fallout, and soldiers were trained with the instruments that they could use to find out if there was in fact any contamination with radioactive particles. They were taught how to wear the defence uniform so that their own bodies would be safe while they did this. It was rather like going into a gas chamber and being trained as to what would happen when personnel took off their gas masks. At this camp Captain Robin Salvesen was given the duty of taking the recruits' platoon, with forty recruits who had never been in National Service to try and bring them up to the standard of drill and training of the rest of the battalion who had served with the regular Army, within two weeks. So Robin was involved with his training sergeants in trying to work out what the training programme should be and organising the everyday drill, so that there was a reasonable standard at a passing out parade.

The next years were all tied up with the cutting down of the defence expenditure in the UK and the 7th/9th Royal Scots were merged and amalgamated with the 8th battalion to become the 8th/9th battalion and the outlying towns were included. Robin commanded the Dalkeith drill hall, which was in the Midlothian company. One of the biggest nightmares was running the bar as the stock had to be checked from time to time and the bar accounts kept, and the officer had to make it quite clear to the corporal in charge of the bar that he wasn't able to get away with various fiddles and fraud. It is quite easy for a barman to give short measures of whisky and make a bit of money on the side, probably getting an extra two tots out of each whisky bottle, by giving people just slightly short measure. Each year the company accounts would be audited, and the Army book-keeping method would be presented for other officers to look at and confirm that the accounts were being properly kept. The only way that Robin could keep these bar accounts was to actually do an hour or two's work at home on the accounts at least every month. He also had to learn the Army system of double entry accounting.

Capt Harold Salvesen, who was the chairman of Christian Salvesen, was amazed one day when he got accounts coming from Dryburgh's Brewery, addressed to Capt Salvesen, East Claremont Street, which had been sent to Christian Salvesen & Co in Bernard Street in Leith. These accounts had been made out to Capt Salvesen without initials. It suddenly impinged upon him that young Robin, who was just a junior in the office, had actually a similar ranking in the Army to himself. He, one day, said, 'I think the time has come when you should stop calling me "Sir" and call me "Harold",' so that was really quite a boost for the young Robin Salvesen.

During the period before the merger with the 8th Battalion it was found that the local Post Office Brass Band found it difficult in getting money for uniforms. A deal was struck where they would become en masse the band for the 8/9th Royal Scots and they all signed up for Territorial Army pay. The Army provided them with Royal Scot uniforms so they could march smartly on parade in their uniform as well as for concerts and dances. So from that time the 8/9th Royal Scots had the Military Band playing the hymns at their Armistice Day Services and in concert at the end of the Service as well – which was very nice. The Battalion could in fact march a full Military and Pipe Band and do a Beating of Retreat which was of a very high standard.

When the Forth Road Bridge was opened to the public the Battalion provided a Guard of Honour for Her Majesty the Queen. At this stage Robin Salvesen was a Captain and was second in command of the Guard of Honour. The chosen soldiers went through the process of rehearsals for the Parade and marching on the new road before it had been opened and on the day of the Parade they lined up beside the end of the bridge where now the money is collected from vehicles. This was planned to be a tri-Service occasion with Royal Navy Ships under the bridge and a fly-past of the Air Force over the bridge; but on the day of the Parade there was fog, and so the aeroplane fly-past was cancelled and the Navy (we understand) had one or two problems of navigation in the Firth of Forth. The Queen took the salute and inspected her Guard of Honour and then took the car across the bridge and back again before going off to her further duties. It was in fact a very smart Parade and the Territorials were honoured to be part of it.

There was another big formal occasion when the Territorial Army was reviewed – all the Lowland and Highland Regiments were reviewed at Holyrood and Brigadier General Macgregor of Macgregor was the Commanding Officer of the whole Parade. Robin Salvesen and his group practised coming by helicopter to do a section attack, with thunder flashes and firing their blank ammunition as a sort of exercise for the crowd to raise the cheers. It was arranged that the platoon should go to Turnhouse Airport to join the helicopter, but on the actual day they went to the airport only to be told that there was too much mist on the hill and for safety reasons the helicopters were not going to fly for the Parade. The Administrator said, 'Oh, it's been arranged that you will get into transport, rush round Edinburgh with a Police escort, go round the back of Arthur's Seat and join in on the road at the entrance near Jock's Lodge. Then you will be able to line up your vehicles and join into the march-past at the right time. So although you won't have been on the Parade and won't have been inspected and won't have been on the Parade ground, you'll actually be there for the march-past.' Robin arrived in an open Land Rover standing to attention and was driven past the Saluting Base and saluted the Queen who was taking the Parade.

Robin Salvesen, as a Major, went to one or two Senior Officers TEWTs (Tactical Exercise without Troops). The Brigadier held these occasions – the first one was at the Hartree Hotel near Biggar and it was a long weekend for all Captains and Majors. One part of the exercise was teaching the Senior Officers how to use explosives and Charles Ritchie, the lecturer at that particular stage, showed them – as some of them had seen already – how to handle plastic explosives. Then they went out for a demonstration in a typical Charles Ritchie manner where he had chosen some big stone that the farmer actually wanted to be blown, laid the plastic explosives, lit the fuse and ran back to hide in a ditch. There was a great bang and of course the big stone had duly been blown up.

The other TEWT was at a hotel near Duns with General Leask in charge and covered an area of the Lammermuirs. The officers were given an illustration on the Sunday morning about the enemy forces having landed and which direction they were likely to come from and how each group were to set up a company defensive zone to oppose this particular attack. General Leask listened to the plans – and then he produced the team solution which was different to anything that had been proposed, but as he explained his solution it was quite clear that there were merits of doing it his way which none of them had really thought about. It was a good weekend and officers learnt a lot from it.

The Brigade Camp that year was in Lincolnshire – Stamford. This was to be the final Camp of the whole Brigade as it was at that time. There were quite a lot of inter Battalion dinner parties that took place so the officers from each group could meet each other. Robin was lucky enough to be invited to accompany the Colonel to the KOSB's Mess Dinner night. The KOSB officers had a terrific meal and circulated the wines, but their tradition was not only to have the port circulated after coffee but Kummel as well and it became an evening where the conversation grew louder and people sat round the table for quite a long time. Eventually the Colonel was ready to go home and Robin was expected to drive him in his car from the KOSB Mess back to the Royal Scots. The following day was out in the fresh air on the Ranges which was thought to be good for everybody. It was at the Stamford Camp that the whole concept of the final merger took place and Robin was asked if he would consider being the Company Commander for the Royal Scot Company in what was going to be 52 Lowland as the only Battalion which was effectively volunteers and Territorials in the future. There was to be a Cameronian Company, a HLI Company, a KOSB Company and a Royal Scot Company, and Robin was to be the Senior Officer of the Royal Scot Company. Major Ronald Ironside, a Royal Scot, was to be the Battalion Second-in-Command and there would be a regular Commanding Officer – so Robin discussed with Lt. Col. Charles Corsar, the Colonel of the 8/9th Royal Scots, which of the existing Officers in the Battalion would form the Company Officers for the new Company and it was determined in fact that two Captains would join him. There were two Captains and three Subalterns so there would be in fact seven officers remaining from the full Battalion. East Claremont Street would be the Drill

Hall as the base for the Company. Eventually Lt. Col. Hugh McKay was made the Commanding Officer of 52 Lowland.

At East Claremont Street Robin decided that he would try to keep alive as many as possible of the old traditions. The company managed to have an occasional dinner night in the Mess and certainly kept alive the Armistice Day Parade and party. It seemed important that in this smaller unit they involved the wives of the six officers – so Robin instituted the idea that officers would have some weekend TEWTs and training exercises and that they would use his home, Eaglescairnie House, as a base for some weekends at which the wives, and their families if they wanted to, would be able to come. There would be a certain amount of social activity and the wives would also get to know each other during the weekend. The TEWTs transpired as a useful exercise, especially when A Company of 52 Lowland became the Ever Ready Company of the 52 Lowland and the first unit in the case of an emergency to be drafted to go off to join the Regular Army in Germany, because at this stage the Russians were considered the main likely enemy and the need to defend Germany was apparent to all.

A Company was to go to join the First Battalion of the Royal Scots for Camp in the summer which meant exercises as a mobile Battalion. The First Battalion Royal Scots were equipped with APCs and carried a whole section of men in the travelling cross-country machine which went on tracks and so a General could move the whole Battalion very quickly. If there was going to be an attack, soldiers would be travelling very quickly over the country and fighting in this mobile role. This of course was the way in which the 1991 Gulf War was conducted very many years later. So one of the weekends at Eaglescairnie was to train the officers and indeed some of the senior NCOs in the sort of map reading and wireless activity which would be required to keep a Company moving across East Lothian in vehicles. This particular training exercise served well when Robin took A Company to Germany to train there. Robin and one of the Sergeant Majors went on a recce to the First Battalion in Germany and spent the weekend visiting Lt. Col. David Young and the Senior Officers and learning what their duties might be in Germany. The Company was to fly from Turnhouse Airport to Hanover and then move by vehicles to Camp. First they had to be introduced to the Armoured Personnel Carriers and learn how to drive and use them. In order to make the whole exercise work the First Battalion Royal Scots provided the drivers for the APCs and then the company were set up to go into some training exercises – before a whole week-long mobile exercise with the First Battalion doing a Brigade exercise.

So it was in at the deep end again with the soldiers from 52 Lowland. One of the things which was really quite interesting was that the soldiers of the 52 Lowland had been used to marching round the Barracks quite smartly and when they saw an Officer, saluting. So the 52 Lowland A Company actually started off quite well and earned quite a good reputation for being a smart bunch. They went across country and did manoeuvres at speed where armed soldiers decanted from the APCs, formed out on the ground and then did attack in line with blank ammunition firing, The ground gained in attack had to be held, so the company dispersed round the area to guard the place against a possible counter attack. The Territorials had several nights out camping and cooking their own meals with the APCs. The feel of doing a mobile exercise and warfare at speed of this kind was really quite exciting.

During this visit to Germany there was actually quite a lot of work to be done outside normal training hours and Robin recollects one of the company's soldiers being hurt and going into hospital, and himself spending one afternoon in a Land Rover visiting this soldier who was worried about his permanent job. His health recovered when his worries were taken away from him to some degree. His company were prepared to give him some extra paid leave because he had been injured for the sake of the country. The other memory was the flight back from Hanover for many of the soldiers had had a night in town and had presents to bring home for their wives and families. They came through the Customs in Turnhouse Airport and the Customs passed all the soldiers through with their kit bags and then when the Officers turned up at the end, having got their men through, they insisted on opening every single one of the Officers' bags and having a search to see whether the Officers had declared their goods correctly. Sometimes rank does not pay a dividend!

One of the Camps at a weekend which Robin organised for 52 Lowland A Company was at Cultibraggen near Comrie in the summer. He wanted the soldiers in his unit to have the opportunity of firing the anti tank guns with which they had been issued. They had 3.5 rocket launchers and a certain amount of ammunition and set up the targets: hanging bits of sacking. It was really remarkably easy to hit the target for the first time; the sights looked really crude but in fact the weapon fired quite a reasonable distance and with great accuracy. The training team also took the men that weekend onto the grenade range. Robin's Company in the volunteers had one or two Regular Army Sergeants and Sergeant Majors to work alongside the Territorial volunteers. but it was quite difficult for them to get used to working with volunteers who all had their own family affairs, their own holidays and their own business commitments, and the number of people who turned up for the weekend wasn't exactly 100 per cent. On the other hand the Regular Army Sergeants were always amazed at the enthusiasm and the time that the volunteers were willing to put into their training, so there were pluses and minuses. The Regular soldiers might have been working in peacetime on a 9 to 5 basis but the Territorials would actually be enjoying it and trying to learn and being very keen to spend the whole period in uniform usefully.

All good things come to an end. As Robin got more senior in his own office job he found that he had to travel out to Japan and Australia and to other places rather more frequently and his family were beginning to grow up and it was quite attractive to spend some weekends at home. The 52 Lowland commitment seemed to become greater all the time and sometimes he was with them three weekends out of four. The other point was that Robin had two Captains and neither of them could get any promotion until he moved on, and so when a new CO was appointed Robin thought perhaps he ought to give these younger chaps an opportunity and so he sent a resignation letter in and finished his Territorial Army career.

CHAPTER 5

Family and Friends

R OBIN SALVESEN went up to University College, Oxford, in 1956. At the age of 21 he travelled down on the train from Edinburgh via the Caledonian station through Crewe and on to Oxford, where he lugged his bags from the station down the High Street to University College and was allocated his room beyond the Radcliffe Quad in one of the buildings which was owned by University College next to the Examination Schools. He shared a set with one of the other new students at the College. Each of them had his own bedroom but they shared a very big sitting room with their own desks – large enough to entertain friends and neighbours. Robin always had some sherry in his room so that he could entertain in the evening, but on the whole the main entertainment was to have either coffee or tea. Quite a lot of work was done in the room because studies and examinations were important.

Robin had been playing quite a bit of rugby before, and early in his career at Oxford he was asked to play in the trial matches for the University teams and got into the College side as a wing forward. In the University team at that time there were one or two International players – David Brace, the Welsh scrum half, was the Captain and Cameron Cochrane managed to get into the team as stand off half. Cameron had been at school at the Edinburgh Academy and was later to become the Headmaster at Fettes College. Malcolm Swan, who was another old Fettesian, was playing at Oxford at that time, and eventually became a Scottish International player. So Robin knew quite a few of the senior players in the University and played a few games for the Greyhound side. In his second year he became the Match Secretary for the University College team.

There were many out-of-school activities, including the Church of Scotland Society, the Iona Society where he met many of the Scots who were at Oxford at the time. In particular he met a Scottish girl from Edinburgh called Sheila Abercromby who had already got her degree from Edinburgh University but was now studying theology. Sheila, in the summertime, played cricket in the Oxford University Ladies Cricket Team and Robin from time to time went to see the match. Sheila bowled and batted for the team and Robin and Sheila got to know each other quite well and used to go on a lot of cycle rides together in the countryside round Oxford just to get a bit of fresh air.

In University College Robin met many of his contemporaries in the Junior Common Room. John Rees, studying law at Oxford, was known in those days as the pocket dictator but he was quite a good centre three-quarter in the rugby side. David Morris, who became Robin's best man later, was studying PPE – Politics, Philosophy and Economics. David went on to be one of the leaders in Peat, Marwick and Mitchell and then left to become the Finance Director of the P & O company, working with Lord Stirling. John Wolstenholme shared digs in the second and third year with Robin; he was rowing in the College boat during that time and gained three bumps during the bumping races with all the College down to watch the race and cheer. This earned a College dinner in honour of the team in the Big Hall at University College. Frank Pearson, who had also been at Fettes, and one of the Prefects at Glencorse House, was up at University College as well. He was a scholar and a hardworking chap. He kept a diary and each evening would look through the jobs he had intended to do that day and all the ones he hadn't managed to achieve he would pass forward in a priority list for the next day. Some of the jobs he intended to do went on and on week after week but Francis was always very busy

The new undergraduates all had rooms in the College, and some of the rooms were beautifully panelled. They met in the Hall for breakfast and again for dinner which was fairly formal with the high table of dons sitting on a platform and the undergraduates with their gowns on at the big wooden tables, served by the stewards. In the second year, John Wolstenholme and Robin had 'digs' down Iffley Road fairly near the University Rugby Ground, with a strange landlady who gave them fairly minimal breakfasts; but the rooms themselves were quite comfortable though the landlady was not terribly pleased when they had visitors in the rooms in the evenings – she expected her house to be quiet by nine o'clock.

In the third year, John and Robin moved out to digs in the Banbury Road and brought in a third companion who was another ex Fettesian called Chris Normand. The Engineering Department was at that side of Oxford. As time went on Robin and John Wolstenholme actually went into the College building very rarely because they both had girlfriends in Oxford and they tended to cook their own evening meal. One of the features there was Sunday lunch – Robin would put a roast into the oven before going off to the Scottish Church.

When Robin first got to University College a group of them found that
the beer that was being offered was English ale, considered by them to be
very watery, so they moved a motion in the Junior Common Room to
purchase Scottish beer, which obtained approval, and that custom has
continued ever since.

During the first summer vacation, Robin went to Canada to be a
counsellor at one of the youth clubs at the Algonquin Park. When Robin
was at Fettes a group of girls from Canada had come to visit Edinburgh and
they put on a show. The Fettes boys had an evening of country dancing
with them and Robin gave a demonstration of sword dancing and highland
fling. He did the various steps of dancing as a demonstration. Robin became
a penpal with a girl called Heather and he continued to write to her during
his time in the Army, and again during his first year at Oxford. The idea of
going as Youth Counsellor to join her at Algonquin Park gelled when he
realised that the fee would nearly cover the air fare. Heather met him in
Toronto and took him to her home, an old mill by the river, for the
weekend before joining the camp. Robin was given his counsellor role and
met the Team Leaders of the 10 to 12 year old group. One of the young
students was a grandchild of the current Prime Minister of the Canadian
Parliament who came from a French speaking family, but all the boys and
girls in the Camp used English as a common language.

The boys were on a mainland part of the Camp and the girls including
Heather were segregated in their huts on an island in one of the lakes but
there was frequent canoe traffic between them and the Counsellors met
each other for parties and evening meals once the younger folk had been
settled down for the night. Robin had many new things to learn, including
how to drive a canoe in the Canadian way with one paddle, kneeling in the
stern of the canoe. It was also necessary for him to have a sufficient
swimming qualification. But Robin had a whole lot of other know-how
from his time in the Army and Nigeria, trekking through the jungle and
setting up camp, and knew various safe procedures to assist life in the wild.
It was rather like a large Scout Camp with many activities for the young
people to participate in during the daytime hours. There were horses to ride
and many things to do with canoes and sailing. Robin did quite a bit of
sailing with one or two of the other Counsellors and took some boys out as
well, and had little sailing races in the dinghies.

After about a week the Senior Counsellors decided there were some of
the boys who weren't settling in terribly well and so Robin and two others
were detailed to take a group of eight to ten boys off with four canoes for

three days into the wilderness. They loaded up the gear with tents and groundsheets and foodstuff for a few days. Each of the boys and the Counsellors had a pack to carry which contained their own clothes as well as some of the stores. This was very similar to the trekking that Robin had done in the Army in Nigeria where each of the soldiers would carry a pack of eighty pounds. For the younger boys at the Camp the weight was kept down to about forty. When the boys were paddling the canoes there were two of them, one on either side, but when the Counsellor was doing it he would give the boys a rest and paddle from the stern on his own. At the portage points the canoe and the packs would be carried from one lake to another, a distance of up to four hundred yards.

The countryside round the lakes was natural forest – many of the trees were maples which hadn't yet turned colour in July and August. The summer sun was shining and it was really very good weather. The group set up a camp at a place where there had been camps before and the boys were shown how to clear the area round the fire so there was no danger of the fire spreading and to build it on a stone bed. They tried to fish for trout in the lake but they never got a bite. By the time they got back to the camp fire, the first night's supper was ready and they gathered round the fire and told stories until the boys looked tired.

The next day followed the same pattern but they camped in a completely wild part this next night. There were a lot of wild blaeberries – blueberries as they called them in Canada – the bushes being rather bigger than on the hills in Scotland and a very good rich crop. So Robin at the camp fire not only made porridge for the next breakfast but also a sort of stew out of the blaeberries – the ones that the boys hadn't put into their own mouths anyway – and at breakfast the next morning the boys were quite keen to have the sweet taste of fruit with their porridge and they tucked into a good breakfast. During the night a pot where the oatmeal had simmered was left outside the tent, and some hungry racoons came and opened the lid of the pot and ate some of the porridge.

The next day they came to a beaver dam. Mr Eastall, the leading Senior Counsellor in the party, said, 'Follow me,' and aimed the canoe at a point in the beaver dam at the end of one lake and going at some speed, the canoe went up and over and through the top of the dam, down the slope at the other side and into the lake next to it. There was a round beaver house, like a large pile of wood, in the middle of the lake, which was quite safe from predators out there.

The next evening at the main Camp there was a big fire set up in the hills and all the boys sat round a huge camp fire and ate a sticky buttery bit of maize, corn on the cob, which the boys just ate with their fingers and got really thoroughly dirty, then a bit of meat and finished up with some ice cream. But then they were singing songs by the camp fire and hearing Indian tales and the whole evening finished up with a big bang with a couple of fireworks, then the boys went back down to the hill to settle down and have a good sleep.

At the end of Camp the Counsellors had the camp themselves for a couple of days – to clear up the area but also to have a bit of fun together as adults and at this stage the girls from the island and the men on the shore, the Senior Counsellors from both parties, had a ceilidh of their own. Robin showed off a bit by getting one of the girls to play on the piano a Scottish tune and he did a sword dance as a demonstration, just using a couple of sticks as swords. There was dancing together in the evening and it was quite obvious that Heather had other boyfriends and Robin wasn't the only boyfriend in her life. The pen pal arrangement between the two of them came to an end at that time, but Robin had enjoyed meeting Heather once again. One of the other events in their last few days was a canoe race, and Robin teamed up with an American man and the two of them, as it were foreigners amongst the Canadians, came 2nd. There was about half a mile canoeing and then quite a long portage, then another quite long paddle with everyone cheering to see who would get there first in the final run-in to win.

Back at Bonnington House, Robin was able to tell his father about his time in Canada. Iver was fairly disappointed that Robin had missed a major part of the grouse shooting that year in the Pentlands but he was in time for the last few days in September.

Iver Salvesen died on 27 September 1957. He was at the height of his powers at the time of his death. It was the night before a shooting day and he had come back from the office at the usual time. Most of the family were away. Evelyn, the youngest one, was only ten years old and at St Monica's day school in Edinburgh. Alastair and Hilary were both away at school and John was down at his farm, Spylaw, near Kelso. So Robin and Marion, the two adults, were the ones who were at Bonnington House, when Iver died. It was very much the usual kind of evening. Robin's father came back from the office and he had his glass of sherry and then they sat down to dinner at 7.30 prompt. They went through to the drawing room to have a cup of coffee. Iver Salvesen sat and listened to the 9 o'clock news after he had his coffee. He ate a black ball, a peppermint sweet, with his coffee then after a little bit of chatter, and after the dog had been taken for a walk, Iver went to have his bath and to bed and then Robin went up to bed as well.

Robin was woken up with noises during the night and Marion came up to his room and gave him a shake and said, 'Come on downstairs, Daddy's not very well.' Robin looked in to see his father who looked absolutely still and silent. Marion said that she had phoned for Doctor Lackie to come out and see him because after his bath he'd not been able to settle and not felt well and she was worried about him. An hour or two later Doctor Lackie had still not arrived so she went upstairs to call her son. Robin immediately said, 'Well I'll call for an ambulance. We'd better get an ambulance if the doctor is not here yet.' So they phoned 999. The ambulance arrived at the door but the next Robin heard was that Doctor Lackie was shown in and Iver was declared to be dead.

The next morning was to be a grouse shooting day and so Robin Salvesen knew that he had to get up early the next morning and start phoning around to cancel the shooting. There was one group of people who were going to be picked up on the way to the shoot so Robin got the car and went off to the garage to go into Edinburgh to meet up with his father's friend and tell him that the shoot was cancelled. The best thing that Robin had learned in the Army, perhaps, was that when there is a crisis just get on and work and work and get things done. He stopped at Elmsley's Garage to get petrol in the car and the old man at the garage said, 'How's your father?' and he said, 'Daddy's dead.' The garage man said, 'Oh, I am so sorry,' and that was the time when Robin first broke down and had to sit in the car until the weeping had stopped before he could drive on into town.

So the next day was full of the hustle of planning the funeral service. The King of Norway, King Haakon, had died the previous week and Iver Salvesen as the Consul General for Norway in Edinburgh was to make the funeral oration during the special Commemorative Service in St Giles on the Sunday morning. Someone else was organised to read the words which Iver had written but none of the family attended the service. Marion arranged with her brother, Logan McClure, for Iver's funeral to take place at Warriston Crematorium, which in hindsight was a bad decision because Iver was at the top of his career and had recently been Master of the Merchant Company and was very well known to the business community in the City of Edinburgh, and the Chapel was really not big enough at all for the crowd of people who wanted to attend and who had to stand all round the Chapel that day at the funeral.

Looking back, Iver Salvesen had really a very short marriage with his wife Marion. Marion went on living for over forty years after he died. They had married in 1933 and by 1940 they were separated by the war. They had probably ten years peaceful life after the war but within that time Iver had been remarkably successful in his business career in Edinburgh – being Treasurer and Master of the Merchant Company and leading that part of the community of the town. He had made a quite an impact on the finances of the Merchant Company, moving investment out of property and land and farms into Investment Trusts and other Stock Exchange investments which gave a better return and better security for the Members of the Company and their pensions. He was also involved in the changes to the Merchant Company schools, when George Watson's separate colleges were joined to make one co-educational school on the south side of the City; and on the north side the Mary Erskine School at Queens Street was moved out from central Edinburgh to Ravelston to a new site and new buildings. These with Daniel Stewart's and Melville College meant the Merchant Company was a thriving organisation with six or seven thousand students in the City of Edinburgh. Much of this education was at a very reasonable price.

Iver Salvesen came to re-build Salvesen Shipping Ventures in 1947. During the Second World War, the coal industry in the United Kingdom has been nationalised. The National Coal Board determined to operate their own marketing and sales to Scandinavia. They never again reached pre-war tonnages. Christian Salvesen and Company had been a major player in coal exports before and after the First World War when they bought the quality of coal required by Norwegian and Danish factories direct from private coal mines. They owned the coal they carried in ships abroad and re-sold it on delivery. Much of the timber carried by sea was also owned and re-sold. Iver had to restructure the fleet and the trade when he returned from his war-time service. He was able to negotiate sales of coke and coke breeze from the gas works in many British towns and export cargoes from Granton, Grangemouth, Aberdeen and Newcastle to the ferro-silicon factories near Bergen and to the steel plant at Mo-i-yana. This formed the basis for export loads while imports were largely timber products including wood pulp.

Shortly after the funeral, Robin returned to Oxford for his second year. Again he was involved in the University trials but shortly after the first two or three weeks of term he was playing in a Greyhound match when he got a severe leg injury and broke a blood vessel and stretched the tendons in his left knee. The University rugby doctor took him under control and gave him a treatment of ultrasonic massage, telling him that he had to rest for a few days. In the next interview the doctor said, 'You really must start moving the knee and the swelling will have to go down – we've got to break it up and move it and you've got to get the blood circulating and the sooner you start bicycling and using that knee the better, however much it hurts – otherwise you'll never be able to flex it again.' It was very difficult to get from Iffley Road up to the Engineering School with a leg that wasn't working. Robin did try to walk quite far and soon got onto his bicycle. This actually brought to an end his career playing rugby because this injury took quite a long time to heal.

Robin very much enjoyed the practical work in the Drawing Office at the Engineering School: Part of the programme at the end of his second summer term was to stay on for a few weeks to do surveying and engineering drawing so he surveyed the parks round the north side of Oxford and drew it all up. He took this further forward during the holidays, and borrowed a theodolite and did a survey for John at his farm at Spylaw – to show the fall of the land and the main structure of the old steading buildings which helped John later to re-build and modernise the cattle courts so that he could put in modern feeding arrangements for the cattle. John not only introduced to the Spylaw Farm the growing of potatoes for seed but also improved the amount of grain that the farmland there would produce each year. Barley was one of the main crops and could be sold as an animal feed – but a higher price was paid for malting barley for making into beer and whisky. He kept quite a lot of cattle out in the open air during the summer but also in the cattle courts in the winter – he used to buy Irish cattle and fatten them at Spylaw. During harvest time, Robin went down to live with him at Spylaw and to cook food for the two. He used to join the harvesters at lunch-time and go out and drive a tractor to bring the grain in from the fields and relieve the tractor drivers during a part of the afternoon shift – and then in the evening the two boys would have dinner together and go to bed. John and Robin shared much of their young lives and were close companions.

During Robin Salvesen's last year at Oxford the most important part was meeting up with Sari Clarke and getting to know her, working together in Banbury Road with Sari studying theology and Robin studying for his exams in engineering. He visited Kent to meet her family and took her sister Vanessa out from school, and met Sari's father as well as her stepfather, before he finally popped the question and asked her if she would marry him. Hilary, Robin's sister, was at finishing school in the Oxford area

and at one of the parties during this last year Hilary was introduced to
Hugh Cairns who was reading theology. Sari and Hugh used to share notes
because Hugh Cairns had to miss some lectures, to play hockey for both
Oxford and Scotland. Then Sari also got her Half Blue. She was one of the
bowlers for Oxford's cricket team and Robin remembers borrowing the car
from John Wolstenholme and going through with a group of friends to
watch Sari and Sheila Abercromby – both playing cricket for Oxford against
Cambridge.

CHAPTER 6

Whaling

AT THE END OF THE examinations in 1959 Robin cleared up all his clothes and belongings, including all the notes of his work, and took the train from Oxford Station on the journey up to Edinburgh, where he was met by a car to take him home to Bonnington House. He had about a week to unpack his undergraduate clothes and to purchase boiler suits and seagoing working gear before travelling to Norway to join the *Southern Venturer*. Between seasons in the Antarctic the *Southern Venturer*, having discharged at Liverpool, would go to Norway to sit at anchor in a fjord there for some maintenance and repair work before going to dry dock in Newcastle before the journey to the Antarctic once again. Robin's first job with Christian Salvesen was to stand by the whaling factory ship in Tonsberg Bay, staying at a boarding house in the village and working as an engineer doing some of the maintenance work during the summer. Tonsberg Bay is a very enclosed bit of water and the whaling factory ship had a very safe anchorage there. Many of the Norwegian crew stayed nearby in the houses round the bay. The engineers who were working with Robin during that summer were nearly all from the Newcastle area and they stayed in a specially built hostel alongside the boarding housekeeper's own home where they had nice bedrooms, simple furniture, and a communal bathroom. The boarding housekeeper made the most wonderful evening meals and packed sandwich lunches for the engineers standing by, to take with them to the ship.

Robin spent much of his evenings while staying there learning Norwegian and could eventually fairly easily read the Norwegian newspapers but he was not good at mimicking and his attempts to speak Norwegian were treated with a bit of a smile because although he was speaking the language as written, it wasn't the way the locals said it, in the dialect in the south part of Norway. Norway's history is an interesting one because the various villages and towns up the coast for many centuries had not been joined by roads, and the people travelled by sea and only in the calm months. The town communities at Bergen and Trondheim and the smaller towns as well had built up as almost separate city states and the language and the speaking of their particular Norwegian tongue was rather

Winter ice builds up on pipes and rigging.

different. One of the first changes King Haakon made was to try to get the people to speak and learn in their schools what was known as the King's Norwegian and, of course, the newspapers followed that instruction pretty well.

The *Southern Venturer*, sitting out at anchorage, was joined by Robin the morning after his arrival, going out in a motorboat launch from the quayside quite near to the chalet as part of a group of about ten other personnel who were working on maintenance either on the deck or in the engine room. The ship seemed huge and the ladder really quite difficult to mount carrying a heavy bag of gear. On the days that followed the first he only had a pack with his lunch in it, but for the first day there was a certain amount of gear so that one could change into a boiler suit for work. He started with a senior engineer opening and cleaning one of the generators in the main machinery room, which was quite pleasant because the main generators were fairly quiet as the ship was needing power only for the ship's lights and services. The other major job was stripping one of the cylinders of the main steam engine and opening up and repairing the valves. It was a very good opportunity for Robin to have a good look round the ship and get to know something about the various pipelines, because as an engineer it is important to know how the systems work in order to react if a problem occurs. During the lunch-time each day, the twenty or so people working on board would go up and stand in the fresh air in the sunshine and eat their sandwiches together. The gulls would come sweeping down for crumbs, doing their normal acrobatics and swooping down to see which one could catch the bread first. In July and August the weather was quite magnificent, with sunshine and very few rainy days.

Working hours were 7 a.m. till 4 p.m. so there was a long summer evening of leisure. The offices in Oslo had very much similar hours so people went to their second homes – usually out of town by the sea – during the afternoon and long, light evenings.

During the centuries before Scottish houses had electricity or gas, candles and lamps were the main source of light in the long winter evenings. Candles made from sheep's fat were cheap but smoky while high quality expensive candles could be made from beeswax. Whale oil and fish oil formed a valuable addition to provide a range of products such as soap and margarine for these animal fats could solidify. Vegetable fats such as olive oil remained liquid until chemical processes, during the Second World War, found a solution which has created a new harvest oil crop – rape seed and linseed. Whaling therefore was a useful industry for Scotland with Leith and Dundee on the East Coast specialising as bases until 1840 when sites were set up further north in Shetland and Newfoundland. Norway had a range of coastal sites for both whale oil and fish oil production. Christian Salvesen and Company only commenced operations as a Ships' Agent in Leith as Turnbull and Salvesen in 1846 and they obtained a licence to open a whaling station in South Georgia, Antarctica in 1909 although they had interests in factories in both Shetland and Newfoundland before the Antarctic venture was initiated. Harold Salvesen was particularly involved in creating markets for by-products – whale meat, bone meal, liver oil and later meat extract.

It is perhaps important at this stage to talk about the whaling industry as a whole in 1960. Christian Salvesen and Company had two floating factory vessels and a shore station so they employed really a large number of people. There was quite a considerable competition. The Norwegians had several expeditions as well and there was another British fleet run by Hector Whaling which had a modern ship called the *Balena* whose Captain was Per Verik. The Captain of the *Southern Venturer* was Harald Myhre. The

A view of Leith Harbour, South Georgia.

Dutch had a whaling vessel called *Willem Barendsz* and both the USSR and the Japanese were also involved. The *Southern Venturer* would expect to catch and process at least a thousand whales during the course of a season. Whalers were paid a basic rate but also, depending on their rank and station, would get a bonus depending on the catch, so many of them went home with a very large pay packet relative to their friends in the Scottish villages. Salvesen's employed, at that time, about 50 per cent Norwegian and 50 per cent British people. The engineering departments were mostly manned by British speaking people, whereas a large proportion of Norwegians would be flencing (i.e. cutting up) the whales on the deck.

The first impression for a visitor to the *Southern Venturer* was her enormous size. It felt as if the after deck and again the fore deck were the size of a football pitch. The whales were drawn up through a hole in the stern and up a ramp by a huge steam winch. The stern deck of the ship was big enough to carry a 100 ft. blue whale. The midship of the whaling factory contained the winches and the derricks for handling the whales and the carpenter's shop. Then there was an equal area of wooden deck before the galley, accommodation and the main bridge. This bridge overlooked the bow of the ship which enabled the navigators to see icebergs and find a route through pack ice.

The senior navigating officers lived in the fore part of the ship near the bridge. Underneath their accommodation there was the galley and the dining rooms for the crew and the officers. Robin was part of the Junior Officers' Mess and fed there, one floor off the main deck, whereas the main body of the crew were in the Ratings' Mess on the lower deck. All the engineers lived at the stern of the ship and during the standby summer they used one of the cabins there to change their clothes before and after work. Above this stern section there was a helicopter deck because Salvesen's were using a helicopter as a means of searching for the whales in the Antarctic. The ship therefore had a very strange appearance in comparison to other ships and did in fact sail slowly – about 10 knots. The engine room was equipped with one huge triple expansion steam engine, which burnt heavy oil. This viscous oil had to be kept heated so that it could be sufficiently fluid to be pumped from one tank to another. If it got cool it would solidify and be almost impossible to move. So the big main engine chugged round at slow revs – 60 revs. The main engine platforms were on three different levels so that maintenance could be carried out and there were metal stairs running from top to bottom of the engine room with platforms at each level. On the second floor up was an engine storekeeper's room and next to that was the main electrical board for distributing the power.

In each watch there would be an officer, a donkey man and a greaser – the donkey man being the Petty Officer, and a greaser the workman and watch keeper who actually knew a lot about engineering but whose duties were to paint and scrape and clean under the instructions of the donkey man or engineer on watch. The generator flat was the noisiest part of the whole of the ship because the three large generators worked at high revs and had turbines to blow sufficient air into the engine to improve the efficiency of the burning of the diesel oil which they used. There were three of these generators in parallel on one floor, of which at most times during seagoing passage two were being used. The engineers had to circulate cooling water so there were pumps and cooling tanks and also, of course, the main ship required circulation of both fresh and sewage water so there were quite a lot of pumps. A ship that was going to be six or seven months away from civilisation needed spare parts for every motor and valve. Because *Southern Venturer* was a factory which would boil up whales

Whale catchers mooring in harbour. Note the crow's nest look-out high up the ship's mast and the gun platform above the bow.

she required to make about 300 tons of fresh water each day so she had a big evaporator plant which would take in salt water and evaporate it by boiling, condensing the steam into distilled water.

During the summer season Robin had spent a happy time going down the fjord in the evenings to have a swim in the nice warm water or going with his friends to have a drink in a pub or to look at the magnificent spruce woods in the area of Tonsberg. Now the *Southern Venturer* would move from Norway to Newcastle for a good paint up of the under part of the ship before she was bound for the Antarctic again and some of the bigger repair work, such as drawing out the main shaft for inspection, could be done in the dry dock at the same time. For this cruise across the North Sea there were as few crew as was safe. Many of the officers who had been standing by had their wives with them and they also had the opportunity of travelling back by the ship to the United Kingdom. Suddenly the English speaking people who had mixed in the villages, gone shopping together, played bridge together, and gone to the beach together became separated *according to rank* for the short passage. The wives of senior personnel used the upper class accommodation in the bridge forward.

Robin had quite a decent holiday in Scotland with his fiancée Sari, and a few weeks of letting his hair down before joining the ship again at Newcastle.

The *Southern Venturer* sailed in October towards the Antarctic. Robin shared a cabin with a very tall young Engineer Cadet, called Tony. He hadn't been to University but had had some training at a Polytechnic to get practical engineering skills. So the difference in background between the two cabin mates was pretty apparent. Robin knew quite a bit about theoretical engineering whereas Tony had quite a lot of practical experience but wasn't trained in the theory to the same degree. There wasn't much room in the cabin that the two shared but luckily, being on separate watches, very rarely were the two men in the cabin at the same time. There was a single table, a fitted clothes cupboard and drawers beneath the lower bed. There was a sink in the room for washing and shaving and that really was the sum and substance of the accommodation.

On the journey between Newcastle and the Dutch West Indies most of the engineers were working normal marine shifts of four hours on and eight hours off, while a lot of the whaling crew who were on passage to the Antarctic, and who would be the crew of the catchers when they got there, worked daylight hours in gangs getting the ship ready for her job. They sailed down the East Coast of the United Kingdom and through the Channel, hitting the first bad weather in the Bay of Biscay where many of the crew felt a bit uncomfortable as the ship started to move a bit more violently under their feet. The lower rank of officers and the ratings had a weekly drink ration, imitating the age-old custom in the Navy, when the crew queued up for their dram of rum each week. Robin's group of engineers however made an application to have a bottle from time to time so that they could go to their cabins and have a game of cards and have their drink together in a more measured sort of way, which was allowed.

When the *Southern Venturer* got to Aruba most people got a chance for a trip ashore, but as usual for those in the Engine Room there was to be a job to be done while the main engine was shut down. Robin managed to get a walk ashore just one afternoon to see the shops and to get his feet onto the dry land before the ship went to the Antarctic, knowing that they would not see a shop or a girl for several months. The crew in fact were rather the worse for wear by the time they joined the ship that evening.

Then of course there was the ceremony of crossing the Equator, when those of the crew who were going across for the first time had to go through the mock hairdressing and ducking which was the normal treatment. A hundred or so men gathered on the deck of the ship to watch the candidates come forward two by two to be sat in a chair and covered in white foam for a mock shaving and haircutting before they were tipped into a rigged pool of water to bathe and that was them 'blessed' as they went past the Equator. Going down past the Amazon River *Southern Venturer* must have been some thirty miles out at sea but the colour change was obvious for the river was discharging very brown and muddy flood water into the South Atlantic. Robin was able to see for the first time the flying fish which rose from the waves at the side of the ship and glided over the surface of the ship for a really long distance – lifting up over the next wave and down into the trough, and later the dolphins playing in the bow waves of the *Southern Venturer*. It was really rather nice after a day's work to go out on a tropical evening and look over the side in the fresh cool breeze of evening and see the dolphins playing in the waves. Also on a tropical evening the crew were shown films on the deck and, of course, being out on sea there were no flies or mosquitoes so it was really very pleasant.

The 1959 Whaling Expedition took to the south young pigs and hens in pens on the main deck. *Southern Venturer* had a very limited amount of storage for food and deep-freezers were hardly customary in the ships built in the 1940s, so Robin's generation was fed with salt fish from barrels, salt beef and salt pork, to supplement the diet that they had. The hens, which gave them some eggs for a period, and the pigs were fattened and ready to eat for Christmas and New Year, fed from the bits and pieces from the galley.

One day Robin went out and saw snowy mountains rising from the sea, a most dramatic looking view arriving at South Georgia. At this stage the watch keepers had not seen very many icebergs. That joy was still to come. Robin was below deck during the harbour entrance. It was quite a tricky narrow entrance into Leith Harbour at South Georgia, but the Second Officer and Navigator Captain Kerr knew the way quite well and took great care to go in during day time. *Southern Venturer* was not in port for very long before she sailed, in company with her eight catchers, in order to start fishing sperm whale to run up the factory before the main whaling season started. In fact they caught some two hundred sperm during this pre-season period. The only sperm whales found in Antarctic waters were the male whales which had been chased out of the main flock as no longer acceptable. The catchers fished near Bouvet Island at the start of the season, towards the end of 1959.

After the new whaling season started the *Southern Venturer* moved on eastward and southward until she met the great icebergs, including an ice sheet which blocked the passage south all day and this measured some 150 miles long. Eventually the ship got to Enderby Land and made a landfall and Robin saw the Antarctic Continent, before she turned and moved towards the west again to join up with other factory ships which were working nearer to South America. In the Weddell Sea they met their tanker with supplies, and it was getting on towards Easter time by the time they got their Christmas mail. It was with great excitement that the whalers saw some very big icebergs and from time to time also saw penguins swimming near them and jumping up onto the ice, sometimes being pursued by a leopard seal.

The sperm whale eats squid on the ocean floor and is a very different kind of whale from the baleen whale which was the main object of this expedition. Squid might appear quite a small prey for a whale to hunt but some of the squid in the Antarctic are really very much bigger than the ones holidaymakers would eat in a restaurant in Spain. A sperm whale has a very large head, about a third of its body length, full of oil which is not edible but which is a wonderful lubricant for clocks and watches. This oil is used in lighthouses because it is wonderful at rust prevention. Unlike many whales, sperm whales have teeth, and these were cut out and preserved for carving and collecting. Very occasionally a flencer found ambergris which was used for fixing high quality scents. This is a very valuable commodity. A sperm whale can dive very deep during its period of feeding and will surface some distance away from where it was last seen blowing on the surface. It is very difficult for the gunner of a whale catcher actually to have the bows of his ship in the right place when the sperm whale surfaces, so that he can quickly manoeuvre the ship and fire the harpoon into it to kill it.

The blue whale, fin whale, and sei whale have baleen which acts as a strainer as they swim through the krill shoals with an open mouth. The baleen filters out the water, leaving the krill in the mouth of the whale so that it can swallow a mouthful of solid matter. They are surface feeders and develop a very thick layer of blubber which contains much edible oil. It is so full of oil that it drips when it is cut or squeezed in the hand. The baleen whale can swim and dive for about thirty minutes before it surfaces again to blow and expel waste air and re-fill its lungs. It can swim as fast as the catcher – some 15 to 20 knots – and has a long endurance at this sort of speed.

It was during the period that the ship was sailing towards Enderby Land that she encountered the first full gale and Captain Myhre thought that the length of the waves was so very large that the ship, if it took the traditional posture and sailed against the wind, could have broken her back, with the bows on one wave and the stern on another. So he positioned the ship

A group of fin whales towed to the factory for processing.

broadside to the main wave pattern and the *Southern Venturer* rolled tremendously from side to side during the period of the gale. However, gales in the Antarctic don't last many hours, and after the wind has fallen down there is enough ice in the area for the sea to flatten again quite quickly. The action of the Southern Ocean is different from the North Atlantic behaviour where a gale is followed by big swells lasting several days.

The crew on the *Southern Venturer* was large enough to require her to carry a specialist doctor, but once away from port and from other ships the crew didn't circulate coughs and colds, and the health of the crew was very good indeed. When the tanker came alongside to replenish the stores, however, it also carried new bugs to the ship, and for a few days quite a lot of people had flu and colds. There were some special cases for the doctor to deal with. One of the crew was finding it difficult to breathe and the carpenter made, effectively out of wood, an artificial lung which kept him alive for some time. The doctor was in radio contact with the main hospital in Cape Town to discuss the case and the advice was that it really wouldn't be safe to try to transport this particular man via whale catcher in the very rough weather existing at that time to take him up to hospital. He eventually reached one, though.

Later in the season Robin Salvesen himself had an operation because he got a chip of metal that stuck into his eye while he was working. The doctor decided that he should try to cut it out. He got one of the engineers to make him a special little instrument and a very sharp little knife to his own design. It was one of the few times during the whole voyage in the Antarctic that the *Southern Venturer* stopped its engines for a time to make the hospital as still and smooth and quiet as possible. Anyway, although Robin had a slight white scar in his blue eye for a time, his eye was certainly not damaged and he was very thankful that the doctor had the presence of mind to do the job there and then so it didn't give him problems in later life.

The crew had to wash their own clothes and it was common practice for the engineers to have a boil-up, once a week, of their boiler suits in the Engine Room. There was a great bucket down there and they put hot water in it with the boiler suits all covered in oil and muck into the drum and then they put one of the steam pipes into it to keep the water boiling for a time. It was left to each member of the crew to clean his own socks and small clothes and do his mending.

During the course of the whaling season, Robin grew to know how the factory worked. The main deck of the ship was a real mess of blood and oil with people working with heavy machinery moving the whales, so if the engineers wished to see the operation they would stand up on the winch platform. On the afterdeck, the whales were pulled up with huge winches which shook and rattled the ship, and especially the accommodation in the after end. The flencers took off the main blubber layer in great long lengths. They would cut from about the mouth a great long slit down the whole length of the whale, then fix a wire for the winch to one end of the strip. Then flencers would assist the winch in pulling off the length of blubber which could be as much as a foot thick of oily fat and strip it up, cutting it off the underlying meat as the winch pulled the strip away from the whale's carcase. This strip would be fed into one of the boilers through a hole in the deck and cut into pieces as it went in. The boiler would boil it until the factory manager thought it was ready and turned down the heat until it was settled when the oil floated on the surface of the water below and he could pump off the two layers one by one. Solid matter would be moved to a different tank to be boiled up and added to the meat and bonemeal as a by-product of the factory's work. Once the main part of the blubber had been taken off, the whale would be moved from aft onto the fore deck where the meat would be cut off and also boiled up to extract another lot of oil. Then the bones would be cut up with huge great bone saws and boiled to produce meal with a high protein and calcium value. This could be used either as a fertiliser or as an animal feed. On the way down to the Antarctic many cargo tanks would be full of oil fuel and on the way north they would be full of edible oil or sperm oil to be sold in Europe. The cleaning of the cargo tanks was an important part of the duties of the crew. *Southern Venturer* had a very large number of separate tanks which is very useful in providing stability for a ship in rough water.

During the season when Robin was on the *Southern Venturer* the expedition caught some fifty-odd blue whales which are up to 130 feet in length – enormous creatures with a huge girth as well and each would produce over a hundred barrels of oil. The catchers killed more fin whales though, often around 70 feet in length, and the sei whale rather smaller. Captain Myhre was Captain of the *Southern Venturer* but also the expedition leader. He instructed the whale catchers where to go each day to look for whales. In reasonable weather, he had the helicopter to use as a search vehicle as well. The factory engineer was a Norwegian, a very large man and very well regarded, and Jimmy Still was the British Chief Engineer who was effectively Robin Salvesen's Senior Officer. Mr Still was fairly remote and busy, often to be seen through his open door working on his records and his bookwork.

Each expedition worked with eight catchers and each of the catching vessels was commanded by a Skipper who was called the Gunner because he also would fire the gun and catch the whale with the harpoon. Very often a man was up in the crow's nest at the top of the mast to search for the signs of a whale blowing – hot breath condensing in the frosty air – and then if they found a whale they would give chase. The gunner had to be fairly careful in choosing whales that were big enough because it was an offence to catch whales below a certain size or to catch whales which were in milk and feeding young. They had to get close enough to shoot the whale – less than a hundred yards from the catcher's bow when he fired the harpoon. The harpoon had the rope attached and had an explosive head so that when it entered the whale the explosive head would burst and in most cases would kill the whale because it would hit a bone and break the nervous system. It would die quickly. In some cases the harpoon would lodge itself in a soft part of the whale's body and the whale would try and run with the rope on holding it. The rope on the whale catcher was threaded through a series of pulleys using the mast of the ship effectively as a fishing rod so that the winch and the ship itself was playing the fish reacting to the tension.

When the Captain was close enough again he would be able to shoot a second harpoon to kill the whale.

Robin Salvesen did a short trip on a whale catcher, the *Southern Laurel*, at the end of the season. She was a war built corvette with four big boilers burning oil fuel for her steam engine. During that period they sighted a whale and chased it for the best part of the whole daylight hours but never got within close enough range to risk a shot. The Captain put on his asdic and the whale heard the 'ping' and ran away in a straight line from it, which might have been a help but in this case every time the whale surfaced to blow it was too far away. When the light faded the *Southern Laurel* stopped and waited in that position throughout the night and early the next morning they again saw a whale blow. They started to chase this one but never caught it so maybe when the *Southern Laurel* stopped for the night the whale also took a rest.

Robin was given a cabin right up in the bows of the *Southern Laurel* just below the harpoon gun. Sometimes the weather was really quite rough with sea breaking over the deck and it was quite scarey to come up from the Engine Room and see the waves crossing the deck. He would think, 'Gosh, I've got to get from here to there before the next wave comes across and hang on to a winch on the way, planning a second run to the door in the forecastle.'

The cabin itself was very small and in the rough sea it was a question of bending knees to wedge them between the side of the ship and the side of the bunk so lying in a dead stupor until daylight – or until the next person banged on the door and said it was time to get up. On the catcher, the crew worked shifts in daylight hours of four hours on, four hours off, and at night time six hours on, six hours off, so that each man was continuously changing shifts as the day went on. However when a whale was harpooned and chased the whole crew had to help to bring the whale alongside to pump air into its stomach and flag it. After catching several whales, one of the catchers would tow all the whales that had been caught to the factory ship, perhaps as many as eight.

On the factory, Robin Salvesen's twelve hour day started with a tap on the shoulder by 'a greaser' who had come up to warn him that his watch was due to start in ten minutes. He would get from his bed and shave quickly and go below deck to start work. Breakfast in the Mess Room consisted of scrambled powdered egg and a bit of bacon and coffee or tea. Robin found that he didn't enjoy tea on board because tea with condensed milk is really not at all pleasant. Coffee was more agreeable. The shift worked during the day and had a break at lunch-time for the main meal of the day and then worked on until relieved for tea. Nearly every evening there was either a film to be seen in the Officers' Mess Room, or else the engineers gathered for a game of cards. Sometimes a group held a ceilidh when someone played a mouth organ or sang some Scottish tunes. The books that circulated round the *Southern Venturer* varied from biographies and serious books to cowboy stories and comics. It was a very happy ship's company. The twelve-hour working days still left plenty time for hobbies and leisure or reading.

The catchers came to the factory ship regularly to be supplied with stores, fuel and food. They would moor alongside the fore end whereas the whales were secured near the stern. If the weather was rough a whale would be used as a fender to keep the two ships apart. Personnel were lifted from one ship to the other in a basket hung from the end of a derrick – a procedure which the Board of Trade would frown at if it happened in the twenty-first century. The crew could get an awful bump when they landed on the deck unless the operator of the derrick was working very kindly and nicely. Stores were loaded and discharged by the basket as well and the fuel pipes were connected up and water and fuel were pumped from one ship to the other.

The production of oil and meal caused a lot of odour on the whaling ship which in the Antarctic could be smelled for quite a few miles and the result of this was that surrounding any whale factory ship there were thousands and thousands of birds. As the waste water was pumped out of the ship there would be little scraps of meat and oil which fed other species. Some of the crew were ornithologists who watched and recorded very many different kinds of birds from an albatross right down to a stormy petrel and went to the Antarctic to take photographs.

There was an office up on the main deck of the *Southern Venturer* and crew could send telegrams home. Robin did send a few on his high days and holidays and people's birthdays – just to tell his friends and family that he was alive and well. Extracts of news would circulate, especially on Saturdays and Sundays when the football scores would be put on the notice board and people would talk about their team at home. Many of the crew had a regular pools investment. They had chosen a series of numbers to use every week which is as good a way of winning or losing as any other.

There were several dirty and particularly dangerous jobs. One of the worst tasks was to clean one of the evaporators and scrape off some of the salt because if the salt accumulated too greatly on the coils in the evaporator the efficiency would diminish. An engineer had to open the doors and cool off the evaporator so that a team could chip off the salt – this was one of the nastier jobs on the ship. The other nasty job was cleaning the tanks of dirty fuel oil and preparing the tank for putting edible oil into it. Robin worked on the meat extract plant, boiling up the blood liquors and concentrating the fluid. There was a very great tendency, rather like in making raspberry jam, for the whole pot to boil over and lose quite a lot of the contents.

Robin went with the *Southern Laurel* to South Georgia, the shore station, where he had time to look at the operation which Salvesen's had had for fifty years. There had been other whaling stations at South Georgia before Christian Salvesen had achieved a licence from the British Government to operate there. The station at Grytviken had been operating for longer, worked by both Norwegians and Argentineans before the Leith company started operating at Leith Harbour, a safe anchorage where a glacier comes down from the mountains to join the sea. The two quayside buildings are the Magistrate's house and the Manager's house, then there is the accommodation for the shore based workers which includes both a laboratory and a hospital. Robin was given a bunk in the hospital for the couple of days that he was ashore because there weren't any wounded and ill people. At Leith Harbour were pens of hens and pigs which were bred and reared so that permanent staff had fresh eggs and meat. The Norwegians had introduced reindeer onto the island of South Georgia which live wild and multiply – feeding on mosses and seaweeds. It certainly does no harm to the stock to cull a few for fresh meat from time to time – a sport for visiting ships.

Very close to Leith Harbour and bay is another small whaling station called Stromness where in 1959 Salvesen's did their whale catcher repair work during the winter season. The over winter repair team had two floating dry docks and some big sheds with spare parts and machinery together with the burning and welding plant. The oil tanks and the church lay between Leith Harbour and Stromness. When the whale factory ship came in, it was an opportunity for a challenge match of football between the people on the factory ship and the people who worked in the shore station.

It was very interesting to see the huge number of stores that were lodged at Leith Harbour: tail shafts and propellers and bits of bronze and brass, as well as the dry docks for repairs of everything that might get broken. Volunteers from the whaling crews were asked to stay down and do a winter working on repair and maintenance.

Stromness, South Georgia. The floating dry docks are ready in the bay and oil tanks line up in rows on the narrow sands below the steep mountain slopes.

Southern Venturer came in to collect the whale catcher crew after the season and travel north again, through the tropics. Captain Per Verik told Robin that he used to sleep for nearly a week at the end of the whaling season because he had been on the bridge for the best part of five months and had very rarely gone to his own cabin for a rest. Other Master Mariners surely would have delegated duty a little bit more than that. Certainly during the time Robin was on the whale factory ship he really didn't see Captain Myhre at all, but he was a junior engineer and not invited to the senior mess.

On the way north the men ripped up the whole of the flencing deck and most of that rotten, dirty, smelly woodwork was thrown over the side. In the Engine Room it was back to the routine of normal merchant ship watch-keeping. In the factory there was much to be done in hosing down and cleaning all the pipelines. It was good to meet warm sunshine and fine weather through the Tropics and see some films on the deck of the ship on a tropical evening. The Senior Officers were busy writing up all the records of the trip and counting the stores. There were quite big queues too for the various people who were recognised as hairdressers on board the ship including the storekeeper in the Engine Room.

In Liverpool Robin went up to the Captain's cabin to say goodbye to Captain Myrhe and thank him for the trip – he had been treated very much as a junior and one of the working men and had no extra perks because of his name.

It would be wrong to finish this account without putting it in the context of the Christian Salvesen Company history. Christian Salvesen and his brother J.T. who had worked in Leith and Grangemouth respectively had been the younger children of a family who owned a sawmill in the south of Norway at Mandal. They had both gone to Business School in Germany before they came to the United Kingdom. In 1846, sailing ships with the British flag really meant that they were able to call upon the Royal Navy for help in case of trouble so Salvesen chose to fly a British flag and operate from the UK.

Christian, who travelled on horseback week by week to meet his brother at Grangemouth, would have passed the developing paraffin industry between Bathgate and Queensferry, so he would have been watching the new industry develop and the export of paraffin from Grangemouth. Indeed he developed the business of selling paraffin and paraffin lamps into Norway. It wasn't a big step to owning a share of the ship which carried the cargo and Christian certainly did this fairly early in his career between 1851 and 1890.

Christian Salvesen almost certainly met the whaling people when he was selling coal to whaling stations and it wasn't long before he owned a share or even had the management of whaling stations himself. He operated certainly in Shetland – Robin Salvesen saw the site in Shetland in 1972 when he first went up there.

The family had whaling stations in Newfoundland as well as Shetland before they got a licence to trade in the Antarctic and it was as late as 1909 before Salvesen's started operating at South Georgia and named the harbour there Leith Harbour – and then 'Christian Salvesen' operated the biggest of the British whaling companies. In its heyday the company was operating two floating factories and a shore base. Harold Salvesen managed to persuade Winston Churchill that Europe would be very short of edible oils after the war so he was able to build the *Southern Venturer* during the war at a British yard, one of the very few merchant ships that was built in wartime. *Southern Venturer* went to sea immediately the war had ended and was joined by the *Southern Harvester* in 1946. It was a big capital investment and a high risk trade. Christian Salvesen and Company for a long period were not able to insure whaling vessels for anything other than total loss and it was only when the company were able to prove a good trading record that a reasonable premium was offered by Lloyds in London.

South Georgia however was quite a good site for a whaling station – a current eastwards round the south of South America forms a whirlpool as it hits a range of undersea mountains – so krill and other floating fishes gather in the stream and congregate to form a feeding ground for the larger fish. Whale fatten as they feed off the krill in this area. There had been whaling stations at both Leith and Dundee in Scotland but they had actually all stopped before Christian Salvesen lived in Scotland and the shore based whaling industry was no longer operating, except in the northern islands. The Salvesens operated whaling in the Antarctic from 1909 until they finished in 1963: quite a short business life for an industry.

Christian Salvesen formed, with his sons, the South Georgia Company as a Limited Company in 1909 and it is that company that formed the basis of the wealth of much of the family who inherited their shares from their forebears.

CHAPTER 7

The *Saldura*

T HE *Saldura* had been built in a Swedish shipyard and was a general cargo ship of nearly 13,000 tonnes. She had been sailing with the Salvesen red, white and blue funnel and British crew for a year and went into dry dock in Amsterdam when Robin Salvesen joined her in October 1960. The hull was found not to be in a good condition – a bit of detective work was necessary to try and find out what had happened. It could have been that the surface of the steel had been damp or that the ship was painted during frosty and wet conditions. Anyway it was decided to give her a thoroughly good scrape down and re-paint with red lead and anti-fouling and a top coat – but at the same time to put anodes on the ship to stop any electrolytic action. The effect is similar to the process in a dry battery with distilled water in the cell – there is electrolytic action between the small particles of zinc or copper within the steel plate, especially in the presence of salt water. Small electric charges float past on particles of dust and molecules in the sea – causing electrolytic action and corrosion of the ship's plates.

It's possible that the Chief Engineer and the staff on the *Saldura* during her first year had not set the highest of standards; certainly when Robin joined her, the Engine Room was in a filthy condition which may have been due to the work in the shipyard where shore gangs opened up some parts of the engine and drew the tail shaft. Extra dirty boots were tramping up and down the clean plating. So there was lots of work to do when the ship left Amsterdam for Cuba to load a cargo of sugar. The crew faced a long ballast voyage right across the Atlantic. The second or third night after Robin had signed articles to legally be a crew member, he, the electrician, and another young officer were able to go ashore after high tea to have a look round Amsterdam. There was a short half mile through the dockyard and over railway tracks to get out of the gates and into the rather scruffy warehouse streets at that part of the busy industrial town. But then the trio came to the bright lights and a rather famous street with a large number of pubs and where girls hang out in the bars. Further along the street the houses clearly became more respectable, the pubs looked more prosperous and the three

Saldura in port and ready to load cargo. Her derricks are set and her ballast water
pumped out, so she rides high.

young men from Scotland found a restaurant pub rather like a British one
with tables and beer. They sat down and had a couple of pints together and
then thought they might move on and try Napoleon brandy. After a time
they thought they'd have a little walk and see what else was going on and
finished up in a night club bar and were surprised to find that there was a
floor show – in fact one of the girls they'd been chatting to appeared in
fancy dress on the stage and as she sang her song she started taking one or
two items of clothing off – a strip show which was not particularly
attractive. After an hour or two in this part of Amsterdam the three men
wandered back along the road to the ship.

The *Saldura* sailed shortly afterwards and Robin started meeting the
other officers and engineers. The Officers' Mess was controlled in a
different way from that which Robin had seen in an Officers' Mess in the
Army. Here on a Merchant Navy ship everyone was given a particular place
to sit. The Captain sat at one table with the Chief Engineer, the Second
Engineer and the Mate (the senior deck officer). Robin, being a Junior
Engineer, sat at another table with Engineers. It felt very strange because
there were very rarely more than three or four officers in the dining room
at any time and they all sat alone at their different tables. There was
however quite a big lounge where they could sit and read a book in
reasonable comfort – or else go to their own cabins – and the officers from

the Deck Department and the Engineer Department did get to meet each other as the voyage went on. It was a shock for the crew to learn as the ship sailed down the English Channel that they were in for a long, round the world, voyage, for the ship was to load a cargo of sugar at two ports in Cuba to be taken to China. The American sanctions, restricting trade with Cuba and indeed China, eliminated the direct route through the Panama Canal so she would have to sail via Cape Town, Durban and Singapore. The Captain on the bridge and the Navigating Officers had to look out the charts and work out their navigation and down in the Engine Room the mechanics were cleaning up the mess that had been left by the shipyard. The Second Engineer dressed himself very untidily and wasn't a particularly clean worker, but he had control of the Engine Room, and the Chief Engineer lived much of his time in his own cabin writing his reports. Robin did day work with one of the donkeymen and was given specific jobs of cleaning and repairing different machinery in rotation: for instance, opening up a pump and cleaning it out. One of the Senior Engineers would look inside the unit and give instructions as to which bits should be replaced.

Once the *Saldura* was south of the English Channel and through the Bay of Biscay and moving southwards towards the warmer weather of the Equator, the climate improved. The cargo ship in ballast had a very smooth passage to the Caribbean. A pilot came on board in Matanzas Bay and the Captain was shown where the anchorage should be. The vessel waited at anchor for two days before a berth was clear for *Saldura* to go into the harbour and then she moored alongside the quay. This was the sole berth in the harbour for a ship of this size and the cargo of sugar came forward and was loaded by the ship's own derricks into the holds. There was a gang of stevedores on board every morning who were nearly all of mixed blood and wore wonderful Spanish moustaches although they had black skins. Some of them were six foot and some only about five foot six but they were strong workmen who could quite easily take a bag of sugar on their shoulders and, with a quick jerk and twist of their torso, lay each bag in the position that it was to be stowed. They filled the hold up with layer on layer of bags towards the tween deck of the ship and stowed it as close as possible up to the roof. Then the tween deck would be closed off and the upper hold of the ship loaded as well.

As usual the Engine Room workers were asked to open up a part of the engine so that it could be inspected as part of the routine maintenance, on a schedule set by the Chief Engineer.

In the port of Matanzas it was possible for the ship's crew to go ashore in

Saldura: *the Officers' Mess with its three tables. Clean but bare of any*
pictures or decoration.

the evenings. On the esplanade they found a great parade of men and
women with rifles doing evening parades and drill. This was General
Castro's way of building up the morale of the nationalist country which
he'd taken over. The Americans had been chased out and their puppet
government replaced. The population did simple basic training as an Army
Cadet Corps, but here there were platoons of young ladies being drilled as
well as older men. Some of the people in the bars invited the Scots to come
home and see their houses and Robin talked to some of the English-
speaking young men and women who frequented the shops in Cuba. Many
of them, because of the American influence, spoke passable English and so
he learned their views on Fidel Castro and the new Government. He
discovered that the Catholic Church was still a big influence on the way of
life in Cuba and also that people who disagreed with Castro had mostly
gone across to live in Florida. The population that was left was on the
whole pro Castro but not communist.

The Americans had been building many hotels, so that Cuba could be a
tourist area for winter holidays for the American people. When Castro took
over he found that agriculture had been rather side-lined and because of the

American sanctions, Cubans had to grow more crops to feed themselves and find markets for cotton, sugar and tobacco. There were still tobacco factories and farms but the road network was not satisfactory and a lot of these recruits drilling on the esplanade were used by Castro to improve the roads throughout the island. The tourist industry was allowed to decline and some of the big hotel buildings were in fact used as schools. In the early days of Castro's power the teaching of the three R's spectacularly improved the population's ability to read and write. Young people were quite keen to go to evening classes because the Nationalist Movement had inspired quite a lot of enthusiasm.

The *Saldura* stayed ten days in Matanzas, loading part of her cargo, and because the water depth in the berth wasn't great enough, she had to move to another bay where more sugar cargo was brought out to the ship in barges. Dockers continued to load with the ship's own derricks and with visiting teams of labour.

When the vessel had finished loading, the Captain took Robin Salvesen with him ashore to meet the Agent who was an English-speaking gentleman of the old school who had owned his own business in the export of sugar in this remote small village. He had his warehouse and his gang of stevedores and barges and tugs to take the cargo from the farms to the ships. When Castro came into power this rather elderly man was told that his business had been nationalised and now belonged to the Government. He said, 'Well in that case it's time that I retired,' and a visiting officer came to interview him and told him very firmly that he should go on working in the business until he was told that he was infirm. If he was going to stop work he would retire to prison. So the best solution was for him to carry on. During dinner together in the restaurant the Ships' Agent talked about the conditions of life in Cuba and discussed the difference in the tally because the ship's officers were keeping a count of the cargo loaded while the exporters were keeping a count as well. There was some disparity between the two figures but the Captain agreed the figure with the Agent so the Bills of Lading and ship's documents were completed in accordance with the contract to carry 12,600 tonnes of cargo to China. All the documents being signed, the ship was able to sail and the *Saldura* proceeded on her journey.

The original Captain was worried by the journey and requested relief so the Chief Officer, Mr Walterson, took over as Captain at Port of Spain until Durban where the ship was joined by Captain Magnus Scott who took command for the rest of the trip. Magnus Scott was a man who Robin was to respect and admire; he later became one of the Salvesen Senior Masters.

Mr Walterson also was promoted to Captain and served with Christian Salvesen ships until he retired to Shetland and became a local authority Councillor.

The first leg of the journey was down to Port of Spain in Trinidad to pick up fuel and water for the voyage to Durban on the east coast of South Africa. The consumption of water was worrying the Captain somewhat and he imposed some rationing so the crew were not allowed to have fresh water baths. As they sailed through lovely tropical weather they could use salt water to wash while preserving fresh water for cooking and drinking. *Saldura* passed Cape Town within sight of the flat topped mountain and passed the 'Roaring Forties' in reasonable weather, a little bit choppy, but by no means bad conditions – and then up the coast to Durban.

It was very close to Christmas time when they arrived and were able to have one evening ashore which allowed Robin a walk on solid ground. Durban had virtually closed for the Christmas holidays and none of the restaurants and shops were open. The Durban people appeared to go to their country houses during the holiday period. *Saldura* moved on from Durban and the crew had special Christmas meals and some opportunities to socialise on board the ship. The Scottish cargo vessel was now moving north again towards hotter weather and higher humidity. The next port of call was Singapore. Here there was no opportunity to go ashore at all – the ship just called in, pipes were connected for fuel and water and so they continued up the China Sea towards Tsingtao.

It was during this trip that *Saldura* encountered the first real storm of the voyage and the seas were really mountainous, Robin had a small repair job right up on the deck above the bridge because during the wind and high sea some of the electrical wires up on this high deck had disconnected. Robin decided the best clothes to wear for this were his bathing shorts which surprised the whole crew. He knew he was going to get wet and it wasn't cold – just very wet. A day or two later they came across two or three American warships who obviously weren't too happy to see a cargo ship with the British flag moving up towards China breaking the sanctions on both Cuba and China. One of them had a bit of a game and tried to get the *Saldura* either to slow down or to change course and came closer and closer, crossing over in front of the bows of the *Saldura*. Captain Scott was shouting on the radio and through the microphone to the Captain of the American ship to 'Make way, make way – don't be so stupid – get out of the way – I'm not going to change course.' Eventually they moved away and left *Saldura* to her voyage in peace.

Captain Scott entered Chinese waters and halted several miles out of sight of land to wait until picked up by a pilot boat. *Saldura* was boarded, not only by the pilot but also by quite a few armed men who went up to the bridge and talked to the Captain while the pilot took over the control of the ship. All the navigation aids had to be turned off and the ship was told to follow the pilot boat very closely. Captain Scott was told that they were going through a minefield and navigation aids were shut off so the crew couldn't really remember what route the ship had followed and there were no buoys marking the minefield – if it existed; it might have been all a bluff. The pilot in fact made a bit of a boob and Captain Scott took over as *Saldura* was getting in towards the berth because he was quite certain that the ship was proceeding too fast – and with a heavy cargo of sugar would do damage, so he put the vessel full astern to slow the ship as she approached the berth. This was a prompt but correct action. The Port of Tsingtao was built rather like Liverpool and Dublin with huge big stone blocks (built by British engineers): a very significant and substantial harbour which would last for years. The *Saldura* discharged here with her own derricks to a huge variety of transport on the quay – anything from hand-drawn carts to railway trains. Some of the vehicles might have been running in the bush in Africa or have been trucks from the First World War. Robin and the rest of the crew were able to go ashore and walk through the town on the dirt roads. Tsingtao had a population of nearly three million but there were only three or four motorcars. It was not considered appropriate for any man to show himself to have more privilege or power – they were all meant to be equal as Communists. The Churches were abandoned and in a derelict condition. There was however a Seamen's Mission ashore where Robin and the other officers and ratings went – it was rather like a NAAFI and provided sausage, egg and chips and a glass of beer. The only other liquor that seemed to be available was a local peach brandy which was fairly alcoholic. In this building they showed films with British sub-titles; one was an adventure story in a Chinese village with Chinese nurses doing very good work and then terrorists came in to upset this calm atmosphere. The propaganda came through in that every ammunition box that the terrorists had was marked 'Made in USA' – (to remind/emphasise) that the USA was the enemy in Chinese terms in 1959 and 1960. Robin was able to buy a nice piece of Chinese silk for his wife.

The whole ship was searched when they got into China. Every man's cabin was inspected and every American magazine was taken ashore and burnt in front of them. Robin was very nearly arrested one evening. He was

Saldura *in the locks of a canal, showing the forecastle and forward deck.*

watching the sunset and idly drawing a little boat which was sailing down
the estuary – the way they had the sails rigged was quite unlike a British
yacht and in the sunset it was really very pretty. A hand fell on his shoulder.
'What are you doing, what's the significance of this picture?' and he was
taken to the Captain's cabin by the Army sentries and interviewed by an
officer who wanted to know why he was drawing this – it was very
significant that he had drawn the skyline. The sketch was taken away and
the Captain was really quite worried that Mr Salvesen might be arrested; it
is the sort of thing crew do not do in a foreign port with sentries on board
and Robin was very lucky just to be cautioned.

     After *Saldura* had been discharged in Tsingtao, the Captain was ordered
by telegram to go to Moji in Japan which was a nice little harbour and
village area. The ship was instructed to have grain shifting boards fitted
because she was going down to Australia to take a cargo of barley back to
Dublin and Liverpool. It was cheaper for *Saldura* to get the shifting boards

fitted in Japan rather than in Australia. So they stayed in Moji for three or four days while the shifting boards were put up and once again there was one evening when Robin and some of the officers could go ashore and have a walk round and a drink. The Japanese welcomed them into their shops with tremendous bows and offered a cup of tea just for being so good as to look at the goods on display – an honoured customer; what a different attitude to the staff in the big chain stores in the UK where no assistant will help you at all – Japanese shopkeepers were honoured by a customer.

It was decided that *Saldura* should next go into Bali to get bunkers for the ship. She arrived as evening was drawing in and sailed up this estuary with jungle on either side. The ship sailed gently and slowly taking soundings – and the Captain was hoping that he would be met by a pilot boat. She went further and further up the estuary with the jungle narrowing on either side of the ship and all the crew could see were little fishing boats here and there. Eventually a pilot boat came out, and the ship was guided to a pier and tied up to bollards on various rather shaky looking structures – with no road apparent, just a pier coming out of the jungle with a pipeline on it. None of the crew got ashore at Bali except the Captain; they never saw a town or the refinery which was over the brow of the hill but they did pump aboard the fuel oil and water to power the next leg of the voyage.

Saldura moved on from there to a lovely little town in West Australia called Geraldton, north of Perth, where she loaded a cargo of barley from big silos on the shore. This didn't take many days but everyone did have the opportunity of going ashore and there was one particular evening to remember – a Chinese dinner with the Ships' Agent's wife. Robin also went ashore on the Sunday to the Presbyterian Church, a very nice experience for a seaman – the only opportunity to worship God communally during a long voyage, apart from in his own cabin and in his own time with his own Bible. Geraldton was a lovely little town. *Saldura* then travelled to Fremantle to complete loading as the water depth in Geraldton wasn't enough to float a full cargo there. Fremantle is the Port of Perth – rather like Leith is the Port of Edinburgh. One of the officers who had been in Robin's Territorial battalion in Leith had emigrated to Australia – a Dr Haltane – and Robin was able to contact him and found that he knew the stevedore director. Dr Haltane and Robin had a car trip round Fremantle and Perth one evening. Robin was able to go to Perth many years later when the Drill Ship *Dalmahoy* operated in Western Australia drilling for oil north of Geraldton. He then spent about a week in a Perth hotel doing the ship's business for the drilling company. Perth has grown to a university city and buzzes with active young people.

For the voyage back from Perth towards Dublin, Captain Scott navigated across to the Suez Canal, arriving in the Red Sea in the lovely evening light – a slightly reddish tinge shining on the desert. The sand in the Red Sea area is a pinkish colour and in the evening sun it's no wonder that it was called the Red Sea because it is quite spectacularly red in the evening sunlight. Is it really a Sea of Reeds as one book suggests? Ships going up through the Suez Canal were congregated in little convoys going northward or southward to segregate traffic in the narrowest parts of the Canal. The *Saldura* joined one of the convoys and had pilots and the navigation lights lit. It appeared that the ship was going through very slowly. Next morning Robin took some of the fuel valves which he was cleaning up onto the deck of the ship to sit in the sunlight and see the camels walk through the desert sand.

Saldura was destined next to go to Greece. Merchant ships going round the world pick up fuel at the best possible price and there was a fuelling depot in Greece which was able to provide her with relatively cheap fuel. The laden cargo ship went into a bay in a Greek island which looked as if it was surrounded by high mountains – almost like a volcanic bowl. In this sheltered water a barge came out to supply the fuel. The diesel engines drove her on through the Mediterranean in very pleasant weather but having passed Gibraltar the vessel met the rougher seas that were the Bay of Biscay and Irish Channel. *Saldura* berthed in Dublin and discharged a large part of the cargo to the granaries (no doubt to make the best Guinness from malted barley) – and then on to Liverpool to discharge the remaining part of the grain cargo at a silo there. Robin was then discharged from the ship and able to go home, having been at sea from October until April, and was home in time to see his first daughter born in Edinburgh.

There were two incidents eight or ten years later in Robin Salvesen's career as a Director in the shipping office which show the worth of experience at sea and knowing that the ship's Captain's life is a fairly lonely one. The first was to do with the small Norwegian ships which traded between Norway, and Scotland and England. The ships phoned in before nine thirty in the morning to speak to the Operations Department and then the Crew Department and Engineers' Department: a very quick call, five or ten minutes, when the office could tell the ship about the next part of the voyage and the ship's Master could tell the office if he needed any supplies or change of crew or had questions. With eight ships reporting in before nine thirty, it was quite a busy time. Anyway, a ship arrived in the Port of Preston and for a couple of days the telephone call to the office was done by the Chief Officer and not by the Captain. Robin Salvesen twigged that there was something strange going on, so he specifically asked the Ships' Agent to go down to the ship and see the Master and talk to him. The report came back in a very confidential way, not wanting to let the ship's crew down. When the agents were asked pointblank if the Master was ill, they said they thought he probably ought to see a doctor. The ship had then to sail round to Ellesmere to load a coke cargo at the mouth of the Manchester Ship Canal with a pilot on board from Preston. When the ship got there, one of the office staff from Salvesen's head office in Leith was there to meet it, and he discovered that the Captain had been in his cabin during the voyage and the pilot and the Chief Officer had taken the ship round. So Robin had to relieve the Captain and get him medical attention and a long holiday. This Captain had mental depression and when he went back to sea, it was as Chief Officer on one of the small ships to see how he'd get on. His confidence didn't return at all quickly, but he had a lot of experience and served out several years more.

The second incident was to do with a Sal class ship, sister ship to *Saldura*, trading round the world – Transatlantic at the time. The nearest point to Britain on this particular voyage was Casablanca and a very senior officer was Captain of this particular 13,000 tonne ship. Robin Salvesen was reading between the lines from the letters he was getting from the Captain and felt that something was wrong and he and Captain Phillip the marine superintendent journeyed out to Casablanca to visit the ship. They arrived there a day before the ship was due and had dinner at a very nice seafood restaurant, very near the lighthouse, and then returned to rooms on the fourteenth floor of their hotel. When Robin woke up it was still dark but he felt he was on board a ship because there was a shakiness as if the ship's engine was vibrating. When he heard a car horn outside he realised this wasn't a ship at all. The lights were turned off, car horns were blowing outside the window; the whole room was shaking and the pictures on the wall were shaking. This was a full-scale earthquake in Casablanca. 'What do you do fourteen storeys up with the electricity off? – do you run downstairs and expect the whole hotel to fall down on top of you? – or do you stay where you are and put on some clothes?' Anyway it calmed down, so Robin thought that he should stay where he was. The next morning Robin discovered that the local people had all gone outside and spent the rest of the night out in the park because they had learnt from the experience of

The 'Sal' class 13,000 ton deep sea fleet had six sister ships often chartered to liner companies and trading worldwide. Crew had accommodation in the stern block as well as amidships.

exactly seven years before that the second shock of a major earthquake is very often more violent than the first one. A day later the ship came in to harbour and the ship's crew reported that during the night they had felt vibrations as if the ship was going aground; they looked at the chart and they knew they were in deep water and couldn't understand this shock wave that had hit the ship. Nearly half an hour elapsed and then a great tidal wave came through and the ship was in a very stormy patch of sea with high waves for a moment or two. The tidal wave had taken much longer to get to the ship's position than the shock wave from the earthquake.

Robin and Captain Phillip visited the Salvesen Senior Captain on his ship in Casablanca and found that he was in fact quite distressed so his relief was organised. The sixth sense had been absolutely right – the tone of the letters that were coming from the Captain had given the office a warning that he was unwell and needed a rest. Captain Phillip organised his relief and this spell of leave enabled the Master to return to work for a further spell of duty.

CHAPTER 8

Coastal Shipping

IN 1963 AN opportunity arose for Christian Salvesen and Company to purchase a Leith based coastal shipping company, A.F. Henry & Macgregor. Robin was working with Hans Hostvedt in the Norwegian department at that time. He lived in Longniddry and almost opposite his cousin Maxwell Harper-Gow (the Chairman) who had his home there as well. Sharing a car on the way back from a grouse shoot, Maxwell started to talk to Robin about the opportunity to work in coastal shipping. He suggested that Robin should work with Willy Ireland, the Director and Chairman of A.F. Henry & Macgregor, for a year to get to understand the business and then take over as the Director in charge when Willy Ireland retired.

Now William Ireland was a character. He was nearly eighty years old. He went to the office each morning in a chauffeur driven car. (He was a widower with a son who was quite a formidable lawyer in Aberdeen.) Willy Ireland had worked in shipping most of his life and had been with A.F. Henry & Macgregor through the both World Wars. This company had close connections with the London & Edinburgh Shipping Company which operated between Dundee and Leith and traded down to London. The coastal shipping part of the business was the bit that was left in 1963. Much of the business of coastal shipping was done through personal relationships such as with Fred Everard, whose family company owned some eighty ships including coastal tankers and many cargo ships. Stephenson Clark was another major power in the coastal shipping field who carried much of the coal for the Electricity Board, with 4000 ton ships carrying coal from the north of England down to London and the power stations in the south. The other major contact that Willy Ireland had developed was with Blue Circle Cement – the CMC. He worked with Charringtons, the coal distributing company who were the main opposition to Stephenson Clark. When his colleagues came from London to visit Edinburgh he would arrange to have lunch with them, very often at Bruntsfield Golf Club where he was a member. He also went up to Shetland and Orkney on an annual trip to fish for trout. He had a business and personal relationship with the builders merchant companies in Orkney which purchased cement from the CMC.

Henry & Macgregor was a small and compact management company. The Contract and Operations department was managed by two men plus a boy. Edwin Davis was the man in charge. Robin initially sat at a desk there with him listening how he fixed the ships and operated the business and was given work doing estimates for the next voyage, settling the bills each day to keep the accounts straight. When any ship was loaded in Scotland he would receive tallies of how much was loaded in the holds. He would have to make out the Freight Contracts and Bills of Lading and tabulate the correct figures for these important legal documents. In the Accounts Department the Company Secretary ruled with one man running the payroll and another running the trading accounts – so there was a small team of three. The Superintendent's Department was headed up by Captain Jack Phillip, the Deck Superintendent, who was to become quite a close friend of Robin Salvesen and worked with him for several years to come. The Engine Superintendent was Mr Alan Benham.

The permanent crew and officers of Henry & Macgregor were supplemented during holiday time by people drawn from the British Shipping Federation. The Shipping Federation office was very close to Henry & Macgregor's office which was near the Customs' House in Leith; men looking for a job could walk round the corner and get an interview.

One further department in Henry & Macgregor was the Agency Department – this was run by Mr Brown with a boy who acted as water clerk who took the mail on a bicycle or on his feet to the various ships and conveyed the Master up to the office to discuss ship's business.

Henry & Macgregor was looking after quite a few ships coming in to discharge or load in Leith and Granton, much the same kind of business as Christian Salvesen along the road, having contacts with some of the major coastal shipping companies and being appointed Agent in Leith and Granton for them. In 1963/64 Henry & Macgregor would be working a six day week – finishing at mid-day on the Saturday. Everyone, the whole staff, would be in Monday to Friday and on Saturday mornings.

The routine started in the morning with phone calls from each of the ships to the Operations Department first and then to the Superintendents. There was a two-way conversation, the ships telling their arrival time at the next port and stating whether they needed any crew changes, reporting the amount of fuel bunkers they had on board and all the other various requirements they might have. The Operations Department would tell the ship what the next voyage and cargo was likely to be and confirm the orders (that they had) given out for suppliers to the ship. The Captains of the ships would then speak to the Superintendents to arrange repairs, maintenance and crew issues.

Henry & Macgregor operated Scottish Cement Distribution for CMC. There were Builders' Merchants and Agents in many of the ports, Lerwick, Wick, Thurso and Grangemouth, and all the cement coming to Scotland would come up by ship; the warehouses were topped up under the control of A.F. Henry & Macgregor. There was a routine 12 noon telephone call between the Sales Directors of CMC in London and Henry & Macgregor to report the state of stock at the various ports and arrange for ships and cargoes to top up the supplies. Often the Builders' Merchants were persuaded to purchase a sufficient tonnage to match the capacity available in the *Dunnet Head* and timed for her next voyage.

Henry & Macgregor kept two small ships, the *St Abb's Head* and the *Dunnet Head* busy from month to month carrying cement cargoes northward from the Thames and very often getting cargoes of stone to take south from a little harbour at Inverkeithing close to the Forth Road and Rail Bridges. They also owned bigger ships for bulk cargoes such as coal, grain or timber – the *Cantick Head* which was able to carry 2,100 tons, the *Kinnaird Head* which carried 2,800 tons and the *Marwick Head*, which had been built by Henry Robb in Leith, which carried a cargo of 2,200 tons. The *Marwick Head* had been intended to be smaller but Henry Robb's had made some design miscalculations. This had the disadvantage that she had to carry a Radio Officer and therefore an extra Cook Steward as well. Her two extra crew made the operating costs more than *Cantick Head*. Willy Ireland had a concept that ships ought to carry multiples of 700 tons, the sort of amount which he reckoned that a gang of stevedores could load or discharge from a ship in a day and so the *Cantick Head* had been built as 2,100 tons. Nothing was worse, in his mind, than a ship at the end of the day having one or two hundred tons left and having to stay overnight, wasting a day when she could be sailing to get her next cargo loaded.

Willy Ireland had met Harold Elly in the Central Electricity Generating Board and he worked with him and Charringtons. They had an annual meeting just before Christmas where they worked out any claims between the two companies and discussed how much they would pay to settle the claim. Rumour had it that quite often after they had had their dinner and their drinks, Willy Ireland would say, 'Well, you know, it's a thousand pounds here or there between us – what about I'll toss you for it,' or, 'You paid last year so I'll pay this,' and come to a conclusion that way. They also regularly saw Eddie Milburn who was the Sales Director of the National

Cantick Head *could carry a full deck cargo of timber and discharge with her own derricks.*

Coal Board based in an office at Washington near Newcastle. It was very important for coastal shipping that the trains of coal were at the loading port at the right time so the shipowner could order up the number of dockers and the stevedores to load cargo when the ship arrived, so it was also important to have a good relationship with the National Coal Board. Eddie Milburn became a close friend of Robin Salvesen and they would go with Charrington representatives to the rugby matches at Murrayfield and Twickenham and have lunch, watch the match and then have dinner together on the days when the major matches were played between Scotland and England.

Gordon Bainbridge followed his father as the Director in charge and owner of Anthony & Bainbridge in Newcastle and his father was a long-time friend of Willy Ireland. Anthony & Bainbridge had good connections with timber brokers covering Russia and Scandinavia and found cargoes for distribution in the North of England. They ran a Ships' Agency company in Newcastle and worked for Henry & Macgregor when their ships were in the area. The ship broking department would be used to try and build up a cargo for the *Cantick Head* or the *Marwick Head* to bring timber from Scandinavia and sometimes even from Russia. Robin remembers a cargo of

Small ships at work in Europe. Timber cargoes to UK ports were a regular feature of Christian Salvesen and H.F. Henry & Macgregor trade.

pit props for Methil and several fixtures of boards and battens for the construction industry in Sunderland or Newcastle. In London the firm of Sidney Cater was the main connection in getting grain cargoes. Each summer grain would be coming into Europe from Australia and the mills and granaries in the various ports often took a transhipment part cargo from the bigger ships discharging in Amsterdam. Sidney Cater used to do the ship broking, bringing the parties together to do that trade. Henry & Macgregor had arranged for their ships to bring in silver sand from the Continent to the glassmaking industry at Alloa near Grangemouth where the stevedoring company, George Palmer, would handle the discharge.

Christian Salvesen used different agents in many of the ports. Christian and Mr Andorsen were relations and business partners in the London firm Andorsen Becker, which later became a wholly owned subsidiary of Christian Salvesen & Co. In Grangemouth Iver Salvesen created Rankine & Salvesen which was a company fifty per cent owned by George Gibson's and fifty per cent by Christian Salvesen. Henry & Macgregor however would use J.T. Salvesen in Grangemouth, the firm created by Christian Salvesen's brother. So the two companies had different connections in the various ports. A.F. Henry & Macgregor was a member of the Chamber of

Shipping and Willy Ireland used to attend their coastal shipping committee where he would meet up with all the main coastal companies.

In 1963, coastal shipping rates were controlled by a 'price fixing' agreement – it was a chamber of shipping tariff and said to be for the benefit of both the cargo shippers and the shipowners. The books with these tariffs in them were freely available and circulated. The Institute of Chartered Shipbrokers' Tariff controlled the agency fees in the ports round the coast of Britain so when ships were moving up and down the coast, the owners of the ships need not argue the rates of charging with the agents because these were fixed figures which had been agreed from year to year. Much the same was happening at the Shipping Federation which was basically owned by the shipowners; it had offices in the various ports which kept a register of people who wished to work on a ship, issuing each crew member with a paybook which was stamped with the ship's name and signed by the Master and he got a reference, just a simple 'very good' or 'good' when he discharged from a ship. So when companies were hiring a man to fill a vacancy as a seaman, the clerk would ask to see his seaman's book. Willy Ireland introduced Robin Salvesen to a wide range of the people in the Chamber of Shipping, the Shipping Federation and in the Baltic Exchange in London. A.F. Henry & Macgregor had connections not only with Sidney Cater who did the grain chartering in London, but with brokers who arranged for the purchase and sale of ships.

In the local area round the Firth of Forth the Leith Shipowners Association met monthly to discuss the relationship of the shipowners with the Harbour Authorities at Grangemouth and Leith, and also at Methil and Kirkcaldy. From time to time there were disputes between the shipowners and the Harbour Authorities. Each port provided tugs and boatmen for bringing the ships in and the scale of pay for these subsidiary services was negotiated year on year between the shipowners and the companies that provided the manpower for these jobs. Robin Salvesen used to go with Willy Ireland to attend the meetings. When his name was proposed for joining the Executive Committee of the Association, he was elected by only one or two votes, as there was some opposition to his appointment.

Very often Everard ships would come in with bagged cement cargoes to fill up the warehouse in Leith which was operated by Henry & Macgregor with a foreman and staff of three men. It always appeared to be very dirty and dusty but it was only walking distance from Henry Macgregor's office beside the Custom House.

Robin hadn't worked for very long in Henry & Macgregor when he started talking about a project of building a new ship for the company and trying to work out the best technology to use in such a vessel. The Salvesen Norwegian line ships (1500 ton) used the ARPA type of steering (automatic steering machinery) so that the officer in charge in the wheelhouse could set the course of the ship at a certain compass bearing and didn't need to have an able seaman holding the wheel the whole time. Automation helped to use men's time and skill more effectively. One of the concepts for the new ship was to introduce a bridge controlled engine so that the navigator wouldn't have to ring a telegraph for a man in the Engine Room to do the speed controls on the engine. So one of the discussions Robin had with the shipbuilders was to investigate different kinds of bridge control and choose a system which was effective and safe. The other concept that had to be borne in mind was to get the biggest cargo carrying capacity possible for a ship which had a gross tonnage of 1599. There was a very good naval architect at Clelland's yard in Newcastle and the owner of the yard was a wonderful character, Kenneth Craggs. Another innovation was a self-tensioning winch. Normally, when the ship was in harbour, a watch keeper was employed and had to keep an eye on the ship all the time to let out the ropes as the tide went out. Robin Salvesen had some interesting sessions with Captain Jack Phillip about the choice of deck machinery for the *Rattray Head* and it was decided to purchase hydraulic winches and derricks. Then Captain Phillip showed Robin the bridge layout for an ideal ship with almost all-round vision so that the Captain could see right along the length of the side of the ship as she was being brought into port. *Rattray Head*'s design incorporated several of these new ideas and the shipbuilders quoted a price. Then for the first time in his life Robin Salvesen had to go to a Salvesen Board Meeting to present the project, to indicate the price and how much money that ship would earn in a normal trading year – and therefore the return on the investment which the company could expect. The price offered by the shipbuilders was deemed to be too great by the Board. Robin was given authority to go into a final discussion with the shipbuilders and to tell them that the authority he had from the Board to buy the ship was about ten per cent less than the price that they had quoted. The reduced terms were accepted and the contract was signed.

Robin Salvesen and Captain Phillip discussed with the shipyard the actual fitting out of the accommodation for the crew on the ships and the colour schemes of the carpets and curtains and they both agreed that a committee of two was a good way to operate these kinds of decisions. They were looking for the best quality they could get for the money. They always chose a carpet which had some design and some variety of colours so that stains wouldn't be so noticeable. They also chose loose covers for chairs in material that could be washed. There wasn't a bathroom or a shower in each man's cabin but a shower between two cabins was arranged. For the first time in a British coaster every man on the ship whatever his rank had his own cabin.

Kenneth Craggs and Robin Salvesen had a discussion about the launching ceremony of the *Rattray Head*. The normal shipbuilders' practice was to have the launching in the morning and then go to the Station Hotel in Newcastle to have lunch together with a large number of guests of a business nature; at the end of the meal they would sing various Scottish and North of England songs together before they broke up to go home. This was the shipbuilders' party, but Robin decided that the shipowners would meet and entertain the shipbuilders in the hotel for a dinner the night before the launch as well.

He particularly asked Harold Salvesen, a retired Chairman of Christian Salvesen and Company, to attend this launching party in Newcastle. So the night before the launch Robin Salvesen entertained Kenneth Craggs, the design engineer and various shipyard representatives and there was a large table of about thirty people in a private room in the hotel; a set meal had been ordered and dinner commenced. At the end of the first course Kenneth Craggs asked Harold Salvesen about his experience in the Antarctic and whaling and shipping during wartime. From that moment on Harold Salvesen entertained the whole of the table who were spellbound listening to him describing the events of his life, the people he had met, and the reasons why various political decisions had been taken. He had had a vast experience in the political and business scene – and had been manager and operator in the British whaling industry, visiting the Antarctic nine times. Many of the whale catchers had been built in the Newcastle and Sunderland area so many guests had seen the models and the ships themselves. It was the most amazing evening and this one man was speaking and the whole table of guests were listening spellbound.

When Willy Ireland retired, Robin had to visit London every month. The coastal shipping tariff rates were coming to an end, partly because of competition from foreign ships but also because many of the shipowners were fixing their vessels on private contracts with the bigger companies like British Steel and the Electricity Board. Tariffs were banned in the United States of America and the British legal system was beginning to look very carefully at this concept as well. The agreement between the shipowners and the agents for fixing a schedule of agency fees lasted for much longer but even it was broken for regular business. Stephenson Clark owned offices in Newcastle, Sunderland and the Thames and were putting ships into their own company's offices. Salvesen's had an arrangement in Aberdeen and Grangemouth and many other parts.

Captain Phillip and Robin Salvesen made it a normal practice to go to Newcastle or Grangemouth and to visit ships which came to a nearby ports. As a courtesy they met the Captain first and asked him to show them round the ship. A tour would first look at the deck machinery and the standard of the chipping and painting and would walk from the bow over the decks. The ship was nearly always loading cargo or discharging, so they would talk about the working of the ship and meet some of the bosuns and able seamen. The Chief Engineer showed the Engine Room, just to see the cleanliness of the ship and how the men got on with each other and whether the ship was a happy place. Then the Stewards would give the normal service and they shared the same meal which would be given to the crew. Nearly always these visits gave Robin new information about the ships and the coastal trade.

It became standard practice for Henry & Macgregor Ships Masters and Chief Officers to take the exams to get Pilot Exemption Certificates, especially in the Thames Estuary but also in the Firths of Forth and Tyne. Ships Officers who had pilot exemption reduced the charge for bringing the ship into port, and in fact under statute the Captain and Master of the ship is responsible for his ship in every circumstance and a pilot is only there as an adviser. Robin had personally seen Masters countermanding the pilot's instructions when he thought a ship was going too fast, because a Master would know his own ship and the response speed of the engine. The pilotage exams are very strict and require detailed study of the depth, tides and dry marks.

One of the next events in the Henry & Macgregor office was the effect of a seamen's strike. There had always been difficulties with the stevedores and dock labour in ports over pay or conditions. When a shipowner put a ship in port he wanted to get its cargo of coal or timber discharged as quickly as possible, so the work of the Operations Department in the office was to make sure that enough railway wagons came alongside so that the cargo could be discharged promptly, or there was enough quay space for timber. Before Henry & Macgregor put a ship into a granary to discharge a cargo of barley, the office clerk would check with the Harbour Authorities as to whether there was space. The profit in trading coastal ships was closely related to the number of voyages which each ship competed in the year and it was essential to keep the ship moving from port to port.

On the whole the Henry & Macgregor coastal shipping crews were really very content with their rate of pay and the fact that they could at almost any time sign off to go home for a holiday or a family wedding. The ships were in and out of port, and as crews were small the men could talk to the Captains and be able to make arrangements. However, negotiations between the Shipping Federation and the Chamber of Shipping determined the rates of pay not only for coastal shipping personnel but also for the big container ships and deep sea vessels which traded overseas. Crews signed on for two years at a time and could only be released from their ship when the ship came back to Europe. The rates of pay became a major dispute between the Shipping Federation and the Seamen's Unions. It wasn't just the conditions of service or the food and the accommodation, but the Unions saw that inflation was moving ahead in the United Kingdom and were looking for more adequate pensions and more adequate rates of pay, and felt that the only answer was to strike. All coastal shipping was brought to a halt – every ship that came into British ports was picketed and the crew, whether they wanted to go to sea or not, were 'got at' by the pickets. Edwin Davis, in the Operations Department of Henry & Macgregor, found that he had no work to do. All his ships were very quickly brought to a halt. The little coastal ships, the *St Abbs Head* and the *Dunnet Head*, were caught in harbour almost immediately. Warehouses were getting more empty as the tradesmen were selling their cement for the building trade and it was not possible to replace it in the sheds. In England, the strike was being broken by lorries taking cement from place to place, but no-one was going to drive lorryloads of cement all the way up to Dundee and Grangemouth. The national dispute brought the fleet to a halt and the company and their men had to wait until central negotiations between the Shipping Federation and the Union moved forward. Life in an office at that time when no work could be done was very difficult.

Robin Salvesen had started going to the Firth of Forth or Leith Shipowners Association meetings and met Roderick McLeod who was a Ben Line Director and one of the Scottish representatives in the Shipping Federation. It was very impressive how quickly his mind worked, especially when it came to rates of pay and anything financial – like a walking computer. Robin also met from the North of Scotland Shipping Company a man called Rex Lewis who attended the Shipping Federation Office and the Leith Shipowners; his company was eventually taken over by P & O but at that stage in the sixties, he was running the ships which carried passengers, cargo and cars between Shetland, Aberdeen and Leith. These ships brought the cattle and sheep, in the appropriate season, for sale to the markets on the mainland. So there was quite a variety of knowledge and different trades within the organisation. The Gibson ships traded a liner service between Leith and Grangemouth and Amsterdam and Antwerp, whereas the Currie Line vessels were trading between UK and Hamburg and Bremen. Currie Line had ships going into Liverpool on the west and to Leith and Grangemouth on the east coast and also a service down to Portugal and Spain which brought wood pulp and timber products to the UK – and oak staves from Spain for making barrels in Leith for the whisky. James Currie was a bit older than Robin Salvesen but he was the next generation of management in the Currie Line and Robin and Sari Salvesen met James and Pamela Currie – both socially and at business meetings in the port.

As time went on the Leith Shipowners Organisation required to send a new representative to attend meetings at the Chamber of Shipping and Robin Salvesen was selected to represent Scottish shipowners there. At the same time Max Harper-Gow decided it was time that he stopped being the Salvesen representative on Lloyds Register of Shipping; he said to Robin, 'You know, this really is the best Club in London – you will meet the Shipowners and the Insurance Companies and Shipbuilders – they have a meeting, then they have lunch together, and you will get to meet quite a large number of people with shipping interests. It is a very good way of networking and building up the range of people you know in the shipping field.' So Robin became a representative to attend the Scottish Committee in Glasgow and the General Committee in London. Lloyds Register classifies ships hulls and engines as safe in design and operation.

A.F. Henry & Macgregor had been members of a Freight Demurrage and Defence Club – the British Steamship Short Trades Association – which had their headquarters in a lawyer's office in Newcastle – Bottrell Roche & Temperley. Robin had been very interested in ship's hull and cargo claims and had done some work on this aspect of shipping, earlier. He had never however worked on the demurrage, freight and defence side of the law of shipping. At the meetings of the British Steamship Short Trades Association many of the coastal and short sea owners met with the lawyers to discuss disputes between shipowners and cargo owners about damage that had taken place and about the short loading of ships or the quality of fuel. There were a whole range of claims which hadn't been in Robin's experience. Willy Ireland and Robin compared notes and listened to reports of cases which changed the law as new events took place. Lawyers would test the wording of a Contract against the events that had taken place, and work out who should be liable for a financial loss. Sometimes very large sums of money were involved. The F D & D Club also got involved in disputes on the sale and purchase of vessels. All this experience and knowledge has to accumulate in the head of a shipowner so that when he comes to discuss a contract for building a new ship, or the terms of the Bills of Lading or the contract to carry cargo in a ship from one country to another, he can influence the terms of contract. In due course Robin Salvesen became the Chairman of the British Steamship Short Trades Association and he learned from these lawyers in Botterell Roche & Temperley, amongst others, very much of his knowledge of the law and practice of running shipping.

Charringtons who were involved in coal distribution, and later in oil distribution in some parts of England, were competing with Stephenson Clark and the Powell Duffron Group. Charringtons had contracts to supply coal to the big new power stations in the London area. They had indeed built their own ship, MV *Sir John Charrington*, powered by coal, as they were in the coal trade. The modern diesel ship proved more efficient than the coal burners. The Henry & Macgregor ships were often chartered by Charringtons and from time to time Charringtons had the opportunity to arrange cargoes for the Henry & Macgregor ships for the power stations in the south. The Stephenson Clark ships, which were carrying nearly 4,000 tons of coal rather than the 2,000 tons of the Henry & Macgregor ships, were profitable at a lower freight tariff. The relationship between Charringtons and Willy Ireland enabled Robin Salvesen to be introduced to this industry which was new for him. He would have lunch with the Charringtons and the Coal Board representatives and talk about the coal trade. Robin put forward his ideas about the new design of the *Rattray Head* and what could be done in making the coal trade more efficient. As the years went by this developed into an idea of buying a second-hand ship, which would carry 5,000 tons and be slightly bigger than the Stephenson Clark ships and therefore competitive. He and Jack Phillip investigated the length and beam and draft of ships which could go into the Newcastle and Sunderland loading ports and discharge at the power stations in London. They discussed a second-hand ship which was on the market at the time, and whether this ship could be used in the coal trade and whether the Electricity Board would take her on charter for that purpose. A proposal to purchase this ship went to the Christian Salvesen Directors who immediately said, 'Have you thought about a new building – with the

Investment Grants available from the Government at the moment, it's tax efficient for Salvesen's to use the free-depreciation allowances from profits in other businesses and the company as a whole will pay less tax. So go away and think again, but think about a new building of the right kind of ship for this particular trade and see how the figures stack up.'

This project developed in the design and building of two ships – the *Dunvegan Head* and the *Duncansby Head*. A shipbuilding yard at Arnhem was looking for work at that time. This yard had a good design engineer who was very willing to talk about this special ship. Jack Phillip and Robin Salvesen provided the dimensions and Schweepswelf De Hoop proposed a ship which could carry over 6,000 tons of cargo, would have single cabins for all the crew and have a bridge controlled engine and self-tensioning winches, but with no cargo gear at all. Robin Salvesen discussed with Harold Elly in the Electricity Board the sort of price he would need for transferring coal from the north, how many voyages there would be per year, and worked out how much the Electricity Board would pay for the freight for shipping coal from Newcastle to London on a ship of these dimensions. The project identified a case to save the Electricity Board quite a lot of money by using a bigger ship and even more if they could use the ship for a large number of voyages in a year. If the ship could be loaded sixty times a year instead of forty-five, the profitability for Henry & Macgregor went up significantly. So Robin got an agreement with the Electricity Board that if he built a ship of this kind they would give him first refusal on cargoes. This negotiation resulted in the building of the *Dunvegan Head*. The Wortleboer family who owned the de Hoop yard became quite good friends during this period with Robin and Sari Salvesen.

It was a tradition in Christian Salvesen that one of the Directors' wives would be asked to launch a ship so when *Dunvegan Head* came ready, Robin put it to the Board that the wife of G.P.S. McPherson (who was a non-Executive Director of the Company) might be asked to do the job and be Godmother to the ship. G.P.S. McPherson had been an impressive centre three-quarter who had played for Scotland against England in the Calcutta Cup Matches before the Second World War. After the War he became a Director of Kleinwort Benson and was a Merchant Banker in London. His sister was the wife of Mr Kittermaster who had been the Headmaster of Cargilfield School when Robin Salvesen was there. Peter, his son, had been a Director of the Ben Line and had joined the Salvesen Board. So Peter Kittermaster and Sheila his wife were invited to the launch as well – which made the whole thing a family party. Sari and Robin flew to Amsterdam and were picked up by a car and taken to the Rhine Hotel, a lovely building right on the River Rhine with the ships, barges and tugs coming past the window; the river was busy and ships were passing all night. The night before the launch the Salvesen party had dinner with members of the Wortleboer family who owned the shipbuilding yard. The Wortleboers suggested smoked eel should be the first course. Sari enjoyed it and wondered whether she could take some home. The following morning Sari found a package of eels lying beside her cases ready to go home with her. The Wortleboer family had already purchased some eels for her to take back to Scotland. This was the sort of relationship between the Dutch shipbuilding yard and the Scottish shipowners. Grandfather Wortleboer was still alive and he had been the owner of the yard throughout the whole war. Robert, the Marketing Director, had married into a family who owned a cigar-making firm, so was also involved with his wife's family cigar-making business. Hans, the older brother, started smoking cigars at 7 o'clock in the morning, almost before he'd had his cup of coffee and breakfast, and was always to be seen with a cigar either lit or unlit in his mouth; he looked after the finance side. Mr Neinhuis, the Operations Director of the shipbuilding yard, was the man with whom Robin Salvesen had developed the contract.

When the *Dunvegan Head* was launched across the stream of the river it looked as if the ship would hit the bank at the other side of the Rhine – but as the bottle was thrown and the ship began to move gently down the slipway gathering speed, then without hitting the far bank, she swung herself in the current, bows upstream, stern downstream, the tugs took control of the bow ropes and there she was – swinging under the control of the tugs in the mainstream of the Rhine. There were great cheers from everybody who watched this performance and the ship bowed nicely to all as she entered the water. After the launch came the speeches and G.P.S. McPherson on behalf of his wife thanked the shipbuilding yard for the work in building the ship; Robin Salvesen made his speech, saying that, of course, at the launch the ship was only half finished and he hoped the shipbuilding yard would finish the job and she would be a profitable ship. It was a very happy occasion and the two families had a very good dinner afterwards.

Robin made frequent visits to the ships. The coastal ships were quite often close to home – at Newcastle, Grangemouth, Methil or Sunderland – and it was quite easy to travel by car to visit the ports. It was very good for the development of business to spend time with the agents and get to know more about coastal cargo movements. Some of the agents were also charterers and involved with bringing cargoes into the ports, either from abroad or on coastal trips. Visiting the ships made Robin wish to go to sea again. It was rarely possible to plan a trip with coastal ships because they might be delayed by the stevedores or by the weather. However, there was one occasion when he took the train from Edinburgh to Newcastle and did a voyage south with the *Rattray Head* with a coal cargo to its discharging station in the Thames. At this time Captain Grant was the master of the *Rattray Head* and she was loading at Jarrow Staithes. Jarrow is above the bridges and upstream of the Newcastle city centre.

Captain James Grant was the Senior Master with A.F. Henry and Macgregor, who enjoyed the opportunity to use his navigating skills by taking a ship abroad sometimes, but he also had to travel frequently to the Thames and Tyne to validate his Pilot Exemption Certificates. These were always difficult tests conducted by the pilots on the detail of the tides and buoys and day marks. A certificate could lapse if pilotage acts were not frequently undertaken. Captain Grant was a superb ambassador when he visited foreign countries and had the knack of making good working relationships by his smile, handshake, and the honest skill in knowing his job.

Robin met him in the afternoon and they went together onto the bridge wing to watch the progress of the loading operation. A train of railway wagons was marshalled and brought forward by a shunting engine to the tipple. Each wagon was lifted and tipped so that the coal spilled out as the side doors opened – pouring cargo into the ship's hold with dust and noise. *Rattray Head* was built with wide holds and small overhangs from the deck. She had been built to qualify as a self trimmer. The operator of the tipple could direct the flow of coal to fill the ship's holds evenly, which helped to keep the ship on a level and also meant that the work of the stevedore trimmers was reduced to a short spell to flatten the top of the coal pile and thus let the Macgregor hatch covers close when each hold was full.

Loading work finished in the late afternoon and the tide was high enough for *Rattray Head* to leave the quay without delay. She was moored with her head upstream and so had to turn as she left the berth. Captain Grant had discussed the manoeuvre with his chief officer and bosun and so the mooring wires had been rigged appropriately, with bow and stern lines, as well as a spring. Captain Grant controlled the operation from the bridge and the bosun, second mate and mate took their stations at the stern and bow ropes, releasing them. The main engine was run slowly astern and the spring wire took the strain, forcing a lever action to bring the bow away from the quay. Some flow from the River Tyne helped as the bow swung out and the ship's turn was completed as the engines moved ahead. The ship was free to sail downstream to pass under the Newcastle bridges and the shipbuilding and repair yards on both north and south banks. *Rattray Head* followed the Fred Olsen passenger and car ferry through the breakwaters but then swung southwards to pick up her course down the English coast.

Captain Grant handed over the bridge to the second mate and took Robin to the Mess Room for tea. There was a choice of hot or cold meat with tea and toast. Coastal ships have the advantage of a regular supply of fresh vegetables and bread and milk. There was one galley on *Rattray Head* providing both officers and ratings with the same choice at their meals. Captain Grant and Robin both enjoyed the evening sail from the bridge and watched the navigating officer check his position regularly with the radar and with the landmarks ashore. There were several passing ships and also fishing boats working in the inshore areas. The pre-determined course had been marked in pencil by a line on the chart but each half hour approximately a cross and a time were added to show the actual progress of the ship. Adjustments could be made to take account of the tidal drift as the vessel made progress on her voyage. During this watch, the bridge party listened to the weather forecast and identified some of the other ships sailing north. There were some interesting messages on the radio as ships were passing calls to give their arrival and departure times.

In the morning, Robin had plenty of time to tour the ship and he spent some of it in the engine room where the noise of both the main engine and the generator were steady and loud. There were separators working to clean the lubricating oil and re-circulate it round the moving parts of the main cylinders. On the bridge, a radio message had confirmed the available berth at West Thurrock Power Station. Robin knew that Henry and Macgregor had a contract with Thames Boatmen who would come out by boat to meet the ship and handle the ropes to moor her. They brought their own radio to call out staff at the appropriate arrival time. Captain Grant was a gentleman of the old school. He had been a Master Mariner and had worked his way up from a junior officer.

The ship came into the power station in the Thames at West Thurrock and was moored in an empty berth waiting for another ship to complete its discharge. Then she was winched along the quay on the ropes between the ship and the quay and took her position under the crane. The driver of the crane was high above the ship and could look down and see what the crane was doing – it was very efficient, for they could pick up the cargo scoop by scoop and swing it ashore, open the crane's jaws and drop the cargo into a reception tank where it filtered by gravity onto the conveyor belts to the pile where it was to be stored. The Superintendent of the power station came on board to have coffee with Captain Grant and met Robin Salvesen. They had a discussion and he invited him to have a look around the power station before going up to London for some meetings.

During the 1970s a lot of industrial action was taking place in the docks and quite often there were strikes for very little cause. Often a whole port would come out on strike in sympathy with a dispute on one ship with one particular cargo; very often these strikes would spread to neighbouring ports and the action could develop to the whole country overnight. It seemed likely that the coal miners were going to come on strike at some stage. Robin Salvesen started discussions with the Trade Unions and the Shipping Federation about the possibility of taking the Radio Officers off the *Kinnaird Head* and the *Marwick Head* because with the new equipment fitted and good voice reception there really was no need for them. To remain competitive, these ships needed to reduce their crew wage costs. The discussions with the Trade Unions got completely bogged down and there was a very clear threat that the Henry & Macgregor ships would be black-balled and would not be able to sail. This was a risk so Robin at one of his regular meetings with the Electricity Board Purchasing Department discussed in detail the way in which he could perhaps reduce the cost of carrying coal to the Thames in these ships if he could reduce the crew. The Electricity Board didn't wish to support Henry & Macgregor and risk a strike which could spread to other coastal ships which were filling up their power station stockyards, especially as there was a likelihood that a miners' strike might occur either the next winter or the year after. They were very anxious to separate a seamen's strike from the dock strike and a miners' strike. It's much easier to handle one at a time. So Robin Salvesen was reluctantly persuaded that he should defer any confrontation and discussion about Radio Officers. Very shortly after this, however, the whole design and manning levels of the *Dunvegan Head* was to be discussed. The bridge controlled engine and bridge controlled ballast might gain the ship an Unmanned Engine Room Certificate, with alarm systems set on the various pressures and temperatures in the Engine Room so that the Captain and engineers would be alerted if there was potentially any trouble. This would enable the engineers on the ship to concentrate on daywork and planned maintenance, rather than keeping statutory watches, so potentially the ship would be able to operate with one engineer fewer. These much more

Troup Head *shortly before launching. She was launched sideways into the water of the canal alongside. A splendid sight!*

important manning arrangements were on the Agenda to raise with the Department of Trade and the Trade Unions. The ships were busy building stockpiles of coal before the expected winter miners' strike.

Discussions took place with the Nautical Colleges at that time because many ships, not only the coastal ships, were getting more automation. It was also thought a good idea to train an engineer to identify faults and conduct simple repairs to the electronics. A programme of new courses at the Nautical Colleges was implemented. Leith Nautical College was one of many which started conducting Electronic Engineers Courses and it became possible for the Radio Officers on the coastal ships to get an electronics qualification. Captain Phillip and Robin Salvesen between them worked out an approved manning scale in discussion with the British Shipping Federation and the Department of Trade, which allowed the new ship *Dunvegan Head* to go to sea with three engineers and a donkeyman in the Engine Room, without a Radio Officer. One of the engineers would be an Electronics Engineer who would be able to do repairs and maintenance to the radio and in the Engine Room. *Dunvegan Head* (at 6,900 tons), a much larger ship than the *Kinnaird Head* (2,800 tons), would go to sea with a crew that was much the same size. This proposal was not opposed by the Trade Unions.

Quite a long time later a signal came through to the office early in the morning that Peter Mellors, who had been the Purchasing Director of the Electricity Board, had been arrested during the night. This caused grunts of amazement and the Agents in Charringtons and other offices who knew Peter Mellors very well were all surprised. Robin Salvesen was asked to go to be interviewed by the Police in London to discuss the relationship between Henry & Macgregor and the Electricity Board. So Robin Salvesen spent an afternoon with Douglas Horsburgh looking through the diaries to see the dates when they'd met and discussed contracts with Peter Mellors which stretched over a matter of five to seven years and they briefed themselves for the sort of questions the Police might ask. Robin decided that Douglas Horsburgh should go with him as a witness. They were taken into a small interview room and two policemen on the other side of the table started asking a series of questions: 'How often they had given Peter Mellors dinner' and 'Whether they had given him other presents' and 'Why had they taken him across to Holland for the launch of the *Dunvegan Head*'. They were able to say that this was a routine thing, that if a charterer was taking on a ship he should inspect the ship and talk about it. Anyway, the Police made notes of places and times and then at the end of the interview the policeman said to each of them separately, 'Is there is anything else you would like to tell us at this stage?' and they said, 'No, I think we've answered all your questions.' 'Is there any other evidence you would like to give us at this stage?' and Robin said, 'No, thank you very much for our meeting – perhaps we should get home.' So that was the end of that and nothing more was heard about it but it was still a huge surprise that the Police seemed to search for evidence that a misdemeanour had been taking place within the Electricity Board.

It is interesting in retrospect to review the extent of thought and action which was actually improving the conditions of the staff on board the ships.

Ships had during this period developed nicely designed cabins with very little difference between the quality of the accommodation used by the ratings and the officers and the petty officers on board the ships. The Captain and Chief Engineer had to bring on board several people to do the ship's business – so they needed a day room as an office. Watch keeping hours were reduced by the unmanned engine with its alarm systems. Watch keeping in port was reduced by the self tensioning winches.

Discussions took place at this time as to whether ships should have a bar on board. In the coastal ships, the men went ashore if they wanted a drink of an evening because there was nearly always a night at the loading or the discharging port. The Henry & Macgregor ships mostly had a Scottish crew and there really wasn't time for them to go ashore or spend a night at home when vessels were loading cargoes in the northern ports. So agreement was made that the crew would get two leave spells a year and would have some additional leave to compensate them for not being able to get home. Deep sea shipowners were providing pensions for their Senior Officers (the Shell Pension Scheme for instance was a very good one) – so it was necessary for the coastal shipowners to compete in some way even though many seamen were very keen to get a job on coasters rather than sign on for two year articles and go to Africa and Australia and China and ports abroad. At least if they were on the coast they were near to their home and their family and men could sign off for a wedding or a funeral quite easily.

Business relationships were also developed by Robin with the Electricity Board and with various charterers in Amsterdam and in London to work the ships during the summer season when there wasn't so much coal being shipped. The Henry & Macgregor ships would load pulp sometimes in south Norway for Grangemouth or Newcastle, or they would load a timber cargo at Leningrad perhaps for Methil or Preston and so the business developed a growing fleet overseas as well as at home. It was however the relationship with the Electricity Board which grew over the time – by reducing the costs of running the ship, carrying a larger cargo with a smaller number of men, making use of the new technology available. The cost of transhipping coal from the North East Coast to the Thames was going down by quite significant figures as the bigger ships were used.

Robin Salvesen was also involved in reducing the cost of shipbuilding by using his contacts in Europe and in Japan to find shipbuilders who would be able to build a modern ship at a competitive cost. He built ships in Newcastle, Arnhem and Groningen and then at a yard in the inland sea of Japan, and used these in Northern Europe.

CHAPTER 9

Ships' Agency

IN THE SUMMER MONTHS of 1960, the year that Robin was to marry Sari Clarke in August, he worked at Walter Runciman's office in Newcastle for two or three months. Runciman's was one of the North of England shipowners which had grown up from the end of the eighteenth century and was a leader of the industry in the Chamber of Shipping, having moved from the coal trade into worldwide cargo ships on the great sea routes of the world. The Runciman family pictures sit in the Chamber of Shipping.

The coal trade grew to feed London in the south and the chimneys of all the houses in Great Britain were smoking, fed with coal fires. Tons of coal were being shipped from the North East down to the Thames and other towns and indeed all over the British Empire. Runciman's was one of the exporters of coal from the North East together with other big names in the area: Common Brothers, Souters, Hargreaves. Stephenson Clarke which was eventually to become part of the Powell Duffron Group had a very large number of ships under their management. Dalgliesh was still a company and Ropner's were trading. Coal was still being loaded at Jarrow, small ships were loading at Dunstan Staithes above the bridges in Newcastle. Newcastle was also a major shipbuilding and repair area with yards at Middle Dock. South Shields was used for the whale factory ships by Christian Salvesen. Swan Hunter on the north side of the Tyne built big ships; Clelland Shipbuilders made smaller ships – and there were several other yards up and down the Tyne. There were huge timber yards with stacks of timber coming in from Scandinavia, lying on the quayside at the end of each summer period – as well as cargoes coming in from Leningrad and the White Sea. Bulk carriers also came into Newcastle bringing iron ore to the big discharging terminal near Jarrow. Newcastle was of course built on the riverbanks with very steep streets running down from the Castle and the Cathedral to the quaysides down below. The high level railway and road bridges allowed ships to go up the river above the bridges but only the smaller coasters could use these quays in 1960 – most of the ships stayed down at the lower end inside the very big breakwater. The Castle was largely demolished to enable the railway to run into the centre of the town.

The Runciman office had quite a modest entrance in one of the steep streets running down on the north bank towards the quayside. During this period Robin lived in a boarding house at Tynemouth – right down the coast at the seaside, a holiday place. He took the bus into Newcastle to work each day. He started as a Water Clerk – going to visit the ships in the Port and taking money and mail to the ships' Masters. This is of course a grand way to discover the local geography of the Port and Harbour, and Robin was sometimes sent out to find his way to a ship down on the south bank of the Tyne. He could travel there by the railway and then walk through the dark streets to the quayside and on board to see the Master, very often having in his coat pockets quite a lot of money for the Master and crew of the ship.

When a ship is fixed for a foreign port the owners of the ship will appoint an Agent to look after the ship's affairs. His first job is to negotiate with the Port Authority for a berth for the ship and sheds for the cargo. The receivers quite often have pre-paid but this isn't always the case; sometimes the cash for the cargo and for its carriage have to be paid before the Agent allows delivery of the goods to the owner who presents his Bills of Lading. Letters came from the various receivers asking for the cargo to be delivered either to train or to lorry or to be laid on the quayside or in a warehouse for distribution later. The Ship Master phones or sends a telegram from the sea to give an estimated time of arrival and the Agent arranges to employ the necessary pilot and tugs as required, and then appoints the stevedores and dockers gangs so that all the cargo can be tallied and discharged from the ship. Cargo is always tallied out of the ship by the dockers so that there is a signed statement of how much cargo has been delivered against the cargo manifest – a list of the goods and names of the owners of packages carried on the ship – a useful paper for the Agent to complete for the payments which have been made for the cargo and its freight. The receivers present a Bill of Lading to the cargo Agents in order to clarify their legal title to the goods. Each day, each ship's Master travels from the ship to the Ships' Agent's office where they get help to solve problems and organise doctors for any men who are ill, or hire engineers and radio mechanics for repairs to the ship. The men going on holiday have to have their travel arrangements fixed up so that they can get to their home port. The Master has to visit the Customs and the Port Office to arrange clearance papers before the ship can sail again. Robin, as the Water Clerk, helped to manage under instruction much of this activity in the area of Newcastle.

He assisted in the loading of a vessel for Cuba. It had a huge variety of

Fairtry II. *Christian Salvesen & Co. developed a factory stern trawler. Robin Salvesen worked on this ship on a voyage from Glasgow to fish off Newfoundland and Greenland bringing the cargo of cod fillets and halibut to Grimsby.*

goods – from sewing needles to pumps and machinery – because Castro was already in control in Cuba and the United States had put up sanction barriers so there was no trade between the United States and Cuba. In 1960 many European countries however were still trading and keen to supply goods to Cuba. The ship had a Spanish flag and a Spanish Master, which was quite sensible because the main language in Cuba is Spanish. Anyway the ship was advertised and cargo came forward to go into the dock warehouse and the office built up a manifest of goods; Robin was involved in the office, taking these orders and building up the manifest with the names of the owners of the cargo and a record of how much had been paid for the cargo and for the freight. The manifest would record the receivers in Cuba so that when the ship arrived Bills of Lading would be presented at the discharging port without delay.

This summer was full at weekends for Robin because he had to travel either from Newcastle down to Kent to see his fiancée or else home to his mother's house at Bonnington where there was a lot of work to do in opening wedding presents and making lists of the thank you letters. When he went down to Brenchley for the weekend with Sari, he arranged a hotel for the family to live at over the wedding period at Tunbridge Wells and started to plan what he was going to say in his bridegroom speech. He

visited, with Sari, the church in Brenchley and had a meeting with the
priest who was going to take the service – for bans had to be read in the
church for several weeks prior to a wedding.

On 5 August Robin enjoyed a family dinner in the hotel and next day
went on to the church to go in with the best man to wait for Sari to come in
her procession with the bridesmaids in their pink dresses. After the
wedding, Robin and Sari were able to walk back on a lovely sunny day
across the village green from the church to the family home and the
marquee that was in the garden there for the reception. The villagers, who
knew Sari well, were there to greet her and cheer her (she sang in the
church choir); she and her sister used to ride round on bicycles and they
knew the local people.

After Robin and Sari left the reception they drove down to Windsor for
their first night, and then they flew to the South of France for ten days
before going to Edinburgh where Robin had to be involved in his sister
Hilary's wedding only a fortnight after his own – and to make a speech
there because Iver Salvesen had died and although John was giving Hilary
away, the lot had fallen on Robin to make the speech. This honeymoon in
the South of France was near both the bridge at Avignon and Arles so there
was some gentle sightseeing for the young married pair. There was
sunshine on the beach and good food, including new tastes of such things
as sea snails which were quite delicious and served beautifully in the hotel.
In southern France there were clear signs of the Roman occupation, big
arenas for bull fights and indeed some of the semi wild white cattle bred on
the salt pans near Nîmes where there was good feeding in the summertime.

Sari and Robin returned to stay in Edinburgh and enjoyed grouse
shooting at the end of August and during September at the weekends.
Robin worked daily in Grangemouth at Rankine & Salvesen's office to get
to know the work of the Ships' Agent there. This meant a morning drive
from the Braid Hills via Bo'ness and South Queensferry up the River
Forth, very much the same route which Christian Salvesen would have
followed on his horse from 1850 to 1890 when, every week, he went to visit
his elder brother to talk about their mutual business. Dan Miller was the
Executive Director in charge of Rankine & Salvesen – a company which not
only did Ships' Agency for outside companies, but which worked for
George Gibson's of Leith. Christian Salvesen & Co operated a rather less
frequent service between Grangemouth and West Norway jointly with
Ellerman Wilson Line; Wilson's finding cargo for the ships in Hull and
Rankine & Salvesen finding the export cargoes from the Grangemouth area.

The Salvesen ships loaded both in Hull and Grangemouth for West Norway where the ships usually stopped at Bergen and Trondheim. Rankine & Salvesen hired warehouses beside their office and there was very often whisky in the bond in the warehouses ready for export to the Low Countries, and also hams which had been imported by the Gibson ships. There was quite a bit of pilferage taking place, so Agents arranged for the whisky to be carried in sealed containers and taken directly from the distillery warehouse to the ship.

There were frequent dockers' disputes and sudden strikes in Grangemouth. The dockers thought up all kinds of reasons for looking for extra money and there was an unhelpful attitude between the dock workers and the employers at that time. One day there was a cargo of toilet seats being loaded by the manufacturer in the port and the dockers threatened a strike because they wanted embarrassment money; they 'didn't want to go home,' they said and 'tell their wives that they had been loading lavatories.' Very often it was clear that the dockers worked slowly during the afternoon to force the owners to pay them a couple of hours overtime between 5 p.m. and 7 p.m. in order to finish the ship and let her sail. If the shipowner and Agents agreed to an overtime payment, the ship actually finished its cargo loading by about ten minutes past five. A few owners were firm and prepared to sail the ship short of fifty tonnes on board rather than pay overtime. They could take the cargo across to Norway and back again if necessary rather than pay the dock workers blackmail.

The Salvesen ships loading in Grangemouth for West Norway carried cargoes such as treacle or second-hand tractors or fire bricks from the Stein factories near Polmont and fireclay moulds for ingots, because in Norway factories were both making aluminium and smelting iron. The clay moulds from the United Kingdom came from Workington to Grangemouth for transhipment up to Moirana in the north of Norway for the steelmaking plant there.

In the sixties, Gibson's were pressing the Port Authority to invest in container cranes at both Leith and Grangemouth for their service to Amsterdam and Antwerp and in due course this took place and Grangemouth in particular developed as a container port.

Robin went to sea again in October 1960 but he was back in Ships' Agency work again on 1 January 1962, when he was sent to work in Liverpool – a firm called Henry Tyrer & Company – a ridiculous starting day because the Liverpool people celebrate a Scottish New Year and don't work on New Year's Day. However, it was a day to find his way to the office and meet some of the people. Robin and Sari hired a house for a year at Neston in Cheshire fairly near to Sari's cousins, the Fletchers. Ferelith was crawling and learning to walk and they often carried her between Scotland and England, sleeping in a carrycot in the car. They really had quite a nice time as for the first time in their married life they were going to be together for a whole year and living in one place. Robin's Aunty B – Burrell – also lived on the Birkenhead side of the river so Robin had his own relations not too far away. Robin travelled from Neston into Liverpool, either by train in the morning, Sari taking him to the station, or else he would take the bus to Birkenhead and go across on the ferry to Liverpool and climb the hill at the other side to the office which was quite near Liverpool Station. He was once again a shipping clerk, working with a team of four people because Henry Tyrer had many different kinds of ships coming to Liverpool. Again he would go to the ships with cash and mail and take the ships' Masters back in the car or a taxi to the office to conduct their ship's business.

Henry Tyrer was a private company, the Senior Partner being a Mr Cutts who was over eighty – but a wise gentleman who was in the office every day. Robin reported to Mr Cutts on many occasions and was helped to learn the business. But Robin normally reported to Mr Harrison, who was the next Senior Director in the Company. Tyrers owned their own stevedoring company and also had subsidiary offices in Manchester and Preston so Robin visited ships at many of the Ports and Harbours and berths in the whole of the Liverpool area. Robin also managed to visit Salvesen ships which came in to load coke at Garston, Preston or in the Manchester Ship Canal for export to Norway. These ships also discharged cargoes of pulp and timber both at Preston and Manchester. Tyrers were Agents for the Ben Line whose ships came in from the Far East to their berth at Birkenhead. They also dealt with the Indian Steam Navigation Company which had regular ships coming in from India with cargoes including tea and memorial stones. They looked after the Currie Line vessels which were loading in Liverpool for Hamburg and Bremen. These very small ships went into a dock very close to the ferry terminal down in the centre of Liverpool itself. They also dealt with the Bowater ships which were brilliantly maintained – almost like passenger liners. Bowater's had their own factory in Ellesmere Port, just at the west end of the Manchester Ship Canal, and they brought in Canadian pulp for making into paper. Once Robin and a colleague went see a Bowater ship and found that the Captain was entertaining a business passenger for the journey across to Canada and they were invited to enjoy lunch at the Captain's table on the ship: quite an extraordinarily good meal was served by stewards. In the Port of Liverpool there were timber ships coming in from Russia and elsewhere leaving stacked timber lying on the quayside. There were also grain ships coming in to the granaries from Australia.

Preston is quite a long way north from Liverpool and is situated on the Ribble. Ships' Captains have to be very careful of the tide and must come in when the tide is high. The port was a big square area, well built in stone, used by small ships which imported timber and pulp cargoes from Scandinavia and exported coke. Preston also had a regular service going out to Ireland. It was an alternative and rather cheaper route to use rather than Liverpool or Manchester, and there was a better supply of labour for the ship which gave a quicker turn round. Preston was used by the small Salvesen ships of 1500 tonnes. It was an opportunity for Robin to go and see the office at Preston and just spend a day talking about the Christian Salvesen trade.

Robin was taken to one of the mid-day meetings between the Port Authority and the stevedores to discuss the programme for the next few days. The Port Authority would allocate berths for the ships and indicate the priority for labour gangs for the various ships. There was usually a priority for the liner ships such as Currie Line and the Ben Line steamers which had to try to sail on schedule, over the bids for gangs for ships carrying cargo such as timber and pulp which came in on an infrequent basis.

Robin was then given the opportunity of working in the Accounts Department in Henry Tyrer to learn about the disbursement accounts which had to be sent to the owners after each ship's visit. The extent of each ship's disbursement account varied both with the cargo it was carrying and also with the length of time it was in port, but at each visit the ship would require pilots, boatmen and tugs. There would be a requirement for money up-front from the companies who weren't regular customers, although the big ship companies like Ben Line or Currie Line would have a current account with Henry Tyrer and a monthly schedule of payments to bring the cash float up to a reasonable level. Then there were all sorts of extras involved: the cost of the stevedores and port charges and telephones and mail, as well as working out the agency fee itself which was based upon the Institute of Chartered Ship Brokers' scale. To calculate the ships disbursement accounts Henry Tyrer had a check-list to go through to make sure their staff hadn't missed out a doctor's bill or some other account for stores or repairs or fuel which had been delivered. The disbursement account would always be submitted to Mr Cutts himself to have a look at before it was sent out to the shipowner and every now and again he pinpointed something that either had been missed out or needed to be amended: a very astute gentleman, Mr Cutts.

The various shipping companies would come and visit their ships in the Port of Liverpool. Ben Line's superintendents would visit the crew and talk to the officers about the next job and what their ambitions were, perhaps going to Nautical College and getting another ticket. They could talk to the crew about their own personal problems. Various shipowners would talk to Mr Cutts in his office and they would usually then go out to lunch together. Foreign visitors would stay overnight in a hotel and see a little bit of Liverpool and Merseyside while they were in the area.

Then came an opportunity for Robin Salvesen when one of the men in Henry Tyrer's office went ill and Robin was asked to take over the Claims Desk, which looked after cargo claims, shortages and disputes, because Henry Tyrer used to do quite a lot of this work on behalf of Ben Line and Indian Steamship Navigation and often for companies involved in the timber cargo as well. Wherever a report of a shortage or damage to cargo occurred, Robin would have to do the initial negotiation with the insurance companies to minimise the cost to the shipowner – and very often proposed settlements for these disputed amounts of money rather than going to a law court to sort out the problem. For instance, if a ship carrying a cargo of timber went through a period of very bad weather and thought the ship might have lost some of the deck cargo, the ship's Master would go to a Notary Public in the Port and 'note protest', which meant signing a form to indicate that at the time the ship first arrived in port he had recognised that there potentially was a damage claim. This of course is treated as strong evidence in a court of law at a later time. The Agent could encourage a ship's Master to take this action. When cargo claims came in a clerk would acknowledge the letter and start investigating whether the claim was a real one, or tried to find out what evidence there was, and whether the person claiming the damage or loss had evidence to support his claim. A shipowner had to look at both sides of the story and some claims took quite a long time to settle. Timber claims were particularly difficult because at the time of the discharge of the ship, the dockers were taking a tally of the cargo discharged. This gave some guidance as to whether there was a major claim or not. Timber claims were usually for shortage rather than for damage but claims on cargoes such as tea or the memorial stones coming in on the Indian ships quite often were to do with damage to the goods, perhaps by pollution or staining, rather than actual loss. Imagine soap and tea being next to each other in the hold and the smell or taste pollution of one cargo with the other! Owners got a letter of complaint and had to collect the evidence to see if there was any responsibility. Normally speaking the shipowner would initially deny responsibility for the claim and wait for the insurance company or the cargo receiver to justify the complaint he had made. Robin took quite an interest in this because it seemed to be a particular skill – he had to apply the brain a little bit to work out how to present his client's case as well as possible. In nearly every case the initial figure and claim for damage would be reduced quite substantially during the course of a negotiation.

One or two major incidents took place during the course of this year. One particular ship had a fire on board and her main cargo was a whole lot of hides which had been damaged by salt water as well as by the fire itself. This cargo was discharged in Liverpool by the dockers who wanted special money for dealing with such a dirty cargo. As the cargo dried out, the hides started cracking during the warm weather as they sat in the shed. This was a major accident and 'general average' was declared, the principle of which dates from early Roman law where every voyage is regarded as an adventure and the risk on the voyage is shared, not only by the ship but by the owners of all the cargo. In trying to minimise the amount of damage which was going on to the hides in the warehouse, Robin was quite anxious that he should identify who owned which parts of the cargo so that he could deliver the least damaged cargo to its owner as soon as possible. It is however necessary when 'general average' is set up to put financial values on all the cargo so that average can be declared amicably and accurately on the loss that each owner has suffered. So when the underwriters came to talk to Robin and Henry Tyrer they said, 'You really cannot hurry these things. You've got to be quite meticulous and before delivering goods to anyone we've got to get proper valuations of it and a bond from the owners to declare that they will pay their share of the costs at the end of the day.' They would say, 'You've not been in the game very long, young man, but you'll learn that you have to have a bit of patience in handling these particular claims.'

Another interesting incident happened at this time. A ship was discharging in Liverpool and the owners had decided to sell it to ship breakers, so the registration of the ship had to be cancelled. As Ships' Agent for the owner Robin had to go to the Customs and Excise and the Department of Transport to declare that this British ship should be taken off the Register because she was going to be broken up. In the format that needed to be signed there was this lovely phrase that should be signed by the ship's 'husband' (or the 'managing owner' of the ship). So Robin had to make a declaration on behalf of the managing owner that the ship wouldn't trade again. Then the ship went to the ship breaker's yard and the numbers were stripped off the main beam of the ship and the ship no longer registered as a British vessel. A rather nice little conversation took place between Robin and his wife Sari that evening about this title of ship's 'husband' – which really describes a shipowner who sends his ship to faraway countries without much in the way of communications but who is still being relied upon by the crew to look after their wages and food, to fuel the engines and to carry out the repairs, deliver stores, and indeed look after the ship in every way. The managing owner is in fact caring for and looking after the ship as a husband would a wife.

The Fletchers were very kind to Robin and Sari while they were staying at Neston and invited them to dinner and introduced them to various people (of their own age) who lived in the area. Willie Fletcher invited Robin to go shooting with him on the marshes on the Ribble Estuary. Very early in the morning they went out to hide in the sand dunes, and hope that they would get geese coming in off the river or ducks going in the opposite direction to the sea. The waiting men had to look inshore as well as out to sea and hoped to see the duck or the geese flying low overhead and have a shot. Willie Fletcher also invited Robin during the winter to shoot wild pigeons in the north of Wales. A whole big area of this countryside was manned by men who each chose a position in the various woods to get the pigeons flighting into the trees in the evening. They had a man in every wood and the pigeons couldn't settle to roost so they would have to circle again and try and land somewhere else. If every wood was manned then the chances were that guns would take the opportunity to shoot at several pigeons during the last half hour of daylight. This was a very successful evening out and Robin came back with seven pigeons, one of the better totals.

Robin and Sari went north to Scotland in August and September 1962 and met the rest of the family and had some time grouse shooting. They left Neston before Christmas time, to go to their new house at Longniddry where Alice was eventually born on Christmas Day. It was a long and happy day because Sari had been able to enjoy the Christmas party with the family and told Robin at tea-time that she thought she ought to go into hospital – and before Robin's relations had finished their dinner Alice had been born.

Robin Salvesen worked for the next two years in ship operating departments and then, as a director of Henry & Macgregor, re-gained responsibility for a Ships' Agent and ship owning business.

Later when Mr Brown was due to retire from Henry & Macgregor as head of the Ships' Agency side of that firm in Leith, Robin decided to merge the two Leith agency departments together. Robert Clarkson, the Salvesen agency manager, would take over as the director responsible for agency work. Henry & Macgregor's agency looked after many of the Everard ships and the smaller coasters and a certain number of foreign owners who nominated as Agents A.F. Henry & Macgregor. The grain broker Sydney Cater would appoint Henry & Macgregor as the agent to look after not only the ship but the cargo too when the ship was coming into Leith. Sometimes Robert Clarkson, Douglas Horsburgh and Robin Salvesen would have lunch together in Leith – in the same way as Robin's father had regularly had a table booked in Crawford's Restaurant. The younger generation used to go to other places – sometimes down towards Newhaven to quite a nice little hotel with reasonable food at a reasonable price, but on other occasions to have lunch on the *Dolphin* Training Ship. The *Dolphin* was managed by Leith Nautical College and was not only a residence for some of the young cadets but also offered training courses for school leavers who were going to become ship's cooks and stewards. Once a week the *Dolphin* served lunch and shipping clerks would eat food that had been cooked by the students and teachers and pay half a normal shop price.

After Robert Clarkson had taken over the management of the Ships' Agency there were opportunities possibly to purchase or merge with either Gibson's or the Currie Line. (Runcimans in fact took over both Gibson's and Currie's and finished up by concentrating the Head Office in Glasgow, so reducing the Leith work in the Currie Line and the Gibson office.) Robin decided that this was not the way he saw the development of Christian Salvesen but later on, in order to limit the cost but also to maintain an agency presence in the Firth of Forth, he proposed the creation of Furness and Salvesen, a fifty-fifty company owned by the Furness Withy Group and Christian Salvesen. Furness Withy were very keen to have a Scottish arm to do forwarding work for their various cargo lines – mostly ships to South American ports from the United Kingdom. So the company of Furness and Salvesen was to look after Ships' Agency and forwarding in Scotland on behalf of the two owning companies. They purchased a transport company called Haig's who operated from Bellshill and for a number of years tried to develop container traffic to Europe. Haig hired the containers and shipped them to destinations in Europe. It was very difficult to get a return cargo for the containers so the management of containers that you'd dispatched abroad was quite complicated. Managers tended to lose track of where they were and so the profit was eroded by the length of the hire period. Haig's went on developing their own local distribution business in the Bellshill area which was profitable and in due course the family bought the company back again.

Furness and Salvesen did get involved with North Sea Oil and managed to get a remunerative contact handling the casing of pipes. Quite a lot of the pipelines between the North Sea oilfields to the mainland had metal pipes put in concrete to hold the pipe on the sea floor. Oil flowing through the pipe reduced the average weight of the pipe system. Leith was a centre for this work in the Firth of Forth area. Furness and Salvesen were involved in importing the pipe and re-exporting it after it had been cased with concrete. Christian Salvesen also had a whisky business exporting to the Swedish wine monopoly. Each year the Swedish wine monopoly personnel wanted to come to Scotland to visit distilleries. Bruce Weatherstone and Bob Clarkson used to go round with them building a programme for the shipments.

There was one good occasion when Robert Clarkson and Robin went to Sweden to talk to the Monarch Line directors whose ships were regularly sailing from Grangemouth and Leith to Gothenberg about moving the whisky on the special size of pallet which the Swedish wine monopoly wanted to use in their underground storage. This storage pallet was smaller than that normally used in the United Kingdom industry. The Monarch Line wanted a different rate of freight to carry the small pallets. Later on business developed for blending and exporting the whisky in bulk from Leith. The raw whisky had to be diluted with water in a very controlled manner in order to bring it down to a strength which was palatable and not too strong for the consumer. Later small ships fitted as wine tankers to carry French wine to North Africa were used for whisky from the Port of Leith to Sweden.

The business of Ships' Agency in the Firth of Forth became less profitable after Forth Ports operated the stevedoring company. Forth Ports since then developed a much more vertically integrated business – by owning tugs themselves to look after the terminal near the Forth Bridge.

Robin got the timing right in buying the controlling interest in John Cook & Son before North Sea oil really developed in 1972. He formed a Board with himself and Bruce Weatherstone, together with Ramsay Pirie and Daniel Stroud – who were shareholders and part owners of John Cook & Son. Ramsay Pirie was related to the Cook family who had been the original owners and Danny Stroud had been the senior manager under Mr Repper at the time of the sale. John Cook & Son owned what effectively was the stevedoring monopoly in the Port of Aberdeen. Cook's did a deal with the P & O company who had regular ships trading to the islands in the north; P & O had three regular gangs, which had special rates and who used their labour to man the ships but also to work in the shore warehouses. John Cook & Son looked after all the other ships that came into the port, providing stevedoring labour force for them.

When North Sea oil supply boats started coming in, there was a need in Aberdeen for a twenty-four hour service and the Aberdeen Harbour Authority opened up the port entrance so that the harbour once again became tidal.

As more and more supply boats came in, the Institute of Chartered Ship Brokers rate for that size of ship just couldn't apply so John Cook & Son quoted a rate for agency work and for stevedoring on the supply boats which gave the company a reasonable return while encouraging major oil companies to use Aberdeen. The company managed to keep the labour force working on flexible terms and the dockers joined a permanent Register replacing casual employment. From that time on, Robin paid regular visits to Aberdeen (about four to six times a year). Very often he would take the train from Waverley Station early in the morning and return the same day on the evening train, which served a very good high tea with the most superb fresh fish and chips on British Rail! As was typical in the shipowning world in those days, managers travelled at weekends and the evening so that they completed all their office work in the daytime. Robin was involved with the Port of Aberdeen in the 70s decade and during development of the American Oil Club in Aberdeen and bidding for contracts from the Americans in the early days of the North Sea oil boom. He was able to persuade Christian Salvesen to invest in the building of an office block, Salvesen Tower, in the Port of Aberdeen – but before it was finally completed Sir Gerald Elliott decided to reduce the capital in property and arranged a partial sale to an institution for a high percentage of the ownership of the office block. The problem later on was how to sell a minority share in an office block.

During the North Sea oil period John Cook & Son had really quite a 'paper factory' of disbursement accounts for supply boats, for up to ten supply boats each day visited the harbour. These generated over three hundred disbursement accounts for owners each month – including invoices for pilots and repairs and all the other eventualities of individual ship visits. It became necessary therefore for John Cook & Son to introduce one of the early computer systems into their office; one of the Salvesen accountants did a very good job in setting it up.

Robin could not arrange licences to operate mobile telephones in the ports to manage a business of this kind. It seems so strange nowadays, when every young person has a mobile telephone, that a port business was unable to get licences to operate business. It would have been so much more easy in the 1970s if the Water Clerks could have reported back on a mobile telephone to the office, instead of having to travel up and down the dockside or else perhaps use a public telephone on the quay. The police objected to private and company mobile phones in case they interfered with the police and emergency services.

John Cook & Son had a problem at this time when competitors started to give gifts to their agents and customers to get special attention. Robin would not allow any staff to accept gifts; and told the customers that the annual staff dinner with a prize draw would welcome raffle gifts. This became quite a talking point in the Aberdeen scene and selected customers and guests were invited to the Aberdeen staff dinner where the prize draw very often included enormous cuddly teddy bears and nice boxes of chocolates and things, rather than the customary cases of whisky. Other companies in Aberdeen at the time were giving annual entrance to a golf club or a set of golf clubs to their American oil field customers in order to get the business from them.

There is of course no doubt that operating, as a young man, as a Ships' Agent in a variety of ports is the most magnificent training for someone who is ultimately to be an owner of ships because he knows in a hands-on way all the nitty gritty of the ups and downs of operating ships and the delays that can occur if some of the cargo doesn't come forward, or a train of coal gets lost, or a doctor is required for a member of crew – all these multitudes of problems which can happen to a ship when she's in harbour. Owners have to appreciate the problems of a Captain of a ship in a foreign port miles away from his home and away from normal communications, perhaps in China or Bali or West Africa, standing on his own and having to look after his ship and crew without relying on assistance from some boffin in Head Office who probably doesn't know the answer anyway. So it was very good training for Robin.

CHAPTER 10

Leith Nautical College

FROM 1965 RIGHT THROUGH to 1985 and beyond Robin was involved with the Dolphin Society and then Leith Nautical College and concerned with nautical education because after all as a Director of a shipping company he was employing Deck and Engine Room ratings and officers.

Robin was working at Bernard Street in Leith when he was asked to join the Dolphin Society as a Trustee. The Dolphin Society owned the training ship *Dolphin*, a wooden sailing ship with a copper bottom which had sailed down to Australia and around the world in her early days. She then became the first submarine mother ship as a hulk in the Thames, an accommodation vessel for early submarines. Later again she was bought by the Dolphin Society and moored in the enclosed harbour in Leith Docks, a dock very close to the new Scottish Office building. On one side were the warehouses for storing whisky; on the other side were the enclosed docks, no longer used by commercial shipping but a very good area for the training of cadets in rowing boats and life saving drills.

Boys from the Shetlands aged sixteen would live on board TS *Dolphin* in wooden cabins and learn their early skills before they went to sea for the first time on merchant ships. There was a resident member of staff who kept the peace and lived on board overnight – this duty being changed from time to time. The galley was equipped for training courses for young cooks and stewards. The Captain in charge of *Dolphin* at that time was Captain Ireland – who ran the pre-sea training of the Nautical College but went on to become a Navigating Instructor and Head of Department in England before returning to Glasgow Nautical College as Principal. He had a very distinguished career. While he was in charge of *Dolphin* he also brought together the plans which Leith Nautical College were developing for a purpose-built College building, although the Governors didn't get planning permission or funding from the Scottish Education Department for some time.

Robin Salvesen learned at the meetings of the Society when they met (four times a year) the costs of operating a wooden hulk and the very

Training Ship (TS) Dolphin *sailing from Leith on her last voyage to Bo'ness.*

regular and large repair bills that were necessary for keeping the *Dolphin* afloat. Quite a lot of this was funded by the shipowners who had bought the *Dolphin* and given her to Leith Nautical College. Captain Harold Salvesen, who'd shown an interest in nautical education for many years, used the funds in the Theodore Salvesen Trust to assist in these operations. It was one of his views that young students who were going to sea should have basic skills in swimming, lifesaving, and rowing boats before they went to sea for the first time. He also had great belief in the Norwegian system where young officers spent their early years as a rating, before being promoted to command; and even shipowners started at sea as a junior and learned their skills at first hand. He was very keen that ratings should be able to become officers and that boys who had had to leave school early should at a later stage be able to go back to College in order to get the academic qualifications for promotion. The Shipping Federation in the United Kingdom was supportive of this attitude and the training for officers in the Merchant Navy was to a large degree sandwich courses where men did a certain amount of sea time and then went back to College for spells before they took their academic examinations towards their next promotion ticket.

Gordon Matheson, Finance Director of George Gibson, became the

Leith Nautical College before the opening day. The picture shows the main classroom block and bridge. Further to the right but out of this picture is the accommodation for resident students.

Secretary of the Dolphin Society and Lord Birsay, a learned Judge who presided at the Land Court in Scotland, took his title from Shetland and was by his accent and behaviour a native of those northern parts, was the President, and he came to annual meetings. In time, Robin became the Chairman of the Dolphin Society – his first active charity job.

Some of the Cadets lived in digs and from time to time there were problems with the landladies. Some of them lived in the Sailors' Home, next to the Martello Tower on The Shore. This was difficult for the staff to administer and the boys in their free time could go to the pubs and restaurants in Leith which was a fairly well-known area for prostitutes – not the ideal place for students fresh from the islands in the 1960s.

Even before Robin was promoted to be a Director of A.F. Henry & Macgregor he had been appointed by the Leith Shipowners' Association to the Board of Leith Nautical College. Tom McGill, one of the Directors of George Gibson and Company, was the Chairman at that time. The Ben Line and Shell and Esso used to send cadets for training and Salvesen's also sent a certain number of cadets to Leith Nautical College. So the shipowners kept a very strong influence in the operation.

It was around 1965 that Mr Callaghan, a future Chancellor of the Exchequer and then Prime Minister, came on an official visit to the *Dolphin* Training Ship and was presented to the Officers and Cadets by Lord Birsay. He met many of the staff and had a look at the accommodation.

The College had four major departments, one for Radio Officers, one for Engineers, and one for Navigators and they also had the pre-sea training courses which included catering. The Board Meetings in Commercial Street took place about once a month and Robin heard about the curriculum and the operating costs. The Principal was an Engineer by trade and training, Ewan Morgan, a Welshman who worked in the Commercial Street office at Leith Nautical College.

Now the Board had plans for a purpose-built College. There was a sudden opportunity offered by the Government which for political reasons took the view that it should help industry to invest in education. Money was available from the Scottish Education Department and a site was purchased between Portobello and Musselburgh near enough to the estuary to have a good view over the river and the ships coming in and out. Robin was appointed to the Planning Sub-Committee and Captain Ireland did much of the work in bringing together the requirements of the four departments for a purpose-built College. It would be built for a five hundred full-time student equivalent but because many of the courses were short ones the turnover of students in a year would be some two thousand, – the majority of them doing three-month or six-week courses. During the negotiations the Scottish Education Department took the view that catering and pre-sea courses would not be financed by them because there was a surplus capacity at the English Colleges in these two areas.

The Sub-Committee's first job was to appoint an architect. Various firms who had built Colleges and Institutions of this type and size were interviewed and their work inspected and J & F Johnson were appointed. It was agreed that the new College would have a simulator on the bridge whereby the officers could work as if it were night outside with windows all closed down and simulate driving a ship on instruments alone They had the radio and radar facilities and received reports from preconceived plans of a ship entering an estuary and various incidents taking place. Later, some very experienced Masters found it so realistic that if offered a cup of tea they would say, 'Not got any time to do that now, can't you see I'm busy?'

The new College was built with a planetarium so that students could see above their heads the stars of a night sky which could be pre-set for a situation south of the Equator as well as northern latitudes and for the

Mr Callaghan in the centre and Lord Birsay on the right in the official photo when they inspected the TS Dolphin *in Leith.*

moon cycle as well. Students could identify the various star and planet groups and learn navigation. There had to be machine rooms for the engineers to train to open up pumps and generators and be shown how to do the major repairs on machinery. The accommodation which was to be built for 260 students in bed-sitting rooms was to be linked to the main teaching block by a canteen facility and, of course, the offices for the administrative staff were needed. Above that was built a library facility and a room for the Chaplains from the local churches to hold quiet study and reflection periods and to console or guide students who had marriage problems or a death in the family. The College was to be built with a swimming pool and a gym which was to be convertible into a Conference Hall. The swimming pool was to teach life-saving, swimming and also the launching of boats. Leith Nautical College used to win prizes in competition for swimming.

After the architect had seen the detailed brief prepared by the staff of the College he developed, in consultation with the Scottish Education Department, a design for the College buildings – bearing in mind the very tight costing which the SED was to allow. The site had to be test bored to see if there were any problems from early unmapped coal mining activity. The Governors decided that there should be extensive car parks and games fields and the Theodore Salvesen Trust put up funds for squash courts beside the swimming pool. The architect advised the appointment of an Engineer Consultant to give him advice on the supply of power and water to the Engineering Labs and to the other classrooms and also to regulate the purchase of heating and air-conditioning systems for the accommodation and teaching blocks. From that time on, the Design Committee started to meet regularly with the architect and the consultants to review progress.

The Scottish Education Department also imposed a new Board structure on Leith Nautical College. It was considered appropriate that the Boards of Colleges of Further Education should have both staff governors and also student governors, as well as Secretary of State nominees and people with a knowledge of academic and financial fields, together with the Union representatives from the officers' and the ratings' Trades Unions. The Board also had to include representatives from the local authorities. The Board suddenly became quite large and Tom McGill, a shipowner, was Chairman. The new Leith Nautical College was planned and built.

Then a very strange situation occurred when the new Board first met in the new buildings and, as a matter of routine, two Members of the Board nominated Tom McGill to be re-appointed as Chairman. The Board, by a majority vote, turned down his appointment. A second motion nominated and appointed George Robertson.

So when the new College building was opened by His Royal Highness Prince Charles, instead of Tom McGill who had planned the building it was George Robertson who was presented to Prince Charles and showed him round the building and presented the Heads of Department to His Royal Highness. It was however a very happy day and after a tour of the main departments and the opportunity for Prince Charles to meet with members of staff and many of the students, the staff and official guests were given a drink in the library in the link block and then proceeded to have lunch together.

The Planning Sub-Committee had to consider the pros and cons of running the catering and cleaning of the College with their own labour or with contract staff and it was agreed they should recruit appropriate staff. This worked very well in the catering department but it became clear that the laundry was not really big enough to run a full team of staff and it was economic to put the sheets and towels out weekly to a commercial laundry in the Edinburgh area. Resident students could use a launderette within the residential block for their small clothes.

The new residential College required a new staffing structure. Janitors were employed for day and night duty as there were 260 students in residence. Miss Johnstone who had been the Principal's Secretary was appointed by Tom McGill to become the official correspondent and the Secretary of the College. This possibly was a mistake and done without due thought as the College Secretary of Colleges of this size usually had either a legal or an accounting qualification. The procedure of advertising and interviews did not take place for this new appointment. Miss Johnstone did an extraordinarily good job in managing the move from the old College to the new and became responsible for the whole administration of this new Residential College – which included the maintenance of the buildings, and the development of the annual accounts and presentation of them to the Scottish Office from year to year. She set up a very good team and it worked extremely well.

Student numbers had diminished to some degree during the time of the building process to around about 480 full-time equivalent. In the new College there was an opportunity to increase the whole scope and size of classes and student numbers so there was a lot of work to do in planning future strategy. Ian Natush, the Head of the Radio Department, was appointed Deputy Principal and he gave considerable assistance to Ewan Morgan in planning the new courses.

After the move into the new building and the selection of furniture and equipment for it, the old buildings down in Leith which had originally been gifted to Leith Nautical College by the shipowners were sold by the Governors who set up a Governors' Fund – a capital fund, the income from which was very useful in supplying equipment on the wish list which had been outwith the budget allowed by the Scottish Education Department.

The Dolphin Society had to determine whether there was a future use for the old hulk – the TS *Dolphin*. Potential hull repair costs were quite enormous and the Governors took the view that although the *Dolphin* had a long and distinguished history, there was very little left of the original ship – she had been modified first of all as a submarine mother ship and then as a College building. So the shipbreakers up at Bo'ness towed the *Dolphin* out of Leith Docks and up the Forth estuary and many photographs were taken of her last voyage. This was a sad moment but interesting too – to see the *Dolphin* actually go to sea again after so many years moored in an enclosed dock.

Some of the Governors approached Robin Salvesen with a request that they should nominate him as Chairman; he agreed to allow his name to go forward and was eventually appointed as Chairman of Leith Nautical College. A lot of new initiatives then took place. It was necessary to increase the student numbers and one of the opportunities arose to work for the Anglo Iranian Oil Company who were using ships with British Officers but Iranian national crew, and they wanted the opportunity to promote Iranian ratings to officers. Leith Nautical College gained contracts for training cadets from both Iran and Iraq. These students needed a specialist course, 'English for foreign students'.

With the development of North Sea oil and the increasing need to carry both oil and gas in tankers, there was a need to train both ships' officers and ports personnel in the safe operation of hazardous cargo. The Scottish Education Department agreed that the College should run a number of self-financing courses and fire-fighting, related to North Sea oil operations, and hazardous cargo courses were included. Mr McGuire, a member of staff at the College involved in the hazardous cargo experience, started taking Leith Nautical College courses to students abroad and staff were sent to do short courses in countries as far away as the Philippines. Leith Nautical College operated distance learning courses which gave sailors on board the drilling rigs or on board ship video programmes to study in their own cabins when off-duty as part of their training course for their next Certificate – quite a revolutionary and new idea.

One of Miss Johnstone's problems as Secretary of the College was to balance the various College accounts. The SED kept tight control of money and ring-fenced grants, separating sums for teaching, for staff wages and for maintenance of buildings and each College had to balance the catering accounts without subsidising it from other sources.

It was also necessary to approve standing orders for the Board. Robin had assistance from the COSLA representative who had access to standing orders used by local authorities and their committees. The LNC board were able to make use of procedures in other places. Robin held discussions with the auditors and the College Secretary to make the administration of the College work in a more comfortable way.

The Principal and Board had to re-state all the rules of disciplinary procedures for both the students and the staff and publish them. Some disciplinary problems took place at this time. The students in the Halls of Residence had parties in the accommodation and damage was caused to some of the bed-sitting rooms and the showers. It became necessary for the

College Secretary to go through the Disciplinary Procedures, interview the culprit, and recover some of the money. One member of staff was suspended after an allegation that he had interfered with another member of staff – not exactly a punch-up but it might have been so – and the Staff Unions took the side of the suspended member of staff. The procedure of the Disciplinary Hearing had to be followed through in a sub-committee, chaired by the Vice-Chairman so that the Chairman of Governors could be available to take an Appeal Hearing if that should be necessary. College work could become time-consuming for a Chairman.

When Ewan Morgan retired the Scottish Education Department appointed Dr Alan Watson as Principal. By 1981 the Scottish Education Department in their wisdom decided upon a review of tertiary education in Scotland and were looking at the statistics of 1975 to 1980. These particular figures were not a fair reflection of the Leith Nautical College's experience and ambitions because during that time College departments were running down the work in Leith and then developing Craigmillar. Having been built for a 500 full-time equivalent the College had already exceeded this and was moving towards 700 with about 2300 students going through in a year. Each discipline had been developing quite a variety of new courses during this time. Dr Alan Watson took charge of the academic staff and his Deputy Ian Natush was proving of great assistance to him. The Secretary of State for Scotland however took the view that there was a surplus capacity for training for nautical education in Scotland. The numbers at Glasgow Nautical College had diminished to quite a large degree and it wasn't very busy, but it was operated by Strathclyde Region, whereas Leith Nautical College was a College of Further Education and directly funded from the Scottish Education Department. So the two principal Nautical Colleges were run at different levels. The academic staff at Leith Nautical College were very keen to increase the percentage of advanced education but the statistics showed that more than fifty per cent were not 'advanced'. British shipping was becoming much more sophisticated with the introduction of automation in the Engine Room, so the actual need for training in the navigating and engineering side was actually becoming nearer degree level. Academic work for the Chief Officer or Chief Engineer or Master's Certificate was close to Degree level work. The staff and the Board of Leith Nautical College were anxious to maintain and develop the new and purpose-built College at Leith for nautical education in Scotland and argued that whereas the Glasgow Nautical College numbers were declining the Leith numbers were rising and forecast to rise quite considerably.

However, as a senior civil servant said in a letter to Robin Salvesen, 'It is sometimes possible to "nudge" the Secretary of State – but after he has made a formal announcement that Leith Nautical College was going to be changed from a directly funded College to a regional College, he was unlikely to reverse his decision.' There was quite a lot of publicity and as Chairman, Robin Salvesen had to put his name to quite a bit of this. The Staff Unions were quite concerned that their Members might lose their jobs because Lothian Region, who wanted the site of Leith Nautical College, was not particularly anxious to continue doing courses for the shipping industry.

Since the early days of North Sea oil in 1972, Robin had been involved as a Member of the Greenwich Forum and during the early 1980s he and Dr Alan Watson arranged for the Forum to have one of its major meetings in the Leith Nautical College building, using the accommodation and catering facilities for a major Conference. The Greenwich Forum had a very wide brief, bringing together experts in all walks of maritime affairs as it met year by year. The Conference would concentrate on different aspects of maritime life in turn – the 'fishing industry' of course was one of the those included as well as 'development of North Sea oil', and the 'development of underwater research'. Ships were beginning to dredge for nodules of minerals in the deep waters of the ocean; and there was a question as to how much research and development should be allowed to take place in the Antarctic area. After the 1939-45 War more and more countries were showing interest in acquiring responsibility for a part of the Antarctic area and already by the 1980s there were fairly strong grounds for recognising that there were seventeen to nineteen countries which had expeditions and bases on the Antarctic landmass. The Greenwich Forum had a wide brief and its Conference in Leith Nautical College, hosted by Robin Salvesen and Dr Alan Watson, was quite successful, with some learned papers presented and developed.

Leith Nautical College was transferred to Lothian Region and it was decided by the local authority to re-name it 'The Jewel and Esk Valley College'. Mick MacGarthy, who had been an NUM leader, was to open the College and Robin Salvesen was one of the invited guests. On the day of the opening, the Students Union determined that they would picket the occasion and not allow any vehicles to enter that day, so the VIPs had to find other places to park in the side streets. It was a different kind of opening ceremony to that conducted a few years earlier by His Royal Highness Prince Charles. When the local MP, Dr Gavin Strang, had had private meetings with the Students Union representatives in the College he discovered that one of the matters of dispute was that although the students were represented on the Board of the College Governors, they hadn't been adequately invited to attend the opening ceremony or the lunches. Gavin Strang did magnificently that day in calming troubled waters and it was quite impressive how he managed to work something out with the College Principal and the Students Union.

The Governors of Leith Nautical College got Counsel's Opinion and moved the money in the Governors' account into a specially made Bells Nautical Trust with the object to support Nautical Education in Scotland. Robin Salvesen through the Trust has been able to keep contact with the Jewel and Esk Valley College since that time. The trust has given grants to both Jewel and Esk Valley College and to Glasgow Nautical College over the years, to encourage Scottish people to gain the Certificates they require to serve at sea. The navigating and engineering certificates for seafarers can only be gained after courses in Glasgow or England. Distance Learning and Hazardous Cargo courses were discontinued from the Craigmillar site.

The Jewel and Esk Valley College didn't remain as a regional College for very long and once again is operating as a College directly funded by the Scottish Education Department. Robin Salvesen, a few years after he had given up the Chairmanship and his Membership of the Board of Leith Nautical College, was asked if he would serve as a Governor of Glasgow Nautical College so went through to Glasgow to several meetings. He found the work there very interesting as they developed their courses. A political review of representation on the Board by the Strathclyde Region took place and Robin's appointment to Glasgow Nautical College was also terminated.

CHAPTER 11

Christian Salvesen Shipping

WHEN PETER KITTERMASTER retired suddenly from Christian Salvesen, Max Harper-Gow asked Robin to take responsibility for the whole shipping division. Maxwell was an inspired leader for the company when he took over as Chairman from Harold Salvesen. He was appointed Director of the Ross Group in which Christian Salvesen & Company had about a thirty per cent interest and also he became a Director of the Royal Bank of Scotland. With this experience of outside directorships, Max was able to bring to Christian Salvesen some of the commercial practices of a public limited company and the private company of Christian Salvesen started to work in the very similar manner to the public companies of that time. Robin Salvesen became one of the executive management team which were mainly looking after the investments of the South Georgia company, but also of the partnership which became the management company of Christian Salvesen. The Group held many shares in the Stock Exchange and direct investment in housebuilding.

The shipping division had been organised in a rather strange way by Christian Salvesen & Co. and Robin wanted to review it. Deep sea shipping had reported to Peter Kittermaster. The Norwegian Lines reported to Hans Hostvedt and Gerald Elliot. Engineering was under Ted Young, who was retiring and handing over to Ken Campion. The crew department still reported to Gerald Elliot as did the purchasing department which was from day to day operated by Roger Pears. The accounts were centralised for the group under Malcolm Bruce but each of the shipping departments had its own accounting function. So the monthly trading accounts were not readily available to the operational managers in the same way as Robin Salvesen had experienced when he had been working in Henry & Macgregor where there was a spreadsheet which showed each month the expenditure break-down and profit from each ship.

So Robin undertook a review of the personalities and skills of the people within the staff. It was quite important that he should be able to sell his scheme to the main board of the company because many of the staff in the existing structure had been appointed by Gerald Elliot and the scheme as a whole had to be approved by the Board.

The deep sea fleet had been initiated by Max Harper-Gow in 1957 after Iver Salvesen died, when Salvesen's had invested in a series of Swedish built ships of 13,000 tonnes. Salvesen's tramped ships across the Atlantic between Europe and America competing against the Conference Lines but their ships also operated on Time Charter worldwide.

The Norwegian Lines had been the responsibility of Iver Salvesen and Cecil Foreman but further ships had been built to complete the series of eight. The *Glitra* was only 1,000 tonnes dead weight but the others were 1,500 tonnes and virtually sister ships.

In the new organisation Douglas Horsburgh became the chartering manager for the bigger ships. Murray Simpson was still operating the Norwegian ships and Edwin Davis working with Derek Tucker in Henry & Macgregor. In the personnel department Captain Phillip and Captain Lowe looked after the crew on all the ships. Ken Campion, Andrew Scrimageour and Mr Robertson and Mr Benham were the senior people in the engineering department looking after the surveys and the repairs and maintenance of the ships. Mr Fairweather, who had been with Henry & Macgregor and Bill Lynch, and who had formerly been a whaling storekeeper in the Antarctic, now looked after the provisioning and stores for all the Salvesen fleet of ships. Roger Pears became Group Treasurer. In the accounts department Mr Henderson looked after Salvesen shipping and Mr Inglis worked with the Henry & Macgregor ships.

Robin Salvesen wished to achieve a monthly managers' meeting of the senior people from each department to review new spreadsheets which showed the monthly expenditure ship by ship under a series of headings which would show the impact on costs from the decisions of the stores, engineering and operations departments. This would give the managers of the whole shipping operation a clear picture of the profit and loss of each ship from month to month. The manager could then see and plan the best time to put ships into dry dock for their main repairs in relation to the trading cycle in the calendar year. Robin, as Chief Executive, felt that he should hold things together and be responsible for business development within the operation. He would also have time to visit the ships and speak to the Captains and also visit the agency offices in London, Newcastle and abroad to build a relationship at a different level from the day-to-day operations. The change had to concentrate all managers' effort on the creation of profit.

The main engine of a diesel ship showing the valves on the cylinder heads and the exhaust. Decking at this level allows the watch keepers to inspect temperature and pressure gauges.

Salvesen's at this time still maintained a London office, still called Andorsen Becker & Co. Mr Gross was a Director of Andorsen Becker and a Member of the Baltic Exchange, skilled in the purchase and sale of ships and chartering, particularly of the bigger deep sea line ships. The Baltic Exchange did not handle contracts for either the Norwegian Lines or the coastal ships. Andorsen Becker was in St Helens Place which was a hundred yard walk from the Chamber of Shipping and also the Baltic Exchange. It was a very useful London office for Gerald, Max and Robin to use, with a quiet room and a telephone.

Robin's new structure had Douglas Horsburgh reporting for all the ships' trading operations activities and Captain Phillip for the operating costs of the ships. Ken Campion led the engineers. Mr Henderson was the Senior Accountant who was able to report at Management Committee on the spreadsheets for the whole shipping operation. Thus Robin had four heads of department in his Edinburgh headquarters.

Robin stayed in his own office in Henry & Macgregor's initially while he studied the performance of the shipping investments. For instance the 13,000 tonne SAL vessels made a more secure income from their Time Charters to the liner companies than they did from the Chimo Atlantic Service where they were trying to attract freight from the Conference Lines. British Shipping had enjoyed, under the care of the United Kingdom Governments, flag preference to British ships trading with the British Empire. The Conferences looked after the trades to India and to Australia. The Conferences effectively fixed the rates charged on cargo and secured the stake of the major liner companies in the trade to the British Empire. A lot of pressure was beginning to develop from the Americans who were not at all keen on price fixing. As time went on the Russian, Norwegian and Greek ships, operating flags of convenience, undermined the power of the Conferences as they increased their share of the market.

When Robin Salvesen took over shipping, Bruce Weatherstone was in charge of the Christian Salvesen Ships' Agency business in Port of Leith where they also owned the Leith Stevedores company of Alexander Orr. Bruce Weatherstone had a very good relationship with the Monarch Line owned by the De Champ family in Sweden who operated regular ships to Leith and Grangemouth. Salvesen's also had interest and ownership in a ship chandler's business in Leith and a transport warehouse in conjunction with an owner of road haulage vehicles called Storage Services Leith. Bruce Weatherstone was committed to re-organise some of these subsidiary companies.

There had been a period of dock and transport drivers' strikes in the United Kingdom. Dock workers offered their services each morning to the stevedores and the men that weren't engaged had to walk up the road with minimum basic pay. This system of casual employment really had to cease and the stevedore companies started to merge so that they could offer permanent employment to their own labour force. Bruce Weatherstone negotiated a change in the ownership of Orrs and 'Forth Stevedores' to obtain the stevedore licence in the Port of Leith.

When Edwin Davis retired, the management team of Henry & Macgregor moved and merged under Murray Simpson to work in the

Bernard Street office of Salvesen and Robin also moved into the Salvesen office again, to an office at the far west end of the building with a smaller office next door for his secretary. Bruce Weatherstone and Ken Campion were working together on the plans for the Salvesen new office at East Fettes Avenue, on a site previously owned by Fettes College, where Bovis were building a speculative office.

It became clear to Robin that the Chimo service across the Atlantic wasn't providing Salvesen's with secure profits. He planned to charter the SAL ships to the liner companies for period charters and to purchase bulk carriers. The first ship to be sold was the *Saldanha* when the Chimo service came to an end. A year later the *Saldura* was sold. Ian Harrison of Harrison Clyde, whom Max Harper-Gow had known from his youth, had developed his own shipping company and Mr Harper-Gow's father had been involved with the Gow Harrison company. Ian Harrison and Max agreed that the two firms might work more closely together. At that time the price of building new ships in Japan was considerably less than in Europe, so Ian had built up a fleet of ships on fairly low capital but with heavy bank loans; he suggested to Max that perhaps they should invest in one of these bigger bulk carriers. So the *Verdala* was built and managed in this way, with Salvesen owning the ship and Harrison's providing the management for her. This relationship grew as Harrison developed plans for smaller ships in Europe. Harrison's were going to put their new small ships into a Norwegian/Dutch pool for the cargo trading arrangements and needed someone to provide the crews and do the management. It seemed logical that Salvesen's should be chosen to do this and they eventually became the managers of the *Voreda* and the *Virgillia*. The pool worked on completely new trade routes. For instance ships which had gone to the Mediterranean with high paying freight cargo returned carrying salt up to Iceland for the drying and salting of fish.

After this purchase of the *Verdala* Salvesen's bought their own ship, MV *Inverleith*. This led to an invitation for Robin Salvesen to go out to Japan with Ian Harrison to the launch of a Clarkson inspired ship, the *Avonbridge* – a very large bulk carrier. Robin was able to meet some of the people that Ian had used in Japan to develop shipbuilding projects with him. He stayed in the Palace Hotel in Tokyo where Clarkson's held a big reception: a magnificent Japanese occasion with many Japanese waitresses dressed in their kimonos wandering round the room bringing savouries and filling the guests' glasses. The next day, the Clarkson party went in a train to the shipyard to see the launch of the *Avonbridge*. As the ship went down the slipway, at the bow of the ship a great big bubble burst and streamers of coloured paper went off rather like a little explosion of fireworks. These streamers blew out behind her in the wind; it was a magnificent completion to the launch.

Initially *Inverleith* stayed out in Far East waters. She had a Hong Kong/ Chinese crew with British officers. She made several voyages between Japan and Australia. Robin stopped off in Singapore and Hong Kong on his way to and from Japan to talk to the agents – Dodwell in Hong Kong – about the engagement of crew and crew problems there. He had a day visiting the sights and driving up into the hills to have lunch and see the development of the island – in clear view of mainland China.

In the review of the Norwegian trade between Scotland and Norway it became clear that the most profitable voyages were bulk cargoes loaded in one port for one port discharge. Hans Hostvedt who had run the Norwegian Lines for Salvesen had a contract with the Ellerman Wilson Line that Salvesen's would run a regular ship, once or twice a month, between Hull and the west coast of Norway. Ellerman's were the agents who would market and sell the service, earning a commission on cargo from the Port of Hull; Rankine & Salvesen would do the same in Grangemouth. In Norway there were agents at Bergen and Trondheim. They also earned commission on the cargo and an agency fee for the ships coming into harbour. Salvesen's, in paying the cost of running the ship, were taking the risk and not always making a profit on the journey – especially if the ships were only part loaded. Robin Salvesen planned to discontinue this service which released some of the Norwegian Line ships for sale. The Norwegian service would concentrate on bulk cargoes such as coke for discharge in Norway and load wood products in the Trondheim area for Manchester or Preston on the return load. From time to time there were full loads of aluminium to take from Norway to Swansea. The key to making a profit was to cut down the round voyage time.

Between 1968 and 1971 Robin negotiated the sale of the Norwegian Line Ships one by one before (only just in time because North Sea oil was developed from 1972) gas works in the UK closed down and little coke was available for export. Pulp cargoes from Norway also declined under pressure from Canada and Finland.

Cement Marketing Corporation decided to open up the limestone deposits at Dunbar and built a new factory there to supply Scotland with cement. So the cement distribution shed in Leith was closed down and small ships which had brought cement up from the Thames were no longer required. The ferry services in the north of Scotland to Shetland and Orkney improved as well.

The sale of *St Abbs Head* to Indonesia was negotiated through Andorsen Becker in London. Robin Salvesen went up to Grangemouth for the final delivery inspection. After the morning inspection Robin went to the office to meet the Indonesian Colonel to make sure that the acceptance was signed cleanly and that the cash deposit was released in London. Robin gave the Indonesian Colonel a good lunch in the Maharata Restaurant in Grangemouth after the hand-over ceremonies had taken place. During the course of lunch Robin asked the Colonel what he would use the ship for and was told it would be for trade within the islands and, of course, if that went a bit slow it was always possible to do a bit of piracy. Robin didn't know if this was entirely a joke; however the Indonesians actually re-sold the ship in Singapore within about a year.

Captain Phillip and Robin Salvesen went directly from a visit to the *Duncansby Head* at Arnhem to see the shipbuilders Van Diepen and the *Voreda* which was being built for Harrison Clyde and which Christian Salvesen was to manage for them. During dinner with Jan Van Diepen and Mr Schmidt from the neighbouring yard, Robin discussed Christian Salvesen & Co's requirements for small ships of under 1,600 gross tonnes and an alternative design to the *Voreda* and *Virgillia*. They explained about the bulk carrier concept for small ships trading in Europe carrying cargoes such as pulp, timber and sand. Mr Schmidt drew various things on the back of an envelope and said, 'We'll talk about that later,' and within the next week or so he came up with a design for a small single-deck bulk carrier carrying over 2,000 tonnes of cargo and outlined the sort of price at which he would be able to sell a ship of this kind. Captain Phillip and Robin were quite interested in this and eventually ordered the *Tod Head* and the *Troup Head* to be built by Van Diepen.

Shortly after that the *Voreda* was completed and Robin Salvesen went across as a guest of Harrison's to the delivery ceremony. The Directors had decided not to have a launching party but to name the ship and take her to sea for the trials all in one exercise. While they were doing the measured mile at an early hour, the fog thickened up and although Christian Salvesen & Co had a Master and Chief Engineer on board, Robin decided that it was not appropriate to take delivery of the *Voreda* in the fog at sea with a crew of shipbuilder's personnel. The shipbrokers were very concerned because they had the champagne bottles all ready to pop and didn't quite know what to do with them if they weren't actually celebrating the hand-over during the

Troup Head *launch – sideways tip into the canal. The water displaced creates a pressure which stops the ship from damage against the opposite bank. An exciting event.*

voyage itself. Within half an hour of this decision the *Voreda* had completed her sea trials and was sailing with a tug in attendance back towards the harbour when a small coaster crossed her bows, collided and sank within about half an hour. The crew were taken off the coaster by the tug and there were no lives lost and no injuries – but it was quite amazing to be in the fog off the coast of Germany and Holland and see this small ship sinking so quickly into the sea. *Voreda* sailed into port and the visual inspection showed hardly a scratch on her paint. The way in which the two ships had struck each other caused one to break – flood the holds and sink. The other had not been damaged at all. Mr Schmidt said to Robin on the shore, 'That was probably one of the best decisions that you will ever make in your shipping career.' The loss of the coaster would fall upon the shipbuilder's insurance policy rather than that of Harrison's who became the new owners of the *Voreda* when she was safely in port.

Salvesen's main agent up in Aberdeen, John Cook & Sons, were looking for a buyer for the company. Danny Stroud would remain with the company and was prepared to act as its Chief Executive, while Mr Repper retired. Robin struck an arrangement which would enable both Mr Stroud and Mr Pirie to have some shares but about 90 per cent would be owned by Christian Salvesen & Co. Robin then had to put this proposal to the Board of Salvesen for their approval. Robin expected that the profitability year on year of John Cook & Sons, which had stevedoring and agency businesses in Aberdeen, would be of the order of £100,000 and would no longer pay Directors' fees to Mr Repper and the Cook family. The figure asked for the purchase was £300,000 – so it was a three-year payback. When it came to the Board Meeting however two at least of the Board voted against it; but by a majority decision Christian Salvesen allowed Robin to buy John Cook & Sons. North Sea oil developed within a very short time and by 1972/73 John Cook & Sons had to do negotiations with the dockers to enable North Sea supply boats to load both day and night. The volume of traffic and the amount of Ships' Agency work in Aberdeen increased dramatically to deliver profit greater than £300,000 each year – so it was a very good investment and one of Robin's better deals.

In the early 70s the banks were prepared to lend shipowners about 90 per cent of the capital cost of a new ship on the security of the ship itself and assignment of charters which were the ship's trade. At the same time, there was an enormous difference between the price of shipbuilding in Japan and Europe and it seemed a good idea to buy ships at these cheaper prices. Robin Salvesen offered to invest in a new ship in Japan. The shipyard wasn't busy and a particular space in the shipyard was available for an order. The shipping management team tried to put together figures which would satisfy the Salvesen Board, but without any fixed contracts and knowing that it would take nearly two years to build the ship, it was really all speculation. Christian Salvesen & Co were looking for a return of about 6 per cent over bank rate. The Group were able to borrow money in both yen and dollars from the Sumitomo Bank in Japan at very low interest rates so the case was to earn 6 per cent over the cost of borrowing money in Japan. Brian Gibb the Group Finance Director and Robin used a new technique with discounted cash flows to show the real return in a period with high inflation but large loans at low interest. The project could finance loan repayments and Group tax was reduced by free depreciation allowances. After a special briefing meeting with the Chairman, the case for a new ship was presented and approved.

Robin travelled to Japan with Captain Phillip and Ken Campion by Japan Air – travelling from London to Moscow and waiting in Moscow Airport for nearly two hours before the plane took off direct to Tokyo. They left just after lunch-time, had their evening meal on the way to Moscow, a long sleep on the trip over Russia and breakfast on the plane before landing in Japan about mid afternoon. Of course their colleagues in Japan wanted to take them out that evening – so they had dinner in two nightclubs at about seven o'clock local time before going to bed in the Palace Hotel at about ten o'clock. Tradition was that people had a fairly early dinner at one restaurant then after the main course you would go on to another restaurant, more like a nightclub, to have coffee and a drink. There would be a little dancing of geisha girls to entertain the foreigners on behalf of their hosts. They certainly saw new forms of cooking and enjoyed trying sushi or deep-fried prawns and other delicious food.

Ken Campion and Jack Phillip helped Robin determine the equipment needed both for navigating and mooring a ship and also in the Engine Room. They were surprised to hear that the shipyard had not worked with Lloyds Register before and was more aware of the rules of the American Bureau of Shipping or Norske Veritas but Salvesen were keen to keep their ships registered with Lloyds and to the Department of Trade specifications. The other surprise was that the standard fitting in accommodation was steel furniture in the cabins of the crew and the officers. The Salvesen team specified wooden furniture with carpets and curtains and a much higher standard of comfort for the crew than the Japanese shipbuilders expected to give. The draft specification went on to a couple of hundred pages and negotiations took a day or two. The principles of the contract and the price then went back for final negotiations through Andorsen Becker and Galbraith Wrightson as ship brokers to negotiate the deal in financial terms between the two companies. Sumitomo Shipyard had a good arrangement with the Sumitomo Bank – so Galbraith Wrightson were able to get a good financial package of loans. Salvesen's expected to get income in dollars rather than sterling, and many of their costs would either be in yen or dollars as they traded the *Inveralmond* on a worldwide bulk cargo trade. It was important to minimise the currency risk and have their income coming in the same currency as loan repayments and operating costs.

Salvesen's built several ships in Japan in the next few years and Captain Phillip and Robin quite often spent a weekend visiting the sights of Kyoto and Niko and their many temples. The next ship was the *Invershin* with the Namura yard at Osaka and they were able to arrange similar loan arrangements.

Robin visited the shipyards both in Europe and Japan at least three times during each construction period. There was nearly always a need to make decisions on the outfitting of the cabins and the colour schemes, as well as

Launch of Inveralmond *by Sari Salvesen showing the view as the ship started to move down the slipway.*

dealing with various technical problems. Quite often the shipyard, halfway through, would say that Department of Trade rules had changed and the yard couldn't construct the ship to their plan without some more money. These meetings helped to hammer out a solution. There would always be a meeting at the time of the launch as well as the celebration party at the delivery and trial trips of the ship.

Sari was asked to launch the *Inveralmond*. The Board of Christian Salvesen used to invite one of the Directors' wives or a daughter to launch the ships in turn and the sponsor was allowed to choose one of her own relations to go out at Company expense to accompany her. Sari had her sister Vanessa with her. First of all Robin and the two girls went to Singapore to break their journey with Sari's stepsister Tessa, who was working and living with her husband there. He worked in an Australian owned cold storage business. They lived in a lovely house with a big garden with someone to help Tessa with her children. Robin noticed that the whole garden area was surrounded by a wire fence and that Tess and John Marriott kept a dog to guard the house. He had been to Singapore a few times and rather liked it because it seemed to be very clean and very safe to walk around. Hong Kong was much dirtier with tradespeople trying to sell things in the street. Singapore seemed a very well-organised place, and the authorities in Singapore were reputed to arrest and charge any person who dropped paper or a cigarette end. John Marriott took Sari, Vanessa and Robin to visit the club and they discussed the family news. Robin visited the shipbuilding and repair yard and made it a business trip as well.

The three travellers then went across to Indonesia where Sari's stepbrother was working for Broken Hill and heading up their tin-mining operation. They saw again the way in which the Europeans lived (almost a complex) outside the main town, in rather nice houses with gardens (and their cars) on secluded roads, whereas the town itself was fairly downbeat with shacks. Robin had strained his back because he'd lifted Sari's heavy suitcases; a girl in a little restaurant by the harbour noticed that he wasn't sitting quite happily on his chair while having his dinner, so offered to give him a massage – it certainly made him feel better in the short term but he was more stiff the next day. Anyway, they enjoyed very nice seafood and the opportunity to catch up with Michael and Helen and the work they were doing.

Rooms were booked in the Palace Hotel, Tokyo where they were met by shipbroker friends and introduced to the banking and shipbuilding divisions of Sumitomo. There was quite a big party for the launch which included Lloyds Register and the bankers. Galbraith Wrightson's representative, Tak Nishikawa, and his wife helped to entertain both the Japanese and the English and everything that was said in the speech or during dinner would be translated for the other parties. Robin started a precedent by inviting the Chairman of the shipyard and the Chairman of the bank with their wives to have dinner with himself and Sari and Tak Nishikawa and his wife. Although the Japanese wives weren't conversant with the English language, it was a very special occasion in a private room in a restaurant where they sat on the floor and were served by geishas.

After the launching of the ship there was a party with many more people

Inveralmond *at sea on her delivery trials and ready for shipbuilders to hand over to Christian Salvesen for her first commercial voyage.*

together in a restaurant where the shipbuilders were the hosts. Everyone sat in their places and didn't eat the food placed before them but had a glass of saki, then the speeches started. Each speech had to be translated into at least Japanese and English, so Robin had to speak one sentence at a time, then it would be translated and he would go on with the next sentence – and all this time the Europeans were waiting for their food and drink. One of the memorable speeches addressed to Robin and Sari was congratulations to them both in having seven children because this was unusual in Japan, and as the speech maker said, 'and with one wife,' bowing at Sari.

Robin and Sari travelled to Australia by air to Sydney. There was a shipping business for sale at Brisbane, so Robin had made an appointment to go there to visit these people who ran a coastal service taking stores and supplies to some of the islands and some of the more remote villages further north. They had built a good kind of ship for this job – it was really self discharging so they wouldn't need to use stevedores. They could unload the ships with their own gear. Brisbane was lovely. They hired a car and drove south through a wonderful jungle area where there were lots of trees and various parrots and coloured birds. They stayed the night in

Sari and Robin Salvesen in Japan in 1972.

travel-lodge hotels (where guests could park the car and get a very nice twin-bedded room) and each had a very passable restaurant where staff served a huge meal of Australian meats and breakfast in the morning. They visited Robin's cousin Joan, on a grass park estate just near Tamworth, rearing Hereford cattle, then at Willowtree they saw Tom and Rosalind Cropper, both first cousins of Robin's. Tom's father had bought Greenhills and Robin and Sari toured round it in a utility truck and saw the kangaroos, the sheep and the cattle feeding in the hilly country. It seemed much drier than the land up at Tamworth. Tom was experimenting with growing crops and he'd been to visit John at Spylaw in Scotland and was now growing barley and wheat. Finally they visited other relations in Melbourne and Adelaide – Peter Morgan and his brother both had estates and property in the south of Australia. They then flew right across the country to Perth and came back to Scotland from there.

There had been two prospects for business in these faraway places: the ferry company in Brisbane and the Electricity Board in New Zealand were looking for coastal ships to take coal from one island to the other to supply a new power station. With the experience that Robin had had with the coastal shipping of coal in Scotland, it seemed sensible to see if Salvesen's could put together a bid for that contract. Robin decided that it didn't really make

Sari Salvesen initiating the launch of MV Inveralmond *by cutting a cord with a silver axe. The cord released the bottle to swing and break against the steel bow of the ship. Then 'chocks away' and the ship slid down the greased slipway.*

any good sense to start an investment so far away unless the growth opportunity was significant.

The second of the ships built in Japan, the *Invershin*, was named by Karen Harper-Gow, the daughter of Max Harper-Gow, and they took out as guest, Eleanor Harper-Gow, Max's mother. The Japanese really did enjoy this and showed huge respect for 'the grandmother' of the sponsor. In fact she was really given pride of place – this rather overshadowed her grand-daughter. It was a very good party and nice to see the Harper-Gow family enjoying the occasion. Robin spent a weekend at Kyoto seeing the main shrines and temples. The pride of Kyoto was cherry blossom in the spring. Each of the shrines had cherry trees planted nearby and the Japanese people actually knotted little bits of paper onto the trees as prayers – so in spring the trees would be flowering beautifully but other times they had these little bits of white paper on every branch so that they looked as if they were flowering with white blossom all year.

Mr Robertson was the Engineer Superintendent who took charge of the construction in Japan. Robin Salvesen engaged a retired Japanese Admiral as the Clerk of Works. He helped particularly by translating and by talking to the Japanese shipbuilding managers to get the requirements fully implemented. *Invershin* in particular was beautifully built and finished. She went to dry dock after a year trading with ore cargoes with a very slim list of modifications or repairs to be done.

Salvesen's had made use of the investment grant for building new ships which was brought in at 20 per cent by the Labour Government when George Brown was the Chancellor of the Exchequer. This applied to ships built for UK companies abroad as well as in British ports. Robin took the view that at between eight and twelve years old a ship required a major overhaul – a sort of half-life maintenance survey and upgrading. Some ships at that age started showing some teething problems. One particular problem was that the ring-main pipes were sometimes made with steel with impurities in it and the salt water going through them sometimes caused the pipelines to corrode. With high inflation at the time it was very often possible to get a price for second-hand ships of this age higher than the original investment. Capital gains were often made from ship investment.

In 1975 because of fast investment in the housebuilding division of Christian Salvesen & Co there was a cash flow problem within the Group as a whole – so Robin was asked if he could find a way to realise some money from the shipping portfolio to help. He negotiated the sale of the *Dunvegan Head* and *Duncansby Head* to the Electricity Board. Robin had built *Dunvegan Head* for about £700,000 and *Duncansby Head* for about £800,000 and then sold the pair of them to the Electricity Board in 1975 for three million. This doesn't take into account the fact that the value of sterling had changed really quite considerably during the six to eight years that the ships had been operating.

Robin investigated opportunities for profit from North Sea oil from 1972 to 1978 – and concentrated on developing the offshore drilling company. He considered investment in supply boats and offshore support craft for the North Sea. Some of these investigations developed into separate companies which were formed into Salvesen Oil Services. In 1976 Robin again put a project forward to the Board to build a large coaster, this time in Japan. There was an opportunity in the inland sea at Hashihama – a shipyard which had done a lot of fairly sophisticated coasters and fishing vessels. This resulted in the building of the *Sumburgh Head*, later on followed by two ships from a shipyard at Miho. All three of these new coasters were very satisfactory and served the company well.

One of the ships which Salvesen's had built for whaling was the tanker *Southern Satellite*. She could carry quite a variety of different types of oil in her many different tanks so could go to the whaling grounds carrying heavy oil and gas oil for burning in the various engines, but also bring back edible oil. She had a double pipeline so that she could load one oil and discharge another at the same time. After a year or two in the Antarctic looking after the whaling ships she was chartered out for a ten-year period to the Ministry of Defence. Then she was used as a Royal Fleet Auxiliary, renamed *Orangeleaf*, manned by the Royal Navy crew and used as a tanker and fleet support ship. This initial contract came to an end in 1968 and Robin and Douglas Horsburgh decided to open discussion through Andorsen Becker with the Ministry of Defence, to see if they would renew the charter for a further period at a higher fee. The Royal Navy had the option of putting the ship back into her original condition and terminating the initial contract – but Robin calculated this correctly as an expensive alternative. Anyway the MOD were very willing to renew the *Orangeleaf* charter for a further period which lasted through to 1978 and Salvesen's earned a reasonable income for that next ten-year period.

CHAPTER 12

Royal Company of Archers

IN 1965 A LETTER CAME advising Robin Salvesen that he had been elected a Member of the Queen's Body Guard for Scotland – the Royal Company of Archers. Some years earlier he had completed the application forms for membership – which included details of his Military Service and his relationship to Members, illustrating that he was indeed Scottish. Several of the shooting Archers living in the Edinburgh area had been 7/9th Royal Scots with Iver Salvesen and they knew both Robin and his father. Tom Grainger-Stewart had married Pansy Salvesen, an older sister of Iver's, and he had actively restarted the shooting of the Royal Company after the Second World War and he had been the officer commanding the 7/9th Royal Scots before Iver Salvesen took this on in the late 1930s. Harold Salvesen, the Chairman of Christian Salvesen, was also a very regular and keen shooting Archer; he enjoyed the matches and the dinners and went to practice sessions in the butts and shooting outdoors very frequently. When Robin joined, both Tom Grainger-Stewart and Harold were keen to introduce him to shooting and loaned him bows so that he could enjoy the first evenings before he owned a bow of his own. Robin went to Stewart Christie's, the tailors, with his father's uniform for fitting and pressing and found that although his father was taller, the uniform in fact fitted him pretty well. He then had to choose colours for his arrows and Robin chose black with two white bands, effectively the funnel colours of the ships in A.F. Henry & Macgregor. In the first years, Robin used his father's butt bow which was quite light but suitable for shooting a hundred feet – the distance of the butts. Then he commissioned Mr Dowson, the bow maker of the Royal Company, to make him an outdoor bow. His bows were made of different woods joined together and laminated so that they were in fact rather more stiff to draw than one made out of pure yew wood. Yew however sometimes doesn't last terribly long because the wood can fracture under compression though it is very good in tension; a bow (when you draw it) has a compression side and a tension side, which gives it spring to cast the arrow the distance that is required.

The first year of shooting was very much a learning process – how to

The Queen's Bodyguard, The Royal Company of Archers shoot a match against The Woodmen of Arden. The Archer shooting the long bow is in the Royal Company uniform and stands beside a clout while he shoots at a similar target 180 yards away.

have the confidence to pull the bow to the full length of the arrow and then stand very steadily, releasing only the fingers so that the shaft would fly straight. The Royal Company practise outdoors in the gardens at Holyrood Palace, by permission of Her Majesty the Queen, and most of the shoots there are at a fixed range of 180 yards; the bow would have a pulling weight of between 54 and 60 pounds in weight. Robin found that 28 inches of length for his shafts was sufficient for the length of his arm – some of the taller Archers could use arrows which had a shaft length as much as 30 inches long.

Outdoor shooting in 1965 started in April with a week's shooting at 60 yards and then a week at 100 yards, before the Archers went on to shoot at the 180 yard length. In the summer shooting was available on Mondays, Tuesdays and Thursdays and Robin went there probably two nights a week. It started at about five thirty and he could get the office work done before an hour and a half shooting, in time to go home for dinner. Tuesdays were the Territorial Army drill night.

Each month the shooting Archers have a match and a dinner. They draw for teams and then shoot a match together and the winning side gets a slightly cheaper dinner than the losing side. The dinner which Tom Grainger-Stewart arranged was fairly simple and could be done by the Company's Officer and his wife, with a waitress to assist them. After shooting they would have a sherry for half an hour and then dinner would be called and there would be soup and a meat course – very often with meat – pheasant or lamb – provided by one of the Archers who had a farm or a shoot. They had claret and a savoury before the coffee and the port was circulated. The regular Archers (about thirty) became pretty good friends, meeting and shooting together. One of the regular shooters was Douglas Nicholson, the Surgeon of the Royal Company, who had been with the 7/9th Royal Scots as Medical Officer in the TA but mainly specialised in doctoring for children. Graeme Warrack, a very big and tall man who wrote about his exploits at Arnhem, was a doctor and a dentist in the practice which looked after the Salvesen family's teeth. Ian Crawford was a senior accountant in Edinburgh. Michael Finlay, another doctor, always felt that he was lucky to be a Member of the Royal Company because he was rather shorter than the regulation 5 ft 9 ins – 5 ft 10 ins minimum height to be on parade for Her Majesty. He was a very well read and interesting man. Peter Bartholomew would score regularly very high scores and in Robin's early days he was certainly the man to try to beat. Tom Grainger-Stewart was quite insistent that Robin should learn how to shoot before he took part in a shoot at a shooting ground where the public were viewing the sport. When the winter shooting started in October, the Archers shot in the butts at 100 feet at a very small target. There were two main prizes: the Dalkeith Arrow which is shot at a white paper probably less than 3 inches in diameter; and the Butt Medal where you are shooting at a bigger paper with colours on it – gold, red, blue, black and white, scoring from five to one in that order. Outdoor shooting started again in summer 1966 and one of the first outdoor prizes each year is the Dalhousie Sword. It is shot at 180 yards at a white target about 30 inches in diameter; the scoring is – two points if you hit the target but if no arrow hits it, the best arrow shot at that end scores one. Each Archer shoots two shafts and then walks up and scores the end and then turns round and shoots in the opposite direction for the second end. Most of these prizes are shot for over an hour and a half and one expects to shoot between eight and twelve ends in order to get the best participant on that particular evening. It was this first major prize of 1966 that Robin was lucky enough to win: the Dalhousie Sword.

In October that year the winter dinner was entitled the Dalhousie Sword Dinner and Robin was presented with the prize there by the Chairman of the evening. About ninety people were sitting round the table all in their best uniforms – green with a white tie and a white stiff shirt with medals, with a quartet playing in the minstrel gallery and a special tune for the winner. He was then asked to make a short speech – Robin in his first year as a Member of the Royal Company having won his first prize had the honour of having to speak at a major dinner. The Dalhousie Sword Dinner is always linked to the military services and the main guests were the heads of the three armed services in Scotland. Robin must have been by far the youngest man in the room and the most junior. So it was quite an undertaking – it was the first major speech he had made since his own wedding and his sister's. As he had won a major prize he was excluded from shooting for the Silver Cock or the Silver Hen which were the outdoor and indoor prizes for people who hadn't won any other – really for beginners.

Robin thought that one ought to hit the big target at 60 yards with most shafts and so he put one up in his garden at home and started practising. The scorebook showed that a competitor had to score at least 80 if not 100 points to win the prize but that shouldn't be too difficult, shooting three shafts at each end. Robin set himself an aim of scoring an average of five points an end to score 80 points and in his second year he achieved a figure of over 80 points but this was not good enough because Peter Bartholomew scored well over 100 points that night. However, Robin came second and felt that he had achieved part of his ambition – he was beginning to shoot more consistently.

One of the major events in 1966 was the presentation of new colours to the Royal Company by Her Majesty the Queen and a very large turnout of Members of the Royal Company paraded and rehearsed at Redford Barracks for this ceremony. Many Archers formed up into three very large contingents and a Drill Sergeant from the Guards came north to help with the inspections and the drill: one of these wonderful men who can shout at the soldiers and yet treat the Officers on parade with respect. Clearly the drill got better as time went on and on the day the Royal Company had to parade at Holyrood and march onto the lawns forming up into a big hollow square and Her Majesty came forward and inspected them, walking right round the ranks of the Archers. The Duke of Buccleugh as the Captain General was in command and Doctor Warr, the Chaplain to the Royal Company, was there to add his blessing to the colours when they were presented. In the evening there was a Ball with some eight hundred people present at the Assembly Rooms and Robin took his wife – Robin, in his full dress uniform, and Sari and the other girls in long dresses with jewels. Most of the dances in the Assembly Rooms were Scottish Country Dances interspersed with Waltzes. It was a glittering occasion with both the Assembly Rooms and the Music Hall open for dancing and the rooms on the ground floor open for both dinner and breakfast later.

In these early years Robin had many commitments including the Territorials so he was shooting to enjoy himself but not getting to shoot so very frequently. The year 1967 however included a special week because the Royal Company of Archers shoot against the Woodmen of Arden every third year and Robin shot well enough by then to be included in the team for the match at Holyrood. It was a gusty day in summer with a strong south-west wind. Robin was lucky enough to score three points for his side during the match – shooting as a pair with James Ingham, a Member of the Woodmen of Arden who was a Royal Navy regular officer. They have met together frequently since that time and often shoot against each other in the matches between the Woodmen and the Royal Company. James Ingham became one of the most consistent prize winners within the Woodmen of Arden. This match is usually a gathering of both men and ladies during a three-day visit. Archers meet and practise on the Thursday then the match takes place on the Friday. On that occasion in 1967 Her Majesty allowed luncheon to be held in the Palace of Holyrood. So, having shot five or six ends in the morning, they had lunch in the Crown Room, a very long and happy meal, and then shot again during the afternoon. In the evening there was a formal dinner, the two teams having a traditional mess dinner in Archers Hall, with minstrels in the Gallery and some speeches – but not too long!

On the Saturday, around forty gathered at Hopetoun in the grounds behind the big house. One of the targets was the other side of the little lake which meant shooting over the water. An individual Woodman of Arden is entitled to win this Royal Company prize. There was a picnic lunch and a shoot again in the afternoon before the prize-winners were presented with their prizes. There were parties in private houses on the Saturday evening before the Woodmen went south again on Sunday back to their normal jobs and duties on the Monday. It is always a very happy occasion with some very competitive days of archery and some glittering dinners and good fellowship.

In 1970 Robin was drawn to shoot with Dr Douglas Nicholson at the Hopetoun Prize. They met having had lunch, shot in the afternoon, and there was a little tent so that the men and their wives could have tea together. It was a lovely sunny day with the beauty of the great Hopetoun

House at one end of the shooting ground. Robin had won an end or two that day but towards the last two ends there were other people with more of a score. Douglas Nicholson said to Robin, 'You know, all you've got to do is to score another point or two at this end and you've won the prize – so, concentrate and have a go at it, stand up straight and take your time and do your best.' With that encouragement Robin indeed got the best arrow at the end and won the Hopetoun Prize. This is the kind of encouragement that a butty can give to his companion. Robin remembers one time saying a similar thing to Andrew Gray-Muir when shooting in the prize at Hopetoun: 'All you have to do, Andrew, is to get a clout,' and Andrew's first shaft was about a bow distance away from the target – just light – and Robin encouraged him again, saying, 'Take the same aim – you'll probably hit it this time,' and amazingly he did and won the prize which Robin felt he had a share in.

Also in 1970 they had another match against the Woodmen of Arden at Meriden, their home ground. Sari and Robin drove down with their latest baby and a nurse. The Royal Company that year was staying at the Warwick Hotel which suited Robin and Sari with a baby because Sari could use the car and get out to the shooting ground to join in the picnics and then go back and have a rest in the hotel before the next dinner. On the first evening, before the Woodmen hosted a cocktail party and met up with the Royal Company of Archers Team, Robin had a practice on the ground and in fact hit the target that night and got a clout which did his morale a world of good. During the match on the following day he certainly didn't shoot as well and didn't score for his team. He stopped at one end and was the best arrow for his side – stopping the other side from scoring a lot more points than they did, but the team got beaten fairly hard in that second match at Meriden. There was dinner in the Hall at Meriden and a dance as well; Sari and Robin danced the Eightsome reel and other dances with the Woodmen and enjoyed all the fun.

Between 1966 and 1976, Peter Bartholomew was quite outstanding and in several years he scored twenty clouts to win the Clout Bowl in the Royal Company – an extraordinary number of times to hit the target at 180 or 200 hundred yards range. He was also very good at winning the butt shooting prizes in the indoor target. He was very consistent and when the Archers shot together on practice nights he used to challenge people there to play for an old-fashioned penny – and actually didn't lose too many because from time to time a good shot beat Peter. But Peter's health didn't do very well for him and in 1975 he wasn't terribly fit. Robin helped to understudy him by running some of the prizes and events. Robin had won eight prizes in the first ten years that he was a Member of the Royal Company and then was appointed Match Secretary to take over from Peter Bartholomew so he started having to attend all the Shoots and to arrange the shooting for the rest of the Royal Company.

During 1975 Robin had helped to plan the 1976 match against the Woodmen of Arden by which time he was Match Secretary. For the first time the Royal Company Team were going to have lodgings in the houses of the Woodmen who lived near enough to the forest ground – this was the first time that the Royal Company had separated and lived in private houses with their opponents. Gordon Simpson, as the Captain, with the Lord Warden was trying very hard to make it fun for the competitors to enjoy each other's company, as well as being competitive; they weren't wanting to have the sort of match where two sides were determined to win and being rude and difficult to each other. The match since that time has been more and more friendly as the competitors and their wives have got to know each other.

The Match Secretary also has to arrange all the Shoots of the Royal Company and there is a calendar of Shoots which are done annually. Robin had to negotiate with the local authorities, such as Edinburgh and Musselburgh, to fit in to the Lord Provost's diary and with other events. In Montrose, Peebles, Selkirk and Biggar there are rather more rare prizes on a rotation of every six years. There is a monthly calendar which has to go out to each of the shooting Members of the Royal Company to tell them about each of the monthly events, including the Match Dinner – and the Company Officer who looks after Archers Hall has to be briefed about the targets, the dates for the dinners and who has won the prizes so that the events can go forward smoothly. Bills have to go out for the Archers' drinks, and at each of the match dinners the Match Secretary sits at a table to collect the cash for that evening's event.

For the major outdoor prizes the Match Secretary of course is involved in negotiating with the host to measure the shooting ground, to get the targets up and to make sure that there are safety arrangements in place so that the spectators don't get too near. So from 1976 Robin had quite a busy time with the Royal Company of Archers and, indeed, because he was shooting much more regularly he also won prizes more frequently.

In the 1970s inflation was moving ahead quite fast and the Royal Company decided to try and cut some of the costs of operating the main events as the Archers would still enjoy their shooting without it costing a lot. For instance at the Queen's Prize the Royal Company had always had a little marquee so that the ladies could have tea and cakes while the Archers were shooting. The Secretary of the Royal Company asked Her Majesty if she could give permission to use one of the rooms in the Palace to serve the tea at that particular prize and she graciously allowed the use of the Equerry's Room and this practice has continued since then.

One of Robin's first negotiations was with Musselburgh where Archers shoot every year, usually in the early part of the summer. Robin visited the Musselburgh Council Officials to discuss how to perhaps reduce the costs of the Shoot. The Royal Company used to have a bus to take the band down to the Racecourse and the Royal Company would park their cars in the car park and take the bus to the shooting ground and then the bus would pick up the band and come back with them – and then at the end of the match the band would march the Royal Company along the street with the Councillors to the old Police Station where competitors would have a very nice tea with the Council. It was thought that the Royal Company of Archers should now discontinue the bus. The Brunton Hall had now been built on the other side of the river so Robin walked the course, as it were, and thought that the Royal Company could march by the back road over the old bridge, past Loretto School playing ground to the Racecourse. They could march back from the Shoot also and have the Pipe Band with them throughout both marches. Robin went, the day before the match, with the Company Officer to measure out the shooting ground beside the old golf course and the Racecourse and place the targets on a bit of sandy ground where there shouldn't be any small stones to break the arrows. Once Brunton Hall was open the Musselburgh Council provided a very sumptuous meal for the competitors and their wives at the end of the match. The prize-winner at Musselburgh is nearly always asked to go to a Musselburgh Club dinner later in the year and join the Council and the Council officials at an evening where everyone can let their hair down a bit and get to know each other. It has been quite a tradition for the Councillors and their officials to play a golf match as well and the winner of the Musselburgh Arrow is often asked to go to that match and dinner on the golf course as well. Of course, some Members of the Royal Company are rather better at golf than others and Robin certainly doesn't pride himself as a golfer. Robin was lucky enough to win the Musselburgh Arrow on several occasions and it was a great joy to go there.

The Salvesen family has a very close tie with Musselburgh because Provost Kemp's granddaughter married Thomas Salvesen, Robin's

After the shoot the Provost of Musselburgh presents the Silver Arrow to Robin.

grandfather, and in fact Pansy Salvesen, Tom Grainger-Stewart's wife, inherited the Bible which was given by Musselburgh to Provost Kemp and later in her life she passed that on to Robin's son Tom, who had been given the name Kemp as one of his middle names when he was christened. At this time the Kemp Bible is sitting at Eaglescairnie waiting for Tom to have his own home. Musselburgh keeps alive many old traditions. It has honoured the Royal Scots by giving them the freedom of Musselburgh so the Regiment can march through the Burgh with drums beating and the men carrying their rifles. The Burgh also gave the Royal Company of Archers the freedom of Musselburgh in the time when Jessie Burns was the Provost of Musselburgh and there was a splendid little parade. Like many Border towns, they have a riding of the marches every year but every twentieth year or thereabouts there is a very special one at which the town of Musselburgh appoints some new Burgesses. These are Musselburgh folk who have done something special for the town and a few Members of the Royal Company who have won the Musselburgh Arrow have been honoured in this way. The new Burgess is presented with a scroll and a bap and the bap has on it the symbols of Musselburgh which of course are the mussel shells. Now Robin, having won the Musselburgh Arrow on a few occasions and knowing officials in the Musselburgh Council, put in his application to become a Burgess of Musselburgh and was honoured in their special week one year. Later in that week he also managed to win the Musselburgh Arrow, scoring seven points that particular night. It was a very hot evening too and as the Archers shot they got thirstier and thirstier. Sari went off with one of the other wives to try and get bottles of water for the relief of some of the Archers who were finding the heat and the occasion quite difficult to bear. But it was a nice night for shooting and Robin found that he could get the range and scored quite a lot of points – so it was a wonderful week.

There was another occasion at Musselburgh where Robin's great friend Pat Playfair Hannay had shot well during the early part of the meeting and had had a winning score. As the afternoon progressed Robin scored a point here and there and at the end there was to be a prize end between Pat Playfair Hannay and Robin. Earlier that year Robin had had a tussle with Pat, the result being that Pat had won the Dalhousie Sword, and Robin was quite determined that Pat shouldn't win the Musselburgh prize end as well. Robin achieved a clout with his first shot at the prize end. He's only ever seen it done one other time. The Musselburgh clout is square which is most unusual because all the other ones are round. The tradition in Musselburgh is a target with a square frame over which originally they stretched a skin – a much older tradition than at other places. The Musselburgh Silver Arrow may well be the oldest sporting prize recorded which is competed for every year.

At the Edinburgh Arrow there also used to be a tea tent for the Archers and their wives. During the time that Robin was Match Secretary it was necessary to make some changes. Edinburgh was changing the shape of the paths or having a football pitch laid out. Robin went out with the officials and decided that the City could move the shooting ground further west to beside Middle Meadow Walk. It meant just a slightly longer march from Archers Hall to the shooting ground, but it was also arranged during that negotiation that the groundsmen would put up rather better safety ropes round the shooting ground to keep the public safe.

One particular day Robin and others were having quite a competitive and closely fought afternoon for the Edinburgh Arrow and Robin was just about to shoot – hoping to win another end in order to contend for the prize. As he drew his bow the press photographer bending down on his knees suddenly said in a loud voice as Robin was drawing his arrow, 'Hold it!' Robin managed not to let go his arrow shaft and he brought his bow down and said, 'You know, this actually is a competition, I can pose for a photo at some other time but we're actually trying to hit the target at the moment,' and so he took his time and tried to settle himself to shoot again. What an extraordinary thing in the middle of an athletic event! The memories Archers have of these shoots.

It was during one of the shoots at Hopetoun that Lord Clydesmuir, the President of the Council, talked to Robin about the shoot for Biggar which was to take place the following year. The Biggar Jug had been presented to the Royal Company by the gentlemen who lived in the houses round about Biggar. Archers had been accustomed to shooting at Coulter House, a lovely little Georgian building. The shooting ground was a very long grass pasture with a row of splendid old trees on either side of it, forming a great avenue. The first time that Robin shot at Biggar there was a bit of a west wind blowing and the arrows lifted above the height of the trees as they were going their 180 yards up the course. The wind caught the arrows and made them drift across several yards, although the Archers themselves were standing in completely sheltered ground. Robin said to Michael Finlay during that shoot, 'How on earth do you manage to get so close to the target when the wind is really very difficult today?' and he answered, 'Oh, I'm aiming at one of the wee windows in Coulter House and it seems to work.' That was a good tip for other prizes and certainly when Robin is shooting at Hopetoun nowadays he quite often aims at one of the wee windows in the big house, especially if there is a wind going across the course. Anyway, the residents of Coulter House went to live elsewhere and the Royal Company wouldn't be able to use the ground again. Ronald Clydesmuir thought that the Secretary and Match Secretary should talk to the Community Council about making the Biggar Jug a community event so that the local people could take an interest in the Royal Company's visit there. Robin took this suggestion up and he and George Burnet, the Secretary of the Royal Company at that time, went down to Biggar during the off shooting season to meet the Chairman of the Community Council. They went out to the field where the Biggar people have their annual fair and decided that they could march there from the centre of Biggar with the pipe band and shoot there. The Secretary and Match Secretary had to provide luncheon for the Pipe Band and for the Members of the Royal Company so they tested the food and service at one or two of the local hostelries. After lunch they met the local Police Inspector to talk about the march through the town, where and when, to get his blessing and ask the police to look after the parade and deal with the disruption for the public and the cars. But the police told George Burnet that the whole of

Strathclyde region had a ban on public marches that year because there had
been trouble at Orange marches. The Police were asked to help.

The Royal Company were allowed to march with a band through Biggar
for the prize that year. They had lunch with their wives at the hotel, then
the march with the Band, the shoot and the giving of the prize; then all the
Archers went home without having an evening dinner together. Having a
more relaxed prize with the wives joining in for luncheon was an
experiment which worked very well and has gone on ever since.

The most recent prize at Biggar was a very happy day for Robin Salvesen
because they marched from their luncheon to the grounds of a private
house to shoot, and have a nice tea party with the kind people who owned
the house. Robin won the first end in the competition with the best arrow,
shooting with a group of three archers at the very end of the list, and as the
prize went on, all three 'Butties' won ends. Walter Riddel-Carre and Bill
Bewsher were shooting quite well and it looked as if Walter Riddel-Carre
might turn out to be the ultimate winner. However the Judges shouted for
the last two ends 'up and down' and Robin managed to get a clout which
was best but Walter Riddel-Carre had a very good shaft at the same end – so
he was catching up. And then at the last end of the shoot Robin again hit
the clout, shooting in the opposite direction. It is rather unusual to get a
clout at each of the last two ends in a major prize and this gave him the
outright winning of the Biggar Jug.

When the Montrose Arrow was shot in 1972, Peter Bartholomew was
Match Secretary and he asked Robin if he would be good enough to take
the policeman who was playing the pipes for the dinner at Montrose, back
to Edinburgh the morning after the shoot and the dinner, together with
Peter himself. After lunch at Montrose they marched out to the shooting
ground. The match started on quite a nice day but with a bit of a breeze,
because its ground was right out on the sand dunes on the seaward side of
Montrose. The match started very well with different people winning ends
but at the third end Robin shot a clout and a half bow and they were both
the best arrows so he scored three points. Gordon Simpson said, 'Really,
that's tremendous – very often prizes are won with three points – after three
ends to have three points is a jolly good score.' Peter Bartholomew got on
form and started winning ends and getting a clout and slowly but surely his
score was the best and Robin was trailing behind. But by winning another
couple of ends Robin also managed to get five points – and the match
finished with the two of them having to shoot a prize end together. Robin's
first arrow was the better of the two, then Peter shot another arrow which

wasn't good and then as they went up it was clear that Robin had won the prize. Robin was told he'd have to make a speech at the dinner after he'd received the prize. There are forfeits to be paid for winning prizes in the Royal Company! So as he changed and bathed before dinner he had to think of what he could say. It all seemed to go all right.

The next day after breakfast Peter and Robin got to their car and were looking round for the Police bandsman because no doubt he'd had a good evening in Montrose. Later, driving through a village in Perthshire, the policeman suddenly said, 'We must stop, we must stop,' and he went into the Police Station. Coming out he said, 'All right, go up left and go up right and we'll stop here.' They went in the back door of a nice little hotel and up to the bar and suddenly realised that the Police bandsman had felt that it was time to have a drink before lunch. It was rather amusing that the policeman went to the Police Station to find out which pub might be open at that time in the morning.

Six years later, in 1978, Robin travelled to Montrose with George Burnet to make arrangements for the match and then went up early to measure out the shooting ground. The Secretary had asked Robin if he would make the speech at the dinner for the Royal Company, to drink the health of the City of Montrose. The Company officer made sure that the targets were in place and that there were some safety ropes to restrict the movement of any crowd. On this particular day there was a much stronger wind and it was blowing right across the course. After lunch as they marched out and got their equipment ready Gordon Simpson said to Robin and others, 'Well, it'll be a jolly lucky winner today with a wind like this because it's gusting – very difficult.' This Robin thought was a good challenge and as it was very much a crosswind you had to aim two, three or four yards away to the side of the target and the arrow would drift across. This crosswind was a lot of fun and Robin managed to enjoy the way the arrows were drifting across and got it right a few times and won a few ends and gained the Montrose prize. He had to do the speech at the dinner in the evening to drink the health of Montrose, and then he had to go up and receive the prize. He was asked if he would like to make another speech as the winner – which he did in a matter of two or three sentences and thanked them all very much for a very enjoyable day and that was greeted with great applause because nobody wanted to listen to two speeches at the same dinner!

In the spring of 1980 Robin felt pretty tired as he'd been travelling abroad quite frequently on business, so he and Sari went up to Ardmaddy Castle on the west of Scotland and had a week's holiday in May. Argyll is awfully nice at that time of year because the midges aren't too bad and the brackens aren't too high. In the Ardmaddy Estate there are one or two small lochs that one can walk to – through the fields and up the valley until you get to the loch near the top of the hill. Robin walked up with a picnic on his back and a fishing rod in his hand to one or other of these small lochs and got a bit of exercise and lots of fresh air and was able to see the ducks nesting on the loch and sometimes even deer as he was fishing quietly. Charlie Struthers had been doing quite a lot of demolition and rebuilding of his house at Ardmaddy and there was a very big beech that had fallen that winter in the park in front of the house. Robin said, 'Can I help with that?' and so it became Robin's project. With an axe and a saw he started cutting the limbs back and piling up the straighter branches ready for firewood. He got quite a lot of fresh air and exercise and went back home to Eaglescairnie feeling better, with the result that during the next fortnight he not only won the Musselburgh Arrow and the Peebles Arrow but also the Queen's Prize. This is presented by Her Majesty herself on the day of the Garden Party at Holyrood House. Robin was told to turn up at Holyrood House with the prize that he had chosen – a silver coffee jug – which had to have on it the Royal Crest, his own Crest and the Royal Company's Crest. After the Queen has presented the prize the silver is inscribed with the fact that it was presented to the winner by the Queen and the date when he won it – because the prize cannot be inscribed before it has been presented. On the day of the Garden Party, Robin in his uniform had to go through the Equerry's entrance into the Palace and upstairs to the Drawing Room to await Her Majesty and then had the honour to be presented to her. As he stood in the corridor of the upper gallery in Holyrood two or three members of the Royal Family came past and congratulated him in a most informal and delightful way. Robin was also presented to the Duke of Edinburgh and to the Queen Mother.

It is perhaps worth recording that Robin has won eighty-one prizes in the Royal Company of Archers at various shooting occasions over the years – which is a greater number than has been recorded on any other person's name in the history of the Royal Company.

The main objective for the Queen's Body Guard is to act as Body Guard for Her Majesty on her visits to Scotland and the main duty is to provide some form of Guard and Reception for the huge Garden Party at Holyrood each year. Both the Queen and the Duke of Edinburgh attend the Garden Party regularly and they each are taken down an aisle in the garden which is marked out by the standing bodies of Archers – the Lord Lieutenants who introduce people who have been distinguished in one way or another or given good service to their country are picked out of the crowd and presented to Her Majesty. People turn out in their best clothes and enjoy a day in the sunshine. There have been days when the weather was rather grey and damp, but the memorable one was when the Archers were instructed to wear their capes because the rain poured down and umbrellas were carried by many guests and everyone got rather wet. There have been some good days and some not so good days but in the heavy clothes that the Archers wear, it is nice to have a cool breeze, although the ladies in their smarter dresses would prefer it to be a hot summer day.

The other occasion for which the Royal Company provides a Guard of Honour is a Thistle Ceremony in St Giles' Cathedral when Her Majesty has a parade of the Knights of the Thistle who are installing a new Member to their ranks. Outside St Giles a Guard of Honour of the Queen's Body Guard form up, having had a rehearsal the day before – they usually go by bus to the Esplanade at the Castle and then march down the hill to take their places in front of St Giles'. Then The Queen will come up the High Street from Holyrood House in her carriage, and draw up in front of the cathedral where she receives the royal salute from the Body Guard before she goes in to the Thistle Ceremony.

CHAPTER 13

Lighthouses

AN ARTICLE IN *Fairplay* magazine described a legal case when British Steel objected to the payment of local lighthouse dues for their ships entering the Port of Newcastle. At that time Trinity House in Newcastle had the right to charge local lighthouse dues on all vessels which entered the Port of the Tyne. The statute actually said vessels which used or passed the lights. British Steel sailed ships from the south up the Channel and believed that they neither used nor passed the local lights on the Farne Islands and around the coast north of Newcastle. They won the case and Robin Salvesen and others using the Port realised that the big colliers also were not using the local lights and they too applied to cease paying local lighthouse dues. Trinity House in Newcastle, like all the other Trinity House organisations round the coast, had been set up by the Master Mariners to look after members who fell on evil times or were injured and needed to retire. They had a group of almshouses and a hall in the Port of Newcastle. Master Mariners from the Port of Leith had built a very beautiful hall, also Trinity House – now a museum owned by Historic Scotland.

Robin's first meeting with the Northern Lighthouse Board in George Street in Edinburgh took place about 1984/85 when, with David Ropner, he listened to the plans for capital expenditure for the Northern Lighthouse Commissioners in the forthcoming year. After the meeting, the Commissioners invited delegates from the Department of Transport and the Lighthouse Advisory Committee to go down to Leith Docks for lunch on board the pilot vessel MV *Pharos* where the crew served a very good meal which went on through fish, meat and sweet to coffee and port. Robin Salvesen was a busy shipowner and needed to get back to his office fairly sharply so he excused himself and went back to work. Not long after that however he was invited to join the Lights Advisory Committee and to take over as Chairman from David Ropner. This meant attending the bilateral meetings of Lighthouse Authorities in London, Dublin and Edinburgh each year and going with the Department of Transport to the wrap-up meeting of the Lights Finance Committee (LFC) which gave advice to the Minister of Transport* on the setting of the lighthouse dues for shipping in the following year.

Robin's first task was to look at the efficiency of the operation of the Lighthouse Authorities. Each of them is set up by statute and has a proud tradition – the Stephensons in Scotland built lighthouses on very difficult rocks, as did Trinity House in England – and the Irish Lighthouse Commissioners.

The Irish Lighthouse Commissioners look after both the Republic and Northern Ireland. They elect new Commissioners themselves and have gathered over the years a very good broad cross-section of skilled folk who look after the safety and navigation in Irish waters.

The Northern Lighthouse Board is set up by statute in a different way, having a very high proportion of Sheriffs and the Lord Advocate as Commissioners. Robin's Grandfather McClure had been a Sheriff and a Member of the Lighthouse Commission many years before. The Northern Lighthouse Board had three co-opted Members by the time Robin was involved in the Lighthouse Advisory Committee, to widen the range of skills available to the management of an increasingly complex and scientific operation.

Trinity House in London has members known as Brethren and a strong connection with the Royal Family. They also have, in recent times, co-opted three Commissioners to join the Lighthouse Board of Trinity House. For many years Trinity House in London operated the Pilotage in many major English Ports as well as the lighthouses.

In 1984 there was significant change in management of the ports, harbours and estuaries around the coast of the United Kingdom. The Forth Ports Authority, for instance, was set up to own and operate five different harbours within the Estuary of the Forth. The pilotage control was vested in the Port Authorities, by a very significant change through Act of Parliament.

The Lights Advisory Committee represents not only shipowners but also the Chambers of Commerce and the Ports in the United Kingdom, offering advice to Her Majesty's Government about the payment of light dues. The LAC was keen that the lighthouse dues charged on shipping should remain as low as possible, while supporting the operations of the three statutory bodies providing aids to safe navigation round the United Kingdom and the Republic of Ireland.

The British Government had seen the necessity during 1984 to set up

---

*In these early years, the Department of Trade had responsibility.

two Commissions to look into the Lighthouse Authorities. The first was by Arthur Young McLelland Moore to review the lighthouse service; it reported in May 1984. A report by Arthur Anderson, on the light dues and their payment, didn't propose any very radical change, but the Arthur Young McLelland Moore report had indicated very considerable short-comings in the operation, management and manning of the Lighthouse Authorities. The result of this was to focus serious consideration on the number of lighthouse tenders and indeed the calibre of the financial control and operations of the three statutory Lighthouse Authorities. One of the major recommendations was that the lighthouse tenders, of which there were nine, should be reduced to a much smaller number and asked whether it wouldn't be better to operate a single management unit for the tender fleet so that the shipping assets, each of which was double-crewed, could be used to greater effect. Robin Salvesen also felt that it would be possible to automate and improve the design of the tenders to provide stable working platforms. The automation of some of the lighthouses had started (by 1985) but the Lighthouse Authorities had decided to take time over this programme. The Commissioners of Irish Lights set themselves a programme of automating two lighthouses a year, whereas the Northern Lighthouse Board decided that they would not require compulsory redundancies of staff. Each lighthouse had at least three men on board and in some cases there were six – to provide two on each watch. Most of their time was spent in watch-keeping and making sure that the generators continued to work: jobs which offered opportunity for modern automation and automatic switching in of alternative power units if there was any failure in the operating unit.

The Lighthouse Authorities have a statutory requirement to provide 'safe navigation' but the Department of Transport and the government had never defined what the Act meant by 'safe navigation' or indeed safe navigation for whom. So each Lighthouse Authority had set up its own criteria for the number of lights and buoys that it should have on station and to provide safe navigation for fishing, pleasure craft and commercial vessels in their area. Nation states are responsible for safety in their coastal zones and most fund this directly. The United Kingdom raise a tax on commercial shipping, known as 'Light Dues' and ring-fence this money in the General Lighthouse Fund. Britain is unusual in having a lifeboat service which is paid for entirely by voluntary subscription, the RNLI. In international terms it is a most strange and unusual situation that protecting life of people on and off the shore should be operated by a charity.

The Kylie report was commissioned in 1987 and reported on the current use of Nav Aids. There are navigation aids such as lights and buoys which are provided round the coast and in the estuaries ashore, visual aids that ship's officers can see as they travel. There are also statutory Nav Aids which each ship is required to carry. Ships over a certain size have to carry one or even two radars. They are required to fit, for instance, direction finding apparatus on the radio sets, and echo sounders so that they can tell the depth of the water underneath the hull. Navigation aids are carried on board the ship to supplement the visual aids from shore and the electronic aids by shore based station or satellite.

The United Kingdom had a choice of going into a European Loran system or to go for the British manufactured Decca navigation system. The British Government decided it would support the Decca system which quoted a price compatible with the Loran system costs. It was known at the time that the Loran system gave the ship operator a greater accuracy and better reliability of performance. The British Government decided to approve the Decca scheme with funds provided by the General Lighthouse Fund. Satellite navigation has become widespread and the receivers can be very small and cheap, providing an accuracy to ten metres if not better. So the actual accuracy of the satellite information is better than anything that seafarers have ever had before, and gives a more accurate position for a ship operator than his chart. It is always a rule of navigation that navigators cross-check their information frequently.

The Lights Advisory Committee commissioned a Dr J.C. Strange to write a report for them on the requirement of Nav Aids round a section of the British coast and he chose to use as his methodology the concept that every merchant ship would check its position with the visual aids every half an hour. So the number of aids that a navigator used would depend to some degree on the speed and size of the ship – so a smaller and slower ship would use more visual navigation aids than the larger ocean-going vessel. The methodology was never accepted by the Master Mariners at Trinity House as an acceptable measure for the number of Nav Aids round the coast but the Strange report did indicate in 1987 that there were approximately three times as many aids as were actually necessary for commercial merchant ships trading up the English Channel.

In 1990 the British Ports commissioned a survey on 'light dues on pleasure craft', to advise the Government on the methodology of charging yachts and leisure craft, and thus share the cost of lights. It was clearly seen that pleasure craft used the lights and buoys as much as fishermen or merchant ships and yet were not paying for the service. The Government is perhaps still reviewing and considering this but no action has yet been taken to bring pleasure craft into the net. One of the problems for the Government is that, unlike France and some other countries, the pleasure craft do not have to register. The operators of fast motorboats do not actually have to have qualifications in order to take their vessels to sea. There are not many statistics to inform regulators on the number of boats or the qualifications of their operators.

Robin Salvesen did a round of bilaterals in 1985 as Chairman of the Lights Advisory Committee. He went to the meetings in Ireland, Scotland and England and then the final meeting with the Department of Transport to consider the annual accounts of the General Lighthouse Fund and to give advice to Her Majesty's Government about the level of light dues. In 1987 the shipping industry was very concerned about the increasing costs which seemed to be coming through in the forecasts from the Lighthouse Authorities. British shipowners and Ports Authorities were not convinced that the Lighthouse Authorities could control their budget and costs. So when the lighthouse dues were proposed in February to the House of Lords, LAC members organised some parliamentary questions. Briefing papers were put forward to quite a large number of peers representing the British Ports Association, which was organised by Nick Finney, and also to those who were known to specialise in British shipping matters in the House of Lords. The Department of Transport received a large number of letters showing concern about the increase in lighthouse dues.

The Lighthouse Authorities have continued to work on research and development during the period and one of the major breakthroughs has been improved light sources. Early bulbs providing light created a lot of heat as well. Readers will know that a light bulb is too hot to hold in the hand. A light source for a twenty-five mile range required fans to keep it cool. The introduction of solar power to the lighthouses and the buoys could never have happened without modern bulbs. It is now possible for lights, giving a range of twelve to fifteen miles, to be designed and powered by solar power, even in the North of Scotland in the winter time. This has been a success story. The new range of modern light bulbs no longer wastes electric power to create heat.

Grey Seal was purchased by the Commissioners of Irish Lights to provide support to their lighthouse tender. She was a second-hand vessel which had operated in the North Sea and had a large crane to lift buoys from the sea to her after deck. The tradition in the lighthouse service had been buoy operations on the fore deck, while navigation control was functioning from a traditional design of ship. Supply boats for the oil industry were built in 1974 with stern operation, all round vision and navigation from a bridge in the bow, rather in the manner of a tug. Robin was invited to sail on a short voyage in Ireland to see *Grey Seal* operate and he enjoyed the chance of informal discussion.

When *Pharos* was built at Ferguson's yard in the Clyde, she had a specification which could allow for her to carry out maintenance of Class 1 and Class 2 buoys and supply to construction projects of remote rock locations. Helicopter operations were expected to lift supplies from her deck. On her trial trip in the Clyde Estuary, Robin saw her performance on the measured mile and also her ability to turn within her own length using her bow and stern propellers in the rougher sea and swell of the Atlantic. *Pharos* enabled the Northern Lighthouse Commissioners to travel on inspection voyages each summer. They could dine well and entertain in style. The Lights Advisory Committee had a duty to limit funding to focused commercial business.

In summer 2002, the Deputy Master of Trinity House invited Robin to join an inspection voyage on *Patricia*. He was able to suggest a period of three days in early July and joined the ship in fog from a small port in Devon. That evening conditions were not suitable for a helicopter flight in the evening. The lighthouse vessel's tender came in to the rock wall and seaweed covered steps in harbour and the passengers with baggage were helped on board. The boat sailed into the dark sea with occasional fog signals from fishing craft. *Patricia*'s lights loomed out of darkness and the sea waves were vigorous, lifting the small boat in a steep swell, especially as she turned round the stern of the larger ship to come under the lifeboat falls in her lee. The whole tender was lifted up to the main deck. Then Robin was told that dinner was ready and could be served in ten minutes if he could put on his dinner jacket quickly. Each day thereafter Robin and the Deputy Master's team visited three lights in the Bristol Channel area. One lighthouse was on an island where the sea birds had nested and hatched their eggs. The adult birds dived at the intruders while the downy chicks ran amongst the deep clumps of grass. There were colourful patches of wild flowers and also the mess and smell of bird droppings rotting in the summer sunshine. The accuracy of the Differentiated Global Position System enabled further corrections to each lighthouse position, so the team measured and recorded readings on their instruments. The unmanned stations need a refreshing flow of air to reduce condensation in the masonry and solutions to such problems were discussed.

The Commissioners of Irish Lights, in working through their plan for a new lighthouse tender, took advice from many shipyards and have provided a vessel which gives a very stable platform, using Flume stabilisers. It can service all the buoys and lights as required round the coast of Ireland. Northern Lighthouse Commissioners have commissioned the *Polestar* which is a specialist buoy working vessel which has already in her second year managed to visit two hundred and forty-five buoys. The replacement for one or other of the Trinity House lighthouse vessels in the future will follow at least part of the designs of *Granuelle* or *Polestar*. A review of the lighthouse Tender Fleet is commissioned which will explore the workload for the next decades and thus future ship designs, and will assist in the creation of manning scales and training for personnel.

The close operation of the Department of Transport personnel with the Lights Advisory Committee during the last several years has been able to influence major reform within the Lighthouse Authorities, and the standard and reliability of the accounting and the budgets and the plans and forecasts is very satisfactory. The purely commercial part of the operation and the financial side of the Lighthouse Authorities, together with the calibre of the people that meet together, have given Robin a lot of pleasure and interest. The investment in new technology which has improved the efficiency of navigational aids and controlled the operating costs has also reduced the level of light dues.

However, there has not been parliamentary time to re-define the meaning of 'safe navigation'. The Lighthouse Authorities themselves review from time to time the number of Nav Aids which they are operating and make recommendations to close one or two of them. Satallite navigation is now so accurate and its cost so low that pleasure craft, fishing boats and commercial craft are all able to have an accurate print-out of exactly where they are on the chart in front of them on the bridge. Some cars and lorries also use this system.

Robin Salvesen was able to bring to the Lighthouse Authorities some of his experience in managing change and especially in introducing auto-mation. The organisations spend less on daily operational and personnel costs. However, the large payroll of the 1980s has left the GLF with a huge commitment to cover the cost of pensions to former employees.

CHAPTER 14

British Shipping

ROBIN SALVESEN had a deep involvement in the ups and downs of British shipping between 1965 and 1989. The first major decision that he took as a Director of Christian Salvesen & Co related to insurance and took place early in this period. The Lloyds Brokers, Holmwood, Back & Manson, and the Salvesen leading underwriter, Henry Chester, asked for a very large increase in insurance premiums for Salvesen's small ships – the Norwegian Lines. Alex Anderson and Robin Salvesen put a plan to the Board whereby the money that they would otherwise pay to their Lloyds Brokers would be put into a special reserve account. The management team could keep their own record of claims against the Policy. This self insurance worked very well for Salvesen's and over the next several years the money accumulated, although there were one or two quite large casualties. One was a grounding of a ship going to Norway. Robin was called at home by a newspaper reporter at about three o'clock in the morning and asked for information about one of the small Norwegian ships. 'What is the name of the Captain?' and, 'Who are the crew?' and, 'Do you know if anyone was hurt?' As Robin hadn't heard about the collision, he stalled. They asked various questions about what the ship was carrying and where she was going from and to, questions Robin certainly was able to answer, but as far as the calamity was concerned he said that of course they had to tell the next of kin first and couldn't disclose any information about the crew at this stage. In fact no-one had been hurt at all and the ship had continued to her normal port of call where some repairs to the hull enabled her to continue.

The Leith Shipowners' Association was quite active in the early part of this period. There were several shipowners in the Port of Leith: the Ben Line, George Gibson, Christian Salvesen and Currie Line, as well as the North of Scotland company which ran ferries from Leith and Aberdeen up to Shetland and Orkney. Other national companies who had their main offices elsewhere paid a subscription to the Leith Shipowners' Association because they used the Ports frequently and wanted to influence it. This Association had the authority to put forward names for the Leith Dock Commissioners and also provided three members to the Firth of Forth

Pilotage Authority and three Governors to the Nautical College. The rates for tugs and boatmen were negotiated with the Leith Dock Commission.

When Robin became a Director of A.F. Henry & Macgregor he went with Willy Ireland to the FD & D Club – Freight, Demurrage and Defence Club – which was run by a firm of Newcastle lawyers, Botterell Roche and Temperley. The Club was called the British Steamship Short Trade Association and looked after coastal ships and small ships that traded in the European area. It gave access to lawyers to look after the defence if any accident should happen to a member's ship and the legal costs were covered by a mutual club. The Board of Directors always had very interesting meetings where lawyers presented current claims and legal settlements in the Court. As English law is basically case law, to keep up-to-date with the various settlements in Court is a very good way of keeping up-to-date with the law as it changes. The Directors were all shipowners and very much commercial men; they only took a case to Court if they thought there was a real chance of winning although they sometimes wanted a test case to clarify law. They would often instruct the lawyers to negotiate settlement at the best possible rate without going to Court and fighting a lawyers' battle.

There was a problem of a virus in diesel oil which seemed to hit ships when oil was kept in the tank on board the ship for any length of time at certain temperatures. It grew strings of fibre in the tank, which blocked the pipes and the pumps. There were quite a lot of claims for damage to ships' engines because of this virus, and the lawyers arranged negotiations and settlement with the supplying oil companies.

Christian Salvesen ships were entered into the North of England P & I Club. Protecting and Indemnity is a form of insurance for risks which are not normally covered in the Hull Policy which was placed with Lloyds through their Underwriters in London. This was a mutual shipowners' club to cover exceptional events and could level out the cost of operating ships. One interesting claim presented to a Salvesen ship was for frost damage to oranges under bill of lading from Hull to Trondheim. The oranges appeared to be loaded perfectly satisfactorily, and as far as the ship's officers were concerned they were also discharged satisfactorily with the right number of boxes. The receivers however alleged that the frost had damaged the oranges during the passage. Robin took the view that as the sea water in the log books of the ship was always above freezing and the oranges had been stowed within the hold, there was no way that the frost damage could have occurred while they were in the care of the shipowner. This argument held and the Club was able to dismiss that claim. Claims were frequent for damage to cargo such as rolls of paper coming from Skien through the Port of Aberdeen; any small tear would often upset several layers of the paper in the roll – this could cause a very expensive claim. The publishers couldn't have a tear in the middle of the *Aberdeen Press and Journal.*

When one of the Henry & Macgregor ships collided with a bridge across the River Medway, Captain Phillip interviewed the ship's Captain and crew and the pilot involved. It was clear that all the signals on the bridge had been turned to allow the ship to go through but the bridge hadn't opened in time – a ship can't just reverse and stop promptly when the tide is flowing. There was an article in a local newspaper about the collision which reported that a car had stalled on the bridge at the time it was meant to open. This was an interesting case because the entire cost of the damage to the ship and the bridge fell upon the car insurance policy.

Although Christian Salvesen and Henry & Macgregor both had a lot of regular seamen on their books they also had to use men from the pool of labour which was operated by the British Shipping Federation who had a register of seamen, each of whom had a Shipping Federation book to show the dates of service with each ship. The Federation had local offices in Leith, Aberdeen and Newcastle which could supply a volunteer to join the crew at fairly short notice. The Shipping Federation negotiated the annual pay claims with the two unions – the Officer's Union and the National Union of Seamen (for the ratings). During the 1960s there were a lot of strikes, not only of dockers but also of seamen. Eventually the big liner companies like the Ben Line and the tanker companies like Shell, Esso and BP put their own seafarers on company contracts, giving them rates and conditions of employment which they negotiated direct with their own employees. As the power of the Shipping Federation diminished, the strikes got less frequent and seamen had more secure jobs, with pensions and defined leave.

When British shipping declined, a merger was arranged between the Leith Shipowners' Association and the Firth of Forth Shipowners' Association – and was re-named the Firth of Forth Shipping Association as members were often Agents representing several owners. When George Brown was Chancellor of the Exchequer and the Labour Government were in power the Association met to brief MPs about the value to Britain of invisible earnings, such things as shipping freights in cross trades. British shipping was trading all round the world and earning money in many different denominations and currencies. Insurance was also a major earner of 'invisible money' for the British economy at that time. George Brown introduced Investment Grants for the British shipowners to build ships (at a rate of 20 per cent) – which reduced the capital cost of British shipping very considerably and the British fleet grew with a lot of modern ships in that period. On one occasion when Robin was Chairman of the Association, a Friday lunchtime briefing opened discussion with Members of Parliament from four political parties who all supported Scottish Developments.

Robin was appointed by the Association to join the Firth of Forth Pilotage Authority. The pilots themselves were self-employed but shared the money (paid for pilotage) between each other in a fairly straightforward way. The Authority consisted of three shipowner representatives and three Firth of Forth Port representatives and three pilots. The pilots paid for a small office with an administrator and secretary to provide the shipowners with bills for services of the pilots and to arrange the operating roster for the pilots themselves. The Committee suggested that instead of looking for more money they should reduce the number of pilots operating in the Firth of Forth and introduce universal licensing for the pilots. At that time some pilots only operated in the Grangemouth area and others only in the Leith area and it seemed sensible to the Port and shipowner representatives on the Board that there should be a universal licence so that the pilots could operate throughout the Firth of Forth. This change took quite a lot of hard bargaining within the pilots' own Committees because not all of them wanted to train for the universal licence; a smaller number of pilots were employed and they shared more money between them when trade grew, with oil terminals in the Firth of Forth.

The Pilotage Association decided that it would be sensible to operate with new fast pilot boats so that they could move the pilots from one part of the estuary to another much more quickly. So two new pilot boats were built in the Clyde with plastic hulls and a much greater speed.

After Robin Salvesen became the Chairman of the Forth Pilotage Association he endeavoured to work closely with the representatives from the Port Authority, so that a fairly united view prevailed. The relationship between Robin and individual pilots, some of whom had been Salvesen Master Mariners, remained at a very high level. It could be said that they trusted each other. However it was necessary to hold enquiries on occasion. There was one potential collision where a big cargo ship sailing from Leith very nearly overturned a yacht. A committee of the Pilotage Authority had to listen to the evidence, including tapes of conversations on the radio at the time of the incident, and to interview the pilot and the Master on the ship at the time. There was another complaint by a shipowner that one of the pilots wasn't in a fit state to do his job; an enquiry had to take place and the pilot was suspended from duty while that case was investigated.

Robin attended the Coastal Committee of the Chamber of Shipping where owners of smaller coastal vessels sat together to discuss mutual problems and, in particular, the book which covered the rates of freight payable for carrying cargo up and down the coast of the United Kingdom. It was a good way to meet the other shipowners in the same line of business including the Everards, Stephenson Clark and Metcalfe Motor Coasters.

When North Sea oil was found in 1972 it became necessary for those interested in developing the North Sea to create a Supply Boat and Oil Rig Committee in the Chamber of Shipping. Because of Robin's involvement with the Port of Aberdeen, and with Salvesen's investment in drilling rigs, he became the first Chairman of that Committee. He was able to discuss with Lloyds Register of Shipping the regulations for such new types of ship within their Register.

Robin took over from Max Harper-Gow as the Salvesen representative on Lloyds Register of Shipping in 1967 and he frequently attended the Grand Committee of Lloyds Register in London, and also the Glasgow (Scottish) Committee where he met the insurance people, as well as the shipbuilders in Scotland. The British Steamship Short Trade Association appointed Robin Salvesen as their Chairman and during that time discussed a merger with the British Shipping Association, a Club which operated very much larger ships trading worldwide. It was, however, agreed that past claims records were very different and it would be difficult to show that the charges to the mutual Clubs would be fair because there was such a long tail of past claims in the books of both Clubs. So that merger didn't take place at that time.

In the late 1960s Ian Harrison, the Chairman of Harrison Clyde and a great friend of Max Harper-Gow, was concerned about the high cost of Lloyds insurance and talked to the North of England P & I Association about the possibility of operating a mutual hull insurance club. Len Harrison of the North of England P & I discussed this with Alec Murray, the Chief Executive, and arrangements were made by them to get umbrella re-insurance for the Marine Shipping Mutual and they were able to offer competitive premiums for British shipowners who had created the club to operate without the very big premiums at Lloyds. The Marine Mutual Shipping Insurance (MMSI) grew as it developed in confidence and shipowner membership increased. The club grew and soon accepted foreign flag ships. North of England P & I wanted to offer members FD & D cover to widen the range of policies and thus cover all aspects of insurance for shipping. In many cases, shipping companies were members of NEPIA as well as either BSA or BSSTA. The financial planning was more complex as each club had exposure to claims and liabilities. Over a period NEPIA could underwrite new business while the outstanding claims and cases reduced. Both BSSTA and BSA ceased trading in 1989. A successful merger.

The Forth Ports Authority was formed by Act of Parliament at the very end of a Government's period of office. The Forth Ports Authority, which merged the management of Grangemouth, Leith, Granton, Methil and Kirkcaldy, was set up by an Act introduced by one Government but had to work under the next one. There were teething troubles for the new Authority and in particular a cash flow problem because compensation had to be paid to the Duke of Buccleuch for Granton Harbour. Methil, Kirkcaldy, Leith and Grangemouth had all been different organisations. Grangemouth started as a railway port with local management but national ownership. The Secretary of State for Scotland appointed Robin Salvesen to the Board in the early years. Management of change was not easy. The development of the land on the sea front of the estuary has taken place much more recently and now the Port Authority is an important property developer. Robin Salvesen stopped being Chairman of the Firth of Forth Pilotage Association when it was taken over by the Forth Ports Authority. The Port Authority now operates its own tugs and the pilotage and other services.

In the early days of the Thatcher Government, Nigel Lawson, as Chancellor of the Exchequer, set in hand the decline of British shipping, taking away many of the tax privileges that British shipping had enjoyed. These included free depreciation allowances and the Investment Grants. The number of British flag ships dropped from some 1,600 to 300.

Robin was Danish Consul in Scotland but also a shipowner and in these capacities he kept in touch with both the Royal Navy and the Merchant Navy in his normal business. He joined the Edinburgh Committee of King George's Fund for Sailors at a time when Sir John Clerk of Penicuik was Chairman and then President of the Scottish Council. There was an Area Organiser in Glasgow and another for the Edinburgh area so fundraising activities were divided on an east-west basis. At that time much of the collecting of money was done by shaking tins in public areas, but the

Edinburgh Committee always ran a very successful Ball in the Assembly Rooms which was the Edinburgh main fundraising event. The Royal Marine Band has become much more available and frequently presents concerts in aid of King George's Fund for Sailors. These concerts help to keep the Navy in the public eye in the remoter parts of Scotland – playing in some smaller towns as well as in Edinburgh and Glasgow.

After Robin became the Chairman of the Scottish Council, two successive Admirals have filled the office of President of the Scottish Council KGFS. Scottish shipowners used to make very significant contributions to the work. Robin merged the east and the west so there is now one full-time Area Organiser working from an office at Rosyth. The Ball moved from the Edinburgh Assembly Rooms, when local authority charges made it expensive to operate, to the Royal Navy Club in Rosyth, where it became more of a family party. The committee decided to move it back to Edinburgh and make it bigger again. There were a couple of successful Balls within Edinburgh and then it moved to Brunton Hall at Musselburgh. The target for fundraising in Scotland has progressively increased and now is something over £100,000 each year. The Royal Navy were able to help in the filming of a James Bond film and the King George's Fund for Sailors was given rights at some of the new showings. The Bond film launch took place on the same night in Edinburgh and Aberdeen, quite a stretch for the organisation but it did raise some very useful money.

The King George's Fund Area Organiser and Robin Salvesen as Chairman monitor the Charities in Scotland which the King George's Fund helps with grant aid. Several charities offer pensions to a list of seafarers in need of extra assistance and it is hoped that this makes their lives a little bit easier. These people have given very good service to the Royal Navy or the Merchant Navy in their working lives. The King George's Fund has also helped the Queen Victoria School at Dunblane with money for welfare for the students; and also ex Army, Navy and Air Force Homes, Scottish Veteran Residences and the Erskine Hospital. There's a Merchant Navy Home at Greenock which receives a benefit from King George's Fund towards modernisation of buildings and extra care for the residents.

Robin had a full programme during the 1970s and many committee meetings. The day-to-day management of the shipping fleet was delegated to teams which operated in Edinburgh. The Nautical College, P & I Clubs, Pilotage and Chamber of Shipping Committees all had executives and secretaries who carried out the tasks set by the committee. Each committee agenda required preparation time and often study or research to identify initiatives which would enforce its work and influence.

Robin was lucky when he chose Ruth Johnston and promoted her as his Secretary and Secretary for the Danish Consulate: a tall redhead who had intelligence, charm and tact as well as the word-processing skills and efficiency to operate the office. Correspondence on return from a visit abroad required a full day to read and annotate and perhaps to delegate. Ruth kept the filing cabinets in order so that previous correspondence could be recalled and relevant papers prepared for forthcoming committee work. Ruth also discussed and arranged travel tickets and currency and gathered a list of telephone calls in priority order together with briefing notes. Most days began with a session with Ruth which included shorthand dictation of letters and preparation of the more detailed memorandum and contract texts. Many of the London committees could be linked so that perhaps six meetings including dinners etc. could be undertaken within two days. Thus the travel was organised for night sleeper trains or by air through Gatwick or Heathrow. Newcastle meetings could sometimes be fixed to include a visit to a ship and there were many occasions when Robin drove through Coldstream and Wooler from Eaglescairnie during the dawn hours.

During this period Robin was able to attend the shoots (twice a week) of the Royal Company of Archers which would mean leaving the office at 5 p.m. to shoot in the gardens of Holyrood house at 5.30 p.m. This switched his mind's concentration completely from business to the consideration of the aim, and the strength of the wind. At home Sari also had a full life with the children and their school runs and also the catering for a large household. Each of the girls and boys grew up with their own skills and personality and Robin would join them in walks and games in the countryside and garden. Sari and Robin both worked with their Haddington churches and met many East Lothian families.

CHAPTER 15

Work with Schools

Governor at Fettes College

CHRISTIAN SALVESEN moved from the Leith office to a building in East Fettes Avenue around 1970. Robin had been a successful student at Fettes, getting his Entrance Certificates to University College Oxford and playing in the first fifteen for more than two seasons. He was surprised to receive a letter inviting him to a Governors' Meeting at the College indicating that he had been appointed to be a Governor at Fettes by the Edinburgh Chamber of Commerce. The first thing Robin did was to telephone a Governor that he knew to find out how much work and how much time this would entail. The Clerk for the Fettes Governors worked in a lawyer's office in Edinburgh and briefed Robin with the details.

One of the reasons he had been asked was that his son Francis, aged thirteen in 1978, was lined up to go to Fettes, and that his second daughter Alice, who had found it difficult working at Queen Anne's Caversham, being so far away from home and who had had a small illness down there, was to go as a day girl into the Sixth Form at Fettes. She stayed with Michael Lester Cribb, the Music Master, at Fettes College and his wife in their own home and so she was almost a boarding girl but could walk to school. She was looked after very well by Mr and Mrs Lester Cribb; of course, the school gave her meals and Alice chose her subjects for University entrance.

When Robin went to his first Governors' Meeting at Fettes College he was surprised to learn that the Governors had very little in the way of reserves of cash – there was a scholarship fund but it was relatively small, and boys going to Fettes with scholarships and foundation places were in fact subsidised by the fees paid by other children at the school. This seemed contrary to the original foundation of Fettes College, where it had been laid down that there should be a number of foundation places for boys who couldn't otherwise afford to go there. Fettes had already started selling some of the school land, quite a lot of it by compulsory purchase: first of all Telford College, then for the Police Headquarters, then for Broughton School. Land purchased for Bovis to build an office block in East Fettes

Avenue (which was later taken over by Christian Salvesen PLC) had belonged to Fettes earlier, as had a part of the Edinburgh Academy playing fields. The earlier Governors had allowed the school's heritage to be cut away at very low values instead of themselves getting planning permission to build houses on the land. Robin looked at the situation as a commercial man. He discovered that most of the other Governors were professionals – lawyers or doctors or academics. The Chamber of Commerce and the Merchant Company of the City of Edinburgh both had the right to appoint Governors to Fettes and there were old boys of the school as Governors as well. Alan Waddell, a stockbroker in private practice, chaired the Finance Committee.

The other surprising thing was that the Headmaster, Tony Chenevix Trench, who had come from Eton, had the entire responsibility for setting the curriculum and choosing the masters who were to teach there, without consulting the Governors. The Governors, therefore, spent their meetings discussing the school fees, not academic strategy. The Bursar, when asked by Robin at a Governors' Meeting if he could see the school budget, answered that 'inflation was growing at such a speed that he could only make a guess at the cost of operating the school and fees were set at about the same level as those of other Public Schools such as Glenalmond, Loretto and Rugby'.

Fettes College had a large square of land, much of which was used for playing fields, and boarding houses, each with its own Housemaster. Boys stayed at the school from the age of thirteen until they left at about eighteen. The prefect system was a central part of the arrangement with senior boys looking after the discipline and doing much of the training on the games field for junior boys. Each House competed with the others and played cricket, rugby, hockey and other games against each other. Games were played against the local Public Schools from Gordonstoun to Glenalmond including Edinburgh Academy, Watson's, and Loretto.

The masters were expected to take part in extra curricular activities and many of them were quite skilful in teaching the various games. There were two full-time music masters, Dr Fairbairn and Michael Lester Cribb, and the music and singing at Fettes were of a very high standard. Classics was considered to be very important to the tradition of the school and was taught by Tony Chenevix Trench and three other masters.

When Robin himself had been at Fettes there had been a Junior School and boys were taken in from the State School system and did a year or two to learn subjects such as French and Latin. By the time they were thirteen or fourteen, they were able to go into the Third and Fourth Form at Fettes Senior School, on a level par with the other boys who came from Prep Schools. Prep School entry to Fettes was about sixty students a year which really was insufficient to support a full-time boarding school of four hundred. There were spaces in the Sixth Form and Fettes had already started taking in a number of girls for two years of Sixth Form studies. This gave the school additional income which involved no additional expenditure. Many of the girls stayed with the masters as part of their families and there were other friends and neighbours who offered bedroom and bathroom facilities for girls.

Much of Fettes life was arranged around the Chapel Services. 'Chapel' was the first thing each morning after breakfast and Prayers was the last activity at night in the boarding houses when the House Master did a set form of reading and a prayer and a hymn before supper and bedtime. In Robin's school days the school divided at the Fourth and Fifth Form level for meals because there wasn't room for the whole school to eat in the same room. When he was a Governor (after an appeal had been undertaken and some more land had been sold) a big modern dining room was built which could accommodate the whole school and this made the whole operation of the school much easier.

There were still quite a number of the masters at Fettes who had been on the staff when he had been a boy at the school. Mr Brewer, a maths teacher, had taught Robin in the Sixth Form, and several others – Mr Cole-Hamilton and Mr Goldie-Scott and the PE Teacher, Ian Sutcliffe, were on the staff still. So Robin had friends within the Staff Common Room and was invited to go there and meet some of them from time to time. Tony Chenevix Trench was a little more distant. He was a pastoral master, taught classics and coached some of the students for university entrance. He was much liked by the boys and girls in the school but was perhaps not strong and healthy – he'd been a Prisoner of War with the Japanese and was a quiet and reserved sort of man, although with a continuous smile on his face. One of the House Masters at Fettes, George Buchanan-Smith, had trained after Glenalmond as a clergyman and he acted partly as Chaplain. He was a loyal friend, almost Father Confessor, for the Headmaster. It is said that Tony Chenevix Trench had stomach pains occasionally and certainly he had to take a day or two off sometimes. He became ill in the second year that Robin was Governor and it was then he agreed that he would retire when he reached the age of 60 in 1979.

The Governors started the process of looking for a new Headmaster.

Robin said the business way to do this was first to work out the job specification before advertising and was told fairly firmly by the Chairman of Governors, Lord Grieve, that 'Governors would appoint the best of those who applied'. Fettes received about eighty applicants for the job and Lord Grieve arranged that the current Headmaster should go through the list of applicants. Tony Chenevix Trench produced a short-list of six or eight names and their CVs were passed round to the Governors. The Governors interviewed only two of them for the Headmaster's job and Fettes appointed Cameron Cochrane.

Fettes did need a good Administrator and the Headmaster chosen had been in the Education Department of Edinburgh for a spell and also the Head of an Outward Bound School. He had knowledge of the administration and structure of the education system. This was important because a lot of the students going to Scottish Universities could gain Scottish Highers as an Entry Certificate. Fettes had always used the Oxford and Cambridge Joint Board which gave the students a very good grounding to do well. In Cameron Cochrane's time the boys and girls in the Sixth Form were able to do Scottish Highers after one year in the Sixth and then Oxford and Cambridge Joint Board 'A' levels in their second year. However, the curriculum was different in many respects and it wasn't always easy for them to study for both these examination systems.

Alice Salvesen settled down at Fettes and really did very well there. She was very happy and made a lot of friends. She was happier to be near home and see her parents more often. Tabitha (Tibi) also went for sixth form studies to Fettes and both girls gained entry to Aberdeen University. Francis, when he went to Fettes, went to Moredun, followed by Tom and Iver, and had a rather more mixed career. Robin and Sari both felt that perhaps they hadn't chosen the best school to suit their boys.

John Arkell was appointed Headmaster of the Fettes Junior School which then occupied Malcolm House and was enlarged. The Junior School was now competing with the Prep Schools and taking boys in at a younger age; this was necessary for Fettes because the Scottish Prep Schools were not sending enough boys and Fettes had to set up its own feeder school. A rumour reached Robin that some Headmasters at the Scottish Prep Schools were recommending that their students should go to an English school rather than Fettes, or indeed Loretto. The Junior School was working very well with John Arkell and his wife in charge and Robin was asked if he would be the Governor responsible to the Board for it – and so he regularly went across the road to chat with John Arkell and support the operation of the Junior School. Discussion focused on whether there should be a house built for Junior School boys to become boarders and a plan was set in motion for improving the classroom space. In 1982 David Clark took over the Junior School which by that stage had its boarding wing. He had been Deputy Headmaster at the Loretto Junior School before he came to Fettes. Again Robin had a good relationship with him and his wife. John Arkell became House Master of the Glencorse Boarding House in the Senior School. John was not quite as successful as a House Master and soon gained a position as Headmaster elsewhere, achieving a lifetime career in the teaching profession.

It was while John Arkell was the House Master at Glencorse that the Governors started talking about having a girls' boarding house in the Senior School. The number of boarding boys was decreasing and yet there was a waiting list for girls wishing to go to the Fettes Sixth Form. So a purpose-built house, Arniston, was duly built with modern accommodation. The other boarding houses had been built before the Second World War and were old-fashioned, with the boys sleeping in cubicles in quite big dormitories and senior ones having very small studies.

The Fettes Governors had to comply with a new set of Fire Regulations which were going to cost a lot of money in bringing Glencorse, Carrington and Moredun up to acceptable standards. There had to be self-closing doors at every level in the main school building. There was a discussion at the Governors' Meeting; Robin suggested that other schools had bed-sitting rooms for the senior students and suggested they consider a review of dormitories at the same time as putting in the fire precautions. This, however, was turned down by the other Governors who thought that the boarding accommodation at Fettes was quite adequate – 'It had been good enough for them when they had been at school and should be quite all right for their children.' However many of the mothers of children inspecting Fettes were quite appalled at the accommodation offered, and this was one of the reasons why the school numbers of boy boarders at Fettes was declining.

It did become clear to the Governors that House Masters at Fettes were concerned and disappointed by a lack of support in discipline cases. Cochrane had taken on external jobs, not only as Assessor for MOD officers' selection, but also the administration of the Commonwealth Games Village. This took him out of the school quite a lot. The Governors considered it necessary to appoint a Second Master to assist Cameron Cochrane with discipline and the curriculum and the actual administration and operation of the school: an expensive undertaking.

Cameron Cochrane initiated a plan for improving the quality of the class room accommodation together with a sports hall, a science lab and a language laboratory. The appeal was for some million pounds and Robin was asked to help the Headmaster to speak to old boys in different parts of the country and various dinners were arranged – but the old boys and parents of Fettes were not in a generous mood at that time, with inflation going up the way it was, to provide a lot of extra money to support Fettes and the appeal raised less than half that required. The main dining hall building was built and a new gym, but there wasn't enough money for the Sports Hall that was planned. Furthermore, in order to do the essential work required in improving the Houses, Fettes had to sell some more land.

The steward in charge of catering retired and a new incumbent was appointed. Governors asked if efficient purchasing could reduce the price of food. It seemed reasonable to seek a discount for bulk purchases of food at Fettes; this initiative resulted in twenty per cent off the cost of meat. Then the new Catering Manager investigated contract cleaning in the school and savings were made in that area as well. Fettes had its own in-house joiner and plumber who were fairly busy and also staff who did a lot of the painting of the buildings; the Bursar had to work out whether this was efficient or whether some of these jobs should be done by outside companies.

When Arniston House was built for the girls, David Weeks, an Episcopal Minister and a member of staff, with his wife Jean was chosen to be the House Master. Jean wrote school rules for boarding girls. There were teething problems and not all the girls settled into the way of life expected of them. One or two girls were asked to leave and the Governors became involved in an appeal from the parents as to whether their child had been treated correctly. Governors have to support their own staff but also have to be seen to be fair.

So the experience that Robin Salvesen had as a Governor of Fettes contained both high and low points. He had the great success of operating the successful Junior School with John Arkell and his staff, and success on the financial side in bringing about annual budgets so that they were actually putting up the school fees to bring in enough income to pay the known costs of running the school for the next year. The Bursar and others were able to control costs. The new girls' House went ahead. But the downside was that although the girls were getting bed-sitting rooms, the schoolmasters in the boys' Houses seemed to feel that giving boys individual rooms could create problems. There was a need to re-paint and decorate the school and bring colour into the dark corridors.

The whole question of corporal punishment came up while Robin was a Governor at Fettes. Robin as a school prefect at Fettes had been required to beat boys on occasion and had felt that this was an unnecessary part of the discipline process. He had found that when he'd called boys to order either on the games field or in the classroom, they complied with discipline. Obviously if someone stepped right out of line, then it was agreed by all parties that some punishment should be applied. The concept of corporal punishment, and the current alternative, 'writing a hundred lines', needed review. There were many better ways of disciplining and keeping a reasonable standard of behaviour. The other Governors of Fettes weren't in agreement and felt there was a need in a school like Fettes to continue to have corporal punishment. Robin was also concerned, partly because of pressure from his own wife, about the standard of decor – the cleanliness and tidiness and the colours used in the school buildings – it was drab and rather dirty looking. Robin felt that 'he was a lone voice speaking' as the other Governors felt that the school was quite adequate. It was the building that they'd been used to when they were schoolboys. After Robin had done two tours of four years each as a Governor he went to the Chamber of Commerce and discussed with them who in Edinburgh was a Member with a boy or girl at Fettes. Robin nominated the name of his successor.

Daniel Stewart's & Melville College

Robin Salvesen joined the Merchant Company of the City of Edinburgh in 1965 when he became a Director of A.F. Henry & Macgregor and felt himself, therefore, to have the qualifications to be a member. He was keen to do this partly because his father had been in the Merchant Company after the Second World War and had indeed been Treasurer and then Master in the early 1950s. Iver and Marion had really enjoyed the time when Iver was Master of the Merchant Company and built a relationship with the schools that were operated by the Merchant Company. Robin was told (by some of the people in the Merchant Company) that Iver had made an enormous impact on the financial stability and strength of the Company because he had been able to arrange for the sale of some of the farms which they had owned, and had put the money into good investments which showed a much higher return to underpin the development of the Merchant Company schools in the City of Edinburgh. George Watson's College was a large school on the south side of Edinburgh and the girls school and the boys school had been combined. Later the John Watson School, a small Prep School near the Belford Bridge, had been absorbed by the Merchant Company and the children had mostly gone into George Watson's College. On the north side of Edinburgh the Mary Erskine School for Girls had a new headquarters at Ravelston and Daniel Stewart's had combined with an independent school – Melville College.

Robin Salvesen went to meetings of the Merchant Company from time to time (about four General Meetings a year). These took place immediately after lunch in the Merchant Company Hall in Hanover Street. Then one day he was invited to meet with Kenneth Ryden in the New Club – this really amounted to Kenneth Ryden saying to Robin, 'I'd like you to join the Court of the Merchant Company as an Assistant – this is in fact a three-year tour of duty.' Robin found out the amount of time that this would require and agreed that he was honoured to be asked. So Kenneth Ryden said, 'Well, you have to find a proposer and a seconder who are Members of the Company to put up your name at a Court Meeting on a certain date.' The Merchant Company is very well organised and although there are four new Assistants each year for a three-year tour in the Court, it never has more than four nominees for these jobs. The Master of the Merchant Company arranges to ask for a cross-section of the Members who would be useful to join by election. Indeed the nominations of Master and Treasurer are never opposed for all these things are arranged behind the scenes beforehand.

When Robin was an Assistant of the Merchant Company the first thing he did was to arrange to visit all the schools and have a guided tour because the three schools were the main part of the Merchant Company's charity work. Some six thousand students in the City of Edinburgh are educated at the Merchant Company's schools. Members of the Merchant Company Court were also Members of the Education Board which looks after the schools. During that first year, the Education Board received a paper which indicated that there was likely to be a reduction in numbers at the schools and discussed how this was going to affect the operating costs. Although George Watson's was co-educational the two north side schools were not. The recommendation of this report was that Mary Erskine School and Stewart's Melville should join together under one Principal and also become co-educational. This caused a bit of a storm and was reported in the *Evening News* almost before the meeting had concluded so somehow the information had been leaked to the paper even before the Court Meeting had taken place. It was an uncomfortable feeling that the discussions were not confidential at all: very unfortunate and not very happy. There was a lot of support by the parents of the girls at the Mary Erskine School for Miss Thow, the Principal, and the number of girls there who passed exams and went to University was very high. It was however true to say that the number of students signing up to go to that school was declining and something had to be done about it. Robin Morgan, the Principal of Daniel Stewart's & Melville College, was appointed to be the Principal of the combined north side schools the following year.

Robin Salvesen was invited to be the Vice Convenor for Daniel Stewart's & Melville College for a two-year period during which he was in the school meeting Robin Morgan and others approximately once each week. Robin Morgan was very keen to involve his Vice Convenor in the operation of the school and to have someone with whom to discuss plans. He involved Robin in the interviews for members of staff, especially when an existing member of staff was putting his name forward for a Head of a Department job (a good thing to have an independent person involved on the panel). In fact on every occasion the interview panel agreed unanimously on who the best candidate should be.

Brian Head was the Head of the combined Junior School under Robin Morgan's leadership; girls went single sex to the Mary Erskine School and boys to Daniel Stewart's & Melville College Senior School. It is quite interesting – when kids are Juniors, the boys and girls walk together hand-in-hand. When they get a little bit older the boys want to play together and girls want to chat together – and then once in the Senior School there are various joint activities and the boys and the girls want to be together – in school concerts or school plays or the orchestra or the combined Cadet Force: dances and parties and other activities.

Brian Head's great skill was in the interviewing of parents and the recruiting of boys and girls for the combined Junior School. The Headmaster put the advertisements for the Open Day at the school into the newspapers and encouraged parents to come and see it, to meet the staff and put their names on the list. Robin Salvesen and Robin Morgan decided to advertise at Christmas time (so that long before the end of the summer term you had a good idea of the intake for the following year). Various other schools objected violently because Robin Morgan had 'jumped the gun' and held an Open Day early. Since that time Daniel Stewart's & Melville College has kept their school numbers up very well indeed. At one meeting a nursery school for the north side schools was planned and then built at the Ravelston site. That was a great success too and Robin enjoyed seeing an even younger group of children there.

One of the big snags at Daniel Stewart's & Melville College and the Mary Erskine School was the quality of the playing fields. Daniel Stewart's & Melville College had playing fields right up beyond the Salvesen office at East Fettes Avenue and on the other side of the Ferry Road, a long way from the school. The playing fields for the girls were in a hollow and all the wet weather drainage from the houses round about Ravelston Dykes ended up there. The Merchant Company set up a study group led by Ian Forbes, an ex Master of the Merchant Company, and a plan was drawn up for the drainage during the summer holidays of the playing fields at Ravelston. Then a scheme was discussed for selling a parcel of land on the north side of the Ferry Road, to convert that playing field site into a housing estate.

The school staff had to consider whether they could make better use of the playing fields on the south side of the Ferry Road and have fewer fields but use them far more frequently so that the school wouldn't suffer. Anyway this was all hammered out and it seems also to have been a success. Some new money was spent on the pavilion to allow Daniel Stewart's & Melville College former pupils also to use the fields.

As Vice Convenor of the school there were meetings each year of the School Board and Mr Macdonald, the Secretary of the Merchant Company, and his Assistant, Judith Sishi, did out agenda notes to enable Robin Salvesen to run the Committee as Vice-Convenor. Sometimes he felt as if the Minutes of the Meeting had been dictated before it took place, but there was a very clear briefing note from Judith which indicated the items on the agenda together with the proposed solution. The briefing note was very helpful in getting a slick meeting to take place but it was also necessary to make sure that everyone had the opportunity to make a comment and amend or change the proposed scheme. Plans were proposed by the Secretariat of the Merchant Hall for 'improvements of the gym at Stewart's', 'for improvements of the science teaching at the schools, and for language teaching'. There was a need for boarding house accommodation at Stewart's and Dean Park House, once the home of Fred and Robin Salvesen, a Great Uncle and Great Aunt, was chosen. The boarding facilities were required because more and more parents were being asked to do international jobs and some of the international oil company and military employers paid the costs to send children to boarding school.

Many of the weekly meetings that Robin had with Robin Morgan started at eleven o'clock and the two Robins visited some of the Junior School classrooms, to watch the lessons and listen to the staff teaching. Sometimes Robin wanted to talk to his Vice Convenor about the possibility of early retirement for a member of staff who was beginning to show signs of age; for teaching methods were changing and it was necessary to get more up-to-date skills available to the school. It was a very good thing to get round and see some of the staff and students and it was quite extraordinary to see how teaching methods had changed since Robin had been at Prep School in wartime.

Robin Morgan made it a habit when he was interviewing members of staff to talk to them about the need for every member of staff to be involved in one of the extra curricular activities, whether on the sports field helping with cricket, hockey, rugby, basketball or squash – or evening clubs for stamp collecting or ornithology or highland dancing. The Principal wanted to get it across to them that they were trying to build 'a whole person education system', so that the boys and girls developed as useful members of society, not just concentrating on passing the next round of exams but having the opportunity to develop skills and interests which would enable them to choose the right career for themselves. Robin Morgan arranged for Robin Salvesen to attend while members of the school were helped to write their curriculum vitae for an application for University. Robin would say, 'What else have you done at school for the last three or four years – is that all you've done – what are your interests? The only thing that the University will know about you is what you write on this form so you've really got to tell them everything and show how good you are.'

One of Robin's duties as the Vice Convenor of the Stewart's Melville College was to attend the Prizegiving and Speech Days and say a few words on different occasions. There were staff concerts and school plays and Robin was encouraged to take Sari to visit the school and join in on these occasions. They discovered during the course of these activities that the combined school staff of Mary Erskine and Stewart's Melville, and indeed the Junior School and the Senior School staff, didn't know each other that well. An opportunity came round when Robin Morgan said to Robin, 'It's normal for the Vice Convenor to have an annual party and to invite all the staff to an end of term drink.' Robin and Sari decided that the best thing to do was to ask all the staff out to Eaglescairnie on a Sunday for a barbecue lunch, bringing their own children with them, and really have an 'Open Day'. Many of the staff came out to East Lothian for the day and their children were able to play tennis and croquet and other games; a couple of members of staff arranged for a treasure hunt for children to go and find all sorts of trees and shrubs and bushes and animals and bring back samples of sheep's wool and things that they'd found – and a prize was to be won.

Some members of the staff (even twenty years later) are still talking about
the day out that they had.

Robin Morgan was very keen that his combined Cadet Force should
offer the opportunity to the boys and girls to learn a little bit about the
Army, Navy and Air Force. He and Robin Salvesen had both been officers
in the Army and were really keen that this training should go on at the
school.

The north side school operated an Outward Bound fortnight for twelve
year old students – to get them out into the country to see Scotland and
learn a bit about canoeing and geography, planting trees and geology, a little
about using a compass and some orienteering. So each May the boys and
girls of that age were taken up to Carbisdale Castle Youth Hostel, to have a
period of time in the country there. Some of the school staff worked on site
for this Outward Bound week – which was a tremendous occasion. Robin
Morgan and Robin Salvesen drove past Inverness to Bonar Bridge. They
saw the boys and girls learning camp cooking and setting out on an
orienteering exercise in little groups with their compasses. They had to find
their way from one of the roads right over the top of a hill and down the
other side to rejoin their bus at a meeting point. Members of staff with
binoculars kept an eye on the direction the various parties were going, to
make sure they didn't get lost. In the evening Robin Morgan and Robin
were down on the roadside, checking up with the staff to see if all the boys
and girls had managed to get in. One or two parties were rather late in
arriving at the rendezvous but they had found the road although they were
tired. They were picked up and taken away for their night's camp.

Carbisdale Castle had been owned by a member of the Salvesen family
for a time and used during the Second World War as the home for the
Norwegian Royal Family who had come to Britain and escaped from the
German invasion of Norway. As Robin's father had been Norwegian
Consul General, Robin knew its history and was very interested to see it
now as a Youth Hostel. In his report about the Carbisdale experience he
recommended a greater use of radio telephones to improve safety and
control of all the staff and students involved.

One of the senior people on the staff of Daniel Stewart's & Melville
College was Roger Sheriff who'd been the Principal of Melville College
before the merger of the two schools. He stayed on as Assistant Headmaster
and was a tower of strength and a great help in managing the administration
of the school.

The Court of The Merchant Company of Edinburgh met for their

'Greeting Dinner' in Merchants Hall in Hanover Street, with a new Master in the Chair to welcome the recently elected Assistants and to thank Robin and his group for their work over three years. It was the custom for the retiring Assistants to present a gift to the Company. There had been a recent re-decoration of the reception area at the Court Room on the first floor. An antique table was therefore presented to complete this room. The final toast at Merchant Company Dinners is to 'The Stock of Broom'. This wild plant which grows like the gorse bushes on Arthur's Seat can usually be found to bloom with some flowers in every month of the year. It gives hope for everlasting strength and renewal.

CHAPTER 16

The Christian Life!

THE IMPACT OF HISTORY is very alive in Scotland for the countryside bears the imprint of humanity in previous generations: standing stones and castles, brochs and Roman Camps or strongholds. The towns are full of churches with towers and steeples and the lowlands and the Border country have derelict Abbeys built when the main source of wealth came from the fleeces of their sheep. All Scots children know that destruction was often caused by invading English Armies and that religion has been a cause of conflict. Some of the monuments have been used as quarries for the later buildings but remote places have awesome and special sites with their own emotional impact. The standing stones at Callanish in Lewis are very large stone circles in a very remote island near the sea and visitors wonder why people lived there and why they built this enormous shrine. There is a site at Kilmartin on the mainland south of Oban which has standing stones placed very low on the ground on a low lying and rather marshy site. Orkney, with a really bad climate and not much in the way of agricultural production, also has very early sites. At Castlelaw in the Pentlands and at Duns further south there are big Pictish circles, defended places where people retired in times of trouble. South of Aberfeldy there are round houses which long pre-date Christianity. They are not damaged because sheep have grazed there year on year – but why did people set up their dwelling places in these places? Perhaps the earlier settlers were seafarers and fishermen but that of course doesn't explain this inland site. Anyway, these early people found that the *sun was important to life* and they marked the shortest and the longest days. This seems to have been a feature for prehistoric man all round the world.

Modern science has proved how very correct mankind was to understand the sun as a source of energy. It can power electric batteries through solar panels. Sunshine enables green plants to fix carbon into their growing leaves and fibres which releases oxygen for animals to breathe. The concept of a God who was a creator and a governor or a High King seems to have created early civilisation and certainly motivated the building of nation states which left their mark upon shrines, pyramids and burial sites. The

Bible contains an Old Testament which starts with a creation story. The New Testament proclaims Jesus and the teachings about love and the care of others, but also the enormous impact of life after death: the good news that Jesus rose again from the dead and the idea that mankind is in the world to 'glorify God and to praise him forever'.

Robin Salvesen was baptised in the drawing room at 6 Rothesay Terrace, one floor up from the entrance at street level. Doctor Warr the minister had brought back water from the Jordan. He knew Iver Salvesen very well. Iver was a regular worshipper at St George's Church in Charlotte Square but his wife Marion had been brought up in an Episcopal family and confirmed into the Church of England at Priorsfield School.

Every Sunday after breakfast the young Salvesen family were dressed up smartly, because they went to church (it was like going to someone else's house) dressed in their best clothes. A very early memory was going from Curriehill House near Balerno to the church at Currie across the river – down a steep hill and up the hill on the other side. Surprisingly, this is where Keith Ross, Robin Salvesen's son-in-law, has now been called to serve as the Minister and to preach, to quite a large congregation in the Balerno and Currie areas. It is not a big church building. The congregation sit in front of and on either side of the Minister so he is close and doesn't need to have microphones to speak to the congregation.

For most of the war, Robin Salvesen lived at Aberdour and the family would walk through the garden, through the back gate, to the Castle. There were some geese and the gander used to put down his head and hiss at passing travellers. Then they went through another lychgate into the churchyard to the church. On Inchcolm island, very close to Aberdour, was the Abbey, still a most wonderful ruin to go to visit, with its own pier. The monks must have fished in the water and their only communication with the shore would have been by boat. Robin Salvesen and his brother John had a governess daily at the beginning of the war and they were brought up on children's Bible stories. One was about baby Jesus and another about baby Moses and at night time prayers were said: 'God bless Daddy and Mummy, God bless brother John and God bless me.' At Cargilfield grace was said at meals and prayers were said in bed before children went to sleep, each of the boys sitting in bed.

After the war, when Cargilfield moved back to Barnton where the school had a Chapel with a library combined. The services were on the whole Episcopalian – it must have been easier for the school teachers to read from a prayer book rather than to ad lib in the Church of Scotland manner of 'praying from the heart'. The Church Services were led by members of the staff of the school, including the Headmaster. Probably about ten per cent of the boys would have been Episcopalian – the vast majority went on Sundays to Cramond Kirk to sit under Rev. Leonard Small. They marched in procession from school for about a mile. The Episcopalians went in the opposite direction across the golf courses and through the village to Davidsons Mains.

At Fettes at the age of thirteen, after a cold bath and breakfast in the main school building, boys had to make beds and get school books ready before the bells rang in the main school for Chapel. In the evening the whole school in their own Houses sang a hymn and listened to prayers read by the Housemaster. On Sundays the main preachers in the Chapel were Masters in the school. The music was a very important part and the whole school met in Chapel on a Sunday morning to sing together and learn both psalms and hymns. Round about the age of sixteen, Robin Salvesen came under some influence from Rev. Bill Aitken, one of the maths teachers, and also Rev. Booth who was the Episcopalian priest and taught English. His class had a very good record of passing English Literature examinations because he could forecast most of the questions which the examiners would ask. Bill Aitken was a good Maths teacher who taught ordinary Maths and higher Maths. Robin and various others went to Confirmation Classes, led by Bill Aitken, going through the words of the Lord's Prayer and the Creed; each phrase focused on a topic for discussion which included sex and marriage, and of course the belief in God the Father, the Son and the Holy Spirit; and redemption and sin. This Confirmation Class went on weekly for a whole term while the Master and the boys got to know each other well. At the end of term, boys were asked if they understood Christianity and wished to confirm their faith publicly.

After the war the family moved to Bonnington House close to Ratho village on the west side of Edinburgh. The local church was in Ratho village, a short drive of maybe three miles, and on Sundays the family would take the car round about half past ten to go to the eleven o'clock service. There were some Sundays when Iver Salvesen was on duty as an Elder and had to be there to greet the people going into Church. On these Sundays the family had to wait around after Church because Iver would have to count the money that had been collected. The Minister in Ratho Kirk was the Reverend Jones. He would enter from the vestry straight into the pulpit and the Salvesen family sat in the gallery directly opposite him. Many of the congregation were at the lower level, sitting in the various pews below the gallery, but families had their own regular seating places in the church. Iver Salvesen had been an Elder at St Giles' Cathedral but found it so much easier to go to the local church at Ratho that he moved his lines there. As an Elder he had the duty before Communion Sundays of going round a district to deliver Communion cards, to remind members that they were invited to go to Church specially on Communion Sunday.

When Robin was at Eaton Hall learning how to be an officer in the Army he used to go to the Presbyterian Church in Chester where all the Scots met each other. Then to Africa, where several of the Nigerian soldiers had been to Missionary Schools (especially the Ibu people). The majority of the soldiers were from the north and they were Moslems. In Lagos, the officers from the 5th Battalion could walk quite easily across the bridge onto the mainland where the main Episcopal Cathedral Church was situated. Robin used to go to Evensong and the Governor General often sat in the front pew. Further back in the congregation both white and black people would be praising God. Evensong was the nicest of the Episcopalian services, with a mixture of prayers and hymns and a short sermon.

The Moslems were particularly active during Ramadan when the men would fast during daylight hours and then feast after dark and the drums would beat. Very often the men were really quite tired in the daytime.

After National Service Robin Salvesen went to Oxford and on Sundays attended the Presbyterian Church which was only a few hundred yards from University College. Here again all the Scottish students met each other and several local families. The Minister was the Reverend Raymond (W.G.) Bailey whose wife Mary gave Sunday tea parties and really encouraged the students, male and female, to go to her house. Students would take turns to go there early and help make up the egg and tomato sandwiches in the kitchen. Raymond Bailey had a wonderful gift of standing up and introducing everybody present; he would go round the room naming people one by one, which College each was at and what he or she was studying. He had a wonderful memory for names and people. He and his wife had three girls, all quite a lot younger than the students.

There was an Iona Society run by the students. Raymond Bailey was the Honorary President and one of the University Professors was an Honorary Official of the Society. The students themselves provided the Chairman and Secretary and other office bearers. They met on a Saturday evening. A few of the members were reading theology but by no means all the people were intending to be full-time Ministers. Robin Salvesen was reading engineering, other friends read French and German. The Iona Society had

A family picture: left to right - Evelyn, Marion, John, Hilary, Alastair and Robin.

programmes each term on some aspect of the Bible or Theology and could draw on leaders who were acknowledged experts in their field – Old Testament or New Testament or prayer, or some aspect of religion. After the lecture and a discussion afterwards, a group would nearly always go to a café for coffee and so the members became friends. Doctor R.S. Lee, the Vicar of the University Church, was a regular contributor. His daughter Rosemary became a member of the Iona Society, as did Alastair Macgregor, now Minister at the North Leith Church. Bill Brockie eventually became an Episcopal Minister and served at St John's in Princes Street, Edinburgh and then out near Tynecastle. Zander Wedderburn, a clever chap, a scholar from the Edinburgh Academy, used to go to the Iona Society; he worked in Human Relations in a big firm in England before returning to be a Consultant in Edinburgh.

When Raymond Bailey moved from Oxford to Scotland, he was called to a church extension charge at Niddrie. A group of his former pupils from Oxford went round from house to house, asking the people on the estate if they would wish to go to the Presbyterian Church and whether they could introduce Raymond Bailey as the Minister to them. Some householders were Roman Catholics and not interested in going to the Presbyterian Church, but others had children and were quite interested in talking about baptising them and going regularly to the Presbyterian Church. Sheila Abercromby and Sari (who was eventually to become Robin's wife) were members of this group, together with Virginia White and Zander Wedderburn. They would make themselves lunch together and then go and visit in pairs.

During the holidays from Oxford, Robin went with his family to Ratho Church. The Reverend Jones decided to use the glebe to make some money and so he introduced pigs and piglets. Of course, keeping a lot of pigs in a small area created a smell which the village disliked, so the minister became unpopular. Ratho Church is very close to the Forth and Clyde Canal.

When Robin went to sea on the *Saldura* he went to church in Geraldton. The people in West Australia were incredibly welcoming to a visiting Scot and one of the people he met was the local agent who had a Chinese wife. They invited the Chief Engineer, the Captain and Robin to dinner at home. The Chinese wife produced a Chinese meal and the officers took a bottle of wine each to help with the party. They sat down and had a full Singapore/Chinese dinner with a course of rice with two side dishes and crab pancakes and some prawns in batter.

After Oxford, Sari and Robin were to marry at the church in Brenchley in Kent – Sari's parents lived within walking distance across a grass square. Leading through the churchyard there was a path through old yew trees towards the church itself. Sari had gathered together some of her theological friends to help with the Wedding Service and the local choir (which she had been a part of) offered their services and led the hymns and an anthem. Dr Chadwick who had taught Sari and was one of the leading theological scholars at Christ Church, Raymond Bailey from St Columba's in Oxford, and, of course, the Vicar of All Saints, Brenchley Church who had served as Dean of Shanghai, led the service together. In the congregation there were several other ministers who were friends of either Robin or Sari.

There was a photographer present who took pictures of the people going down the avenue of yew trees towards the church. Robin and his best man, David Morris, stood at the front of the church and waited while the bride and her bridesmaids walked down from the house across the grass square and into the building.

Family and friends walked through the village in sunshine to the reception in a marquee in the garden. Robin and the best man had to make their speeches – and then Sari and Robin were very pleased to get into a car and go off for the honeymoon.

Robin and Sari lived for a year in Neston on the Wirral after they had their first child, Ferelith. Aunt B Burrell, who was married to Jack, a lawyer in Liverpool, lived quite near and visited them at weekends. Aunty B and her little children used to go to the Congregational Church which was nearly opposite their house. This was more like a Presbyterian Church than the Episcopal Church, with hymns and prayers and a sermon. After that year Robin and Sari moved to Longniddry where he would go to the village Presbyterian Church (and Sari would worship at the Episcopal Church at Gullane). Sari used to go to the early service while Robin looked after the children, then Sari would take over the children while Robin went to the 11 o'clock service.

They met up with Roland Walls and Eric Stevenson, part of the community at Rosslyn Chapel, on the south side of Edinburgh. Roland Walls was the leader of this group who lived together almost as monks but worked in industry and had prayer meetings. Robin and Sari used to go from time to time to join in with the community and have discussions with them about the Christian life.

Once they were fairly settled at Eaglescairnie in East Lothian, Robin attended the Parish Church at Bolton for a short time. The three big houses, Lennoxlove, Coulston and Eaglescairnie, had by tradition pews in the gallery. The Duke of Hamilton used to go with his row of boys to sit in pews below the gallery. The Broun-Lindsays came from Coulston where they have lived since the twelfth century, including the period of English occupation of Haddington. It must have been quite difficult to keep control of land and house when visiting armies were conquering the area. Anyway, the Broun-Lindsay family are still there and it is wonderful that that should be so. Lady Broun-Lindsay was a local councillor. Her husband had been a Governor General in India and the house was full of ivories and other artefacts. Lady Broun-Lindsay had a distinguished career within the community of East Lothian throughout the Second World War, involved with the Red Cross and local hospital, and was still (1965) a Member of the East Lothian Council. She had an immense impact upon the community life and spirit of the region. Bolton Church was given individual communion cups. It seemed rather divisive that some of the congregation should use the common cup and sit in one corner of the Church while the rest of the congregation used their own individual cups.

Sari at this time worshipped at Holy Trinity Church where Aeneas Mackintosh ministered. He spent tremendous time and energy restoring the church buildings and getting to know the people in the big houses round about Haddington and he became a good friend. Then he was called to join the pioneering team at St John's Church in Princes Street and the Rector at Holy Trinity became Alan Johnson. Later on, under the leadership of Bishop Alastair Haggart, Aeneas was asked to do the training of non-stipendiary ministry in Edinburgh and Sari with her degree in theology and her interest in doing something specific in church work, joined as co-tutor. The training group used to meet for weekend sessions – living at Eagles-cairnie, helping to serve the meal and wash the dishes, between working sessions to discuss theology and learn about Christian ministry. So Robin and Sari had several visiting Bishops and senior clergy at Eaglescairnie to lead the training sessions. Many of these students eventually became ordained as Deacons or as Priests within the Episcopal Church of Scotland.

There are certain highlights in the Church life when each person takes vows. The first is Confirmation and for Robin Salvesen this happened at Fettes College after chapel on a Sunday evening when the group who were going to be Confirmed were lined up to take their vows and then receive their first Communion. When the bread and the wine are served one thinks very carefully about the words from the Bible. 'This is my body shed for you,' and perhaps considers of the bread which is food to give strength and energy and the wine which perhaps represents the Spirit. God speaks to each of us through the Spirit and some of us can listen to this. So mankind get the gift of both the strength to carry out God's wishes and the Christian ideas, which motivate. At a Christian Wedding Service husband and wife are again taking vows and promises. The gathering of friends and family support the two who are going to be married, and join in prayers. Man and wife promise to love and cherish each other, to obey and to share for better and for worse, in sickness and in health – and it is important throughout life to remember these particular occasions. Later children are brought to be baptised and then vows are renewed.

Robin Salvesen used to try to be home in the evenings in his busy business life to say prayers with the children at bedtime and to read Bible stories to them. The habit of regular community worship helps.

When Aeneas Mackintosh was at Holy Trinity he met up with David and Alny Younger who had children of the same age as his and Mary's. They not only ran the Sunday School in the Church Hall at Holy Trinity but also started a primary school there for their children and those of other families, called the Compass School. All of Robin and Sari's children went there and the school continues to this day though in a different building in the West Road in Haddington,.

Robin Salvesen's connection with St Mary's started as an occasional visitor when James Riach was the Minister. The choir and the tower of the Church had been open to wind and weather for four hundred years and the congregation used the nave with a small organ in the gallery at the west end. Around this time the Duke of Hamilton with Duchess Elizabeth organised the renewal of a whole group of buildings near St Mary's; they bought the old Mill and Haddington House and set about a restoration programme. The Lamp of Lothian Trust was founded. It sponsors concerts within St Mary's; it restored this whole group of buildings, and created a Youth Club and an Arts Centre. The restoration of St Mary's was becoming possible; funds were going to become available and loans could be obtained. The Earl of Wemyss visited Robin one evening, to ask for a contribution towards the restoration. Robin had very rarely been to services at St Mary's but when he learnt that many of the people were putting some money into it, he became enthusiastic about the project and the vision. He wasn't much involved with the restoration and didn't become a member until Alisdair MacDonnell became Minister. Then Robin joined the Congregational Board. The work suited Robin quite well because the Congregational Board is responsible for the finance and the buildings (which also included the Manse and the Church Hall) – these were areas in which he had skills to offer.

After about a year on the Board, Robin was asked if he'd allow his name to go forward for consideration as an Elder. Alisdair MacDonnell led some ordination classes. This group met about six times to discuss the work of an Elder and went to St Giles' Church in Edinburgh to see how Elders helped to conduct the Communion Services and serve the congregation. An Elder's duty also requires him to have a group of houses to visit and care for. Another duty is to attend to Kirk Session Meetings and discuss the way in which St Mary's worships, and assist the Minister in conducting worship in Haddington. Alisdair MacDonnell asked Robin to take the Chair of the Congregational Board, and Robin also chaired the Finance Committee for some time.

After the restoration, St Mary's had a very big building to maintain with very little in the way of funding. The congregation had a large debt to pay back to the local authority. The Kirk Session decided to have a stewardship campaign which involved Elders going around all their districts asking members for a commitment to invest their time, talents and money for the good of the church and offering a system whereby they could sign up a covenant either of annual donations or as weekly envelopes. This certainly helped the finances of St Mary's. The church was also lucky enough to receive quite a large number of legacies which has really transformed its financial stability.

There was a Quinquennial Inspection of the buildings after the restoration had been complete. Robin was Chairman of the Board when it received this report which showed that some of the stonework and the roof of the nave, the 'un-restored part' of the Church, was requiring significant repair and the estimate was some £40,000. A pair of contractors put up their own scaffolding and worked gently round the church, when the weather was suitable. However, the only way to finance this was to apply for a Grant from Historic Scotland. Robin and his small Committee looked at the conditions attached to the Grant, one of which was that the church must be open on a regular basis to the public. The foundation of the Promotion and Management Committee as a sub-committee of the Congregational Board of St Mary's was the result. The Board determined that the church should open in the summer months and recruit a gang of volunteers who would welcome visitors and show them round. Christine Milligan, the wife of the Treasurer of St Mary's Church, was Secretary and first organiser of the P & M Committee and the Board agreed to pay some expenses in the initial year to finance stock for a shop to be opened in the church. Christine asked Doctor Eric Stevenson for an interpretation of the building and he made a group of architectural drawings which are still on the pillars in the church so visitors can see what it might have looked like during the various phases of its life: as a Roman Catholic Church with side aisles; with a screen across the middle of the Church and a choir at one end and the nave at the other; its restoration in the days of John Knox when it was a square shape and only the nave was used for worship. Christine Milligan then arranged (with David Levison, a retired Minister) production of audio-tapes in several languages that visitors could carry round with them. They designed, and the Congregational Board financed, leaflets for the visitors. The P & M Committee have been able to repay all this investment. Robin was closely involved with this programme and felt responsible for the commitment to open the St Mary's building. Money raised from visitors and tourists should go to build up a Property Fund.

Later on it was necessary to arrange for wheelchair access to the Church, which was only possible through the north door because there were so many steps down to the Church at the west side. In the year 2001, St Mary's had over a hundred volunteers from all denominations helping with the opening of the Church and the welcoming of the visitors.

The Lamp of Lothian which completed the restoration of the Mill and the Boys Club also runs six regular concerts in the Church each year, with very good orchestras. Her Grace Duchess Elizabeth became the President of the Friends of St Mary's, a non-denominational group who are friends from all over the world. They arrange the Licht Fair, an annual sale in the Church building itself and Alisdair MacDonnell being a keen violinist has always given a musical contribution. The P & M Committee have a Dedication Service for volunteers at the beginning of the year and a close of season party as a thank you to the people who have been helping so much during the course of the summer. St Mary's had radio recordings made by the BBC of some special events, and has appeared on the Sunday evening 'Songs of Praise'.

The Reverend Clifford Hughes created a family 9.30 service which became a very much a lighter kind of Christian experience – a shorter service which children, parents and grandparents and others could all enjoy as a family service. After the family service there are classes for children in groups while the parents drink coffee and tea and stay on for the second service if they wish to do so. The St Mary's community is busy, and four other groups are active. There has been a group of mothers and toddlers meeting in Newton Port, a 'New Club for people not only to meet but to go to shows and theatres in Edinburgh', a 'Drop-in Group for older people to get together', and a 'Group which works together and makes things for a sale of work in Newton Port Hall'.

The next part of the restoration programme started when the Kirk Session was told that Lammermuir Organs, working at Athelstaneford, would offer to build an organ at a price of about £30,000. The Kirk Session and the Board approved this scheme and the contract was drawn up with Mr Rickaby. Duchess Elizabeth very sensibly asked questions about who had consulted them and chosen the type of organ; she knew who to consult about the size of organ and the scope of it for St Mary's. She felt that for the sake of the concerts that she and the Lamp of Lothian were regularly running, St Mary's should actually have a bigger organ than that which the Kirk Session and the Board had ordered. The end of the matter was very acceptable because the church was able to purchase the bigger organ and Duchess Elizabeth, by then the Dowager Duchess of Hamilton, raised the additional funds for the Church through her connections in the City of London and in the art and music world. The big new organ was installed in St Mary's about a year later than forecast.

During Rev. Clifford Hughes' ministry, the Society of Bellringers wrote to the Minister and Kirk Session indicating that St Mary's Church could purchase a set of eight bells from Dunecht in Aberdeenshire. These bells had been in the stable block tower and had not been used a great deal; the tower had rather fallen down and The Hon. Charles Pearson, who had recently inherited the Estate, was not intending to re-install the bells. The Society of Bellringers were anxious that this set of bells should be kept in Scotland. Although there are about fifteen thousand church bells ringing peals regularly in England, there are only four or five sets of bells in the whole of Scotland. The first problem was to determine if the church tower could actually carry the weight of a set of bells. Luckily the Dunecht bells are not hugely heavy. It became a matter of consultation between Duncan Beaton, a retired Civil Servant and an Elder of St Mary's, and Robin Salvesen as to whether the Congregational Board could raise some of the money for putting a set of bells in the Church. The Board decided its funds should not be used for this purpose – but they were not unwilling to accept the bells if they could be funded from some other source. An application for a Lottery Grant went forward in due course from the Friends of St Mary's – all Duncan Beaton's work – but this first approach was rejected. Duncan Beaton and Robin Salvesen couldn't find a satisfactory reason why it had been turned down at a time when many English churches were getting Lottery funding for bells 'for the Millennium'. It was thought to be a good thing for all the church bells in England to ring out to celebrate the year 2000 and so many were getting funding for renewing and restoring their bells. Mr Beaton drafted a letter to appeal against the decision that Lottery funding was going to be denied. A formal reply stated that the appeal had not been successful but the Lottery Board looked at the case again and offered a 70 per cent grant. It was necessary to provide a local contribution and Robin Salvesen himself was very happy to put up a tranche of money to assist and enable the bells to be installed. The bells are rung before the 9.30 service every Sunday. At least thirty people immediately applied to learn how to ring the bells and a team of eight or ten meets every Sunday.

John McVie, a local lawyer and Town Clerk and an Elder at St Mary's, offered his writings and memoirs to St Mary's and asked the Kirk Session if publication of the whole story of the restoration of St Mary's would not be a good project. Clifford Hughes and Robin Salvesen formed a small committee and thought that they should look for an author who could bring together John McVie's work with an historical account of St Mary's since its original foundation and bring it up to date to the year 2001. Lord

James Douglas Hamilton, who had written some books on his own family history, was approached, but was too busy, and suggested the name of Dr Rosalind Marshall. She had been the author of a book about Mary Queen of Scots and also was writing about John Knox, who had a strong Haddington connection. Clifford Hughes, John McVie and Robin Salvesen met Dr Rosalind Marshall to discuss the matter. The East Lothian Library Service showed an interest in developing this book, which would service the tourist industry and the local community, and this enabled the publication in 2001.

As an Elder, Robin Salvesen was given a district of fifteen houses for pastoral care and later as he retired from some business he took on a second district as well. An Elder is expected to hand round the annual accounts of the Church and the Church Newsletter as well as to encourage people before each Communion Service to come to Church and join in with the community worship. This also gives a personal contact which most Elders come to thrive on – of actually visiting and getting to know a group of the congregation. After a round of visits an Elder often comes home feeling refreshed and restored by his conversation with other Christian people in their own homes, finding that their life and their ability to cope with every day life is an inspiration. So instead of being a chore, it becomes a very valuable restorative.

There is a great value in a Christian upbringing, knowing the Bible story, knowing how Jesus would want us to live our life, and how Jesus taught his disciples. All these things help us to run our business and our lives – and perhaps make the lives of the people we live with in our community grow better as the years go by.

The theme of a church connection throughout the years of the life of Robin Salvesen is related in this last chapter, to illustrate perhaps the need he felt for support from the Creator God.

Failure and success are both difficult for a frail human to handle correctly and the Christian pilgrimage takes all men on a difficult journey with a variety of temptations. As a Boy Scout learns to do his best and a soldier works to serve his Queen and country, so also Robin tried to manage change and to bring about a life on earth more closely towards the image outlined by Jesus in his teaching and example.

Psilocybin Mushrooms

Tips and Tricks to Grow
Magic Mushrooms of Premium Quality

EDWARD LEWIS

Table of Contents

Introduction

Have you ever thought about growing your own magic mushrooms but got discouraged because you didn't know how to start? Do you even know their proper name? Psilocybin mushrooms, also known as "shrooms," are surprisingly easy to grow. And because it's always more cost-effective to do it yourself, interest in grown mushrooms has - well - mushroomed! However, like anything that is cultivated, there are certain conditions and environments needed to be successful at growing your own. As with any other mushroom species, the psilocybe thrives in a humid climate, which is the first thing you need to create from the moment you start incubation. While their active substance content depends on soil preparation and taking the necessary steps to avoid contamination, the fungus' benefits have been confirmed scientifically.

As you will learn, paying attention to hygiene is critical when growing your magic mushrooms. And this isn't just because you want to get the best quality possible but also to avoid cross-contamination between different mushroom strains. Misidentification of the incubated species is a serious issue and can have dire consequences. Since the spores do not contain psilocybin, misidentification can go unnoticed until the end of the fruiting process, when you gather the fruit. Fortunately, you can prevent this by being extra cautious about your hygiene. For the same reason, you will need to ensure any equipment you are using is suitable for (and preferably designed) the specific purpose of handling mushroom spores.

To help you understand how to choose the proper strain, this book offers a comprehensive guide on the different shroom species. It includes a thorough discussion of the levels and types of active substances mushrooms contain, laying the foundation for the rest of the process. Keep in mind that not all shrooms have health benefits, and several have specific medical uses, so you must choose yours carefully. Moreover, the equipment, the rest of the materials you need, and the cultivation method will depend on the qualities and requirements of the chosen strain.

Having learned the basics, you will be able to master the art of growing premium quality magic mushrooms safely and efficiently. The book will also introduce you to the intricate language of shroom cultivation, including the most commonly used terms for each step of the process, shroom parts, equipment, and much more. Having learned the basics, you will be able to master the art of growing premium quality magic mushrooms safely and efficiently. You will learn how to differentiate between the strains and decide which cultivating methods suit you the best. After some time and practice, you can tweak the process you are using safely. That said, it's always recommended to work with smaller batches. This way, you can always start from scratch without losing too much time and resources if you make a mistake.

The only way to take advantage of the helpful information and cultivation tips you'll be given in this book is by getting your mushrooms (or spores) from a reputable source. Due to legal and financial reasons may represent another challenge for those wanting to save money on cultivating their own shrooms. However, by doing adequate research on the sources, you can save yourself many headaches. The same applies to the equipment. Whether you buy a ready-made kit or get each piece separately, you must ensure they come from a manufacturer with a reputable background.

Chapter 1

What Are Shrooms?

If you are interested in getting into the process of shroom cultivation, you might have an idea of the benefits, but not just how many there are. This first chapter will help you answer that question - but not before providing a comprehensive insight into what shrooms actually are and why they've gained so much popularity.

Also called magic mushrooms, shrooms are just like any other mushrooms, except they contain a psychedelic substance called psilocybin. When this naturally occurring substance enters the body, it's converted to another compound called psilocin. The latter enters the brain through the bloodstream and can change perceptions, triggering shifts in thought processes and mood.

Initially considered nothing more than a hallucinogenic drug, the use of psilocybin was controversial for a long time. However, according to recent studies, the compound has become a valuable tool for helping people overcome hard-to-treat and traumatic mental health conditions.

Psilocybin is only present in the fruit of the shrooms - and not in the spores - so the latter is for cultivation only and not for its medical benefits. Despite this, more and more people are interested in buying the spores and want to enjoy the benefits of growing their own mushrooms at home. Spores are also easier to find, even if the initial investment into the necessary equipment may be substantial. But how does a mushroom grow from its spore?

The Life Cycle of Psilocybin Mushrooms

Since shrooms look and reproduce like any other mushrooms, their life cycle is pretty much the same. Mushrooms are classified as fungi, which means they propagate through spores. The reproductive cycle of a mushroom starts with a mature mushroom releasing its spores - and ends with the next generation of mushrooms developing into adults with spores ready to reproduce. The end goal of this process is also the same as with any other biological entity capable of reproduction - the survival of species. However, before getting into the reproductive cycle of shrooms, you must understand how shrooms are built.

When you look at a mushroom, you will see that it consists of a stem, a cap - and seemingly nothing else. Many people fail to realize that these structures are only the end product of a mushroom. The functional parts are found beneath the mushroom. Here, shrooms grow a complex network called mycelium - the part that keeps the fungi alive, thriving, and moving on to the next phase. Mycelium is a tight network of cells living under the ground and represents the fruits of mushrooms. In a controlled environment, this extensive root structure can grow as large as you allow it - but in the wild, it can take over vast territories. Through its mycelium, a mushroom takes in nutrients and will enter symbiotic relationships with other species. The shrooms' interaction through their mycelium is a factor you'll need to pay particular attention to during cultivation to avoid cross-contamination with other spores and chemicals.

However, despite looking and behaving like the root system of plants, mycelium isn't considered a root, no matter how confusing this sounds. These fruits are similar to flowers and fruits of flowering plants - as they carry the spores - the reproductive units of fungi. By growing mushrooms, you are, in fact, growing mycelium. The mycelium makes it possible for the shrooms to produce spores that drop onto the soil when the mushroom reaches adulthood. Once a spore finds a moist and digestible home, it germinates and starts to break down digestive material in its environment. In addition, unlike plants that thrive through photosynthesis, mushrooms get their nutrients from digesting organic material and using water from their environment.

The life cycle of a magic mushroom varies between each species and strain. It can range from one to two days up to several weeks. While the mycelial network of certain species can exist for many years, you will probably have to renew it occasionally to renew its psilocybin content.

Below you'll find a more detailed description of each stage of the shroom's life cycle. Reading it will help you understand how your shrooms develop from spores to adulthood and learn which processes need special attention.

A Mature Mushroom Drops Its Spores

If the fruiting parts of mushrooms are like the flowers and fruit of plants, spores are like seeds. They represent the primordial stage of a mushroom's life cycle and its basic reproductive unit. Unlike the seeds of a plant, the spores of magic mushrooms are always asexual, which means there is no differentiation in male or female spores. There are, however, differences in the size and chemical composition of the spores between the numerous psilocybe species. These qualities may also affect the duration of a mushroom's life cycle.

When a mushroom reaches maturity, it releases its spores from its gills - the tiny openings you can see on the fleshy part under the cap. Millions and millions of spores are released every day in every mycelium - and will travel through the air looking for a place to germinate. When the spores find the ideal environment for germination and other spores - they will move on to the next phase - mitosis. While they contain all the necessary nutrients for growing a funding body, they will also need the right amount of water and nutrients to germinate.

Spores Meet Compatible Spores and Form a Hyphae

Mitosis begins when spores meet compatible spores and fuse to begin the foundations of hyphae. The hyphae are the first functional units of the next generation of shrooms. They contain its genetic material and the cytoplasm, where nutrients needed for the survival of the spore are stored.

Hyphae are tiny white fibers made from long tubular structures. When they join forces, they can create an entire mycelium in a matter of seconds. Unlike spores, hyphae can be male and female - as their typically labeling as + and - indicates. This differentiation allows them to fuse in the first place and proliferate into a complex mycelium, which will develop into a fruiting part later on.

Hyphae allow the fungal units to absorb nutrients from their environment. After successfully spreading out through the soil, hyphae will absorb and transport the necessary nutrients throughout the mushroom, including the various stages of its life cycle.

Mycelium Originate from the Fused Hyphae

Compatible hyphae will soon start fusing as they absorb the nutrients from their substrate. They form a complex network of mycelium cells, which is both the most fertile and functional part of the soon-to-be new shroom. This network will allow the fungi to interact with their substrate and permanently integrate the mushrooms into their natural ecosystem.

Mycelium cells act as an interface between the shroom and the soil, including the microorganisms inhabiting it and nutrients. They interact with plants and organic materials interlinked into the mycelium network. The more complex, the more nutrients the shroom will have access to.

In the wild, mycelium interacts with over 90% of the plant species around them. However, this isn't the case when growing mushrooms at home. When farming mushrooms with specific properties - like the magic shrooms - you must make sure they have enough nutrients to develop these properties.

When the mycelium begins its growing process (and form the fruiting body of the mushrooms above ground), the shrooms already have all their active compounds, including psilocybin. In addition, the soil you use relies on the mycelia for purification, which helps create good quality shrooms. And by the time they are fully developed, mycelia contain all the nutrients required to continue a mushroom life cycle and move onto the next developmental stage - the hyphal knot.

The role of the mycelium is to provide continuous support for the entire mushroom. It helps balance the nutrient ratio within the substrate. This allows cultivators to provide all the nourishment required for developing spores, the fundamental units of the next generation of shrooms.

One of the reasons mycelium can do this is its ability to break down all the organic material in its surroundings and absorb nutrients. The process also enriches the nutritional value of the entire ecosystem, creating more nutrients for the mycelium to thrive on, which results in a symbiotic relationship between the mycelium and its environment.

The Formation of the Primordia

As the growth of the mycelium advances, it slowly forms a cluster of bumps called a hyphal knot. This marks the development of the new mushroom -or what we see is the new shroom with a naked eye. These new mushrooms are known as primordia - and already contain the material needed to grow into adult fungi, including spores.

The primordium then moves into the next stage called pinhead. This new structure soon evolves, and the mushroom sprouts upwards from the mycelium. As the pinhead matures, it rises above the substrate, whether it's soil or the half- decomposed organic material it lives within.

This is the phase that you, as the cultivator or forager, can track while forming your mushroom beds or observing magic shrooms in the wild. At this point, you can physically see the emergence of what will soon become a mature fruiting body.

Growth of the New Mushroom

When the hyphal knot and the pinhead are formed, the mushroom starts to mature and grow in size. This fruiting new body is what you will see as the actual shroom - complete with the characteristic stem and the cap all mushrooms possess.

The fruiting body also consists of scales and gills. The latter is where the spores of the new generation develop, ensuring the continuation of the life cycle. The maturing of the gills is a crucial stage in shroom development as this is when spores are released.

However, it must be noted that not all hyphal knots and pinheads will produce mature mushrooms - and this is where the environment comes in. Environmental factors play a huge role in whether the fruiting body will develop or produce spores.

The Cycle Continues

Once the next generation of adult mushrooms develops its spores, it becomes capable of reproduction. As the spores from this generation fall to the ground and find their own compatible counterparts, fertilization occurs again, and the cycle continues by developing new hyphae. This final stage of the shroom's life cycle means that the mushroom is now fully grown and is ready to be harvested. The sooner it's harvested, the more viable spores it will contain, and newer shrooms can be produced in the subsequent generation. Once the new adult mushroom releases its spores, its own life cycle is completed and decomposes.

What the Life Cycle Means for a Cultivator

Understanding the life cycle of mushrooms is crucial as it allows you to pay attention to each step of the cultivation. Keeping the above stages in mind, you will need to:

- Obtain spores produced by adult shrooms

- Make a substrate for the spores to germinate

- Inoculate the spores

- Incubate the hyphae

- Place the shrooms in fruiting conditions

- Provide the perfect environment for pinhead formation

- Follow up with the growth mushroom

- Make a spore print by collecting the spores from your adult shrooms

While the germination of the asexual spores and the mycelium development usually happens pretty quickly, for your shrooms to develop the fruiting part, a very delicate balance of environmental conditions will be needed.

That said, the length of the entire growth period depends on how well you pay attention to each development stage of the mushrooms. For some psilocybe, this last phase will take longer to complete than for others. The specific strain you are using will also affect how long it takes to grow your shrooms. While it's true that the mushroom's mycelium represents the epitome of its life cycle, the fruiting part is what you truly want to achieve. After all, this is where the next generation of spores is produced.

Reasons for Growing Magic Mushrooms

As the medical benefits and research results on the safest dose of magic mushrooms seem to outweigh their psychedelic effect, the stigma around psilocybin has slowly dissipated. Combined with the increased media attention the potentially transformative impact of psilocin has attracted, the general public's sudden interest in magic mushrooms isn't at all surprising. After all, there are plenty of reasons someone would opt for cultivating shrooms at home instead of buying them.

It Costs Less

The cost is the primary reason many people opt for growing shrooms at home. Whether you live in an area where magic mushrooms are considered an illegal substance or not, you will get them from either a dealer or a dispensary. Both of these sources are too scarce to satisfy market demand. This means the price is driven by the supplier and is generally high, to the extent that they can be out of reach for those people suffering from chronic illnesses who rely on psilocin for relief.

Psilocybin spores, on the other hand, costs much less than mature mushrooms - simply because they don't contain the active substance. A small packet of spores costs a fraction of the price of the fungi. Moreover, with the right equipment and procedure, you can produce more than 100 times the quantity of mushrooms you would get for the same price. Of course, for this, you will need to invest in high-quality equipment, but due to the cost-saving potential of the home-grown shrooms, you will soon get the money back.

You Can Find Plenty of Information on the Topic

Thanks to the media attention and rise in market demand for information, you can now find plenty of information on growing shrooms. You don't have to finish courses on the topic, yet you will find a supportive community sharing tips and tricks on cultivating magic mushrooms safely and about the different health benefits they provide. With all this information and support, the lack of experience doesn't have to mean one will fail when trying to grow their shrooms. For this reason, more and more people get encouraged to try it themselves - and those who follow the step-by-step instructions from reputable guides succeed.

The Best Option to Build a Supply

Whether you are new to psychedelics or not, you will want to use (and grow) them as safely as possible. Given that shrooms are illegal in most countries, you get them by picking them yourself, a dealer, or growing them yourself. Picking magic mushrooms in nature is not only inconvenient but highly risky. Several poisonous species look exactly like the ones containing the beneficial psilocin. Misidentifying the species can be fatal, making identification crucial. However, learning how to identify them can take years to master.

Buying shrooms from a dealer can be equally risky, particularly if you are a new consumer. If you don't know how to find reputable dealers, you may have an unsafe product for consumption. Not all dealers correctly identify the different mushroom species either, or as a novice, you will rarely know what exactly you are getting. Some species can vary widely in their psilocybin content. In the best case, you may not even get the benefit you want. In the worst case, you will get poisonous mushrooms or magic ones with toxic mold on them. Dealers may handle other psychedelic substances as well. These can contaminate the shrooms, and you will be consuming much more than you've bargained for.

Those who want to avoid paying a high price for their shrooms may also resort to getting them from the dark web. This means potentially exposing themselves to scams, delays, added costs, or their order being intercepted by law enforcement. And this is all in addition to the same risks buying from a dealer carries.

Growing mushrooms at home, therefore, seems to be the most sensible option, even if it means a significant initial investment. However, after getting all the supplies and equipment you need and researching the process, you can produce a supply that:

- Is the right strain

- Has the right amount the psilocybin?

- Hasn't come in contact with other toxic chemicals

- Doesn't contain mold or spores from other pathogens

- Is readily available whenever you need it

By growing your own mushrooms, you don't have to rely on blind fate or whether all those people who handled your mushrooms exercised proper hygiene and other precautionary measures. You will know the exact strain you are taking and what it contains. Cultivating is, without a doubt, the safest way of obtaining magic mushrooms.

The Tricky Legal Landscape

While growing, selling, and possessing magic mushrooms is still illegal in many countries and states, selling spores is not. As mentioned before, spores do not contain the psychedelic compound psilocybin. Therefore, they aren't considered illegal substances. This means that you can freely buy the spores, and you have much better chances of getting away with cultivating mushrooms in smaller batches than if you need them regularly.

Chapter 2

The History of Shroom Cultivation

Now that you know what shrooms are, we will take a trip back in time to learn the history of this interesting mushroom. People have been using shrooms for centuries for medicinal or ceremonial purposes. When we say centuries, we mean it since historians believe people have been using magic mushrooms for over 12000 years. According to historians, cave paintings of Psilocybe mushrooms in Europe and North America date back to 9000 B.C. These paintings may suggest the existence and use of magic mushrooms back then. Archaeologists also found a painting of mushrooms in Northern Australia that dated back to 10,000 BCE. There were also rock paintings found in Spain dating back to prehistoric times.

Various religious myths belong to the Toltec and Aztec Mayan cultures that mention a certain mushroom that the serpent god Quetzalcoatl bestowed upon their ancestors. The Aztecs also used a hallucinogenic drug called Teonanácatl which means "flesh of the gods," in their rituals. Some historians believe this drug may have been shrooms. The Aztecs used magic mushrooms in various spiritual and religious ceremonies for healing, numbing pain, celebrations, and divinations.

Historians believe many ancient cultures used shrooms but can't determine exactly what they used them for. Some believed that ancient civilizations used magic mushrooms to connect with a higher power or to simply bond with one another. What we've discovered about ancient cultures and using shrooms is thanks to the records they kept in their myth and art.

Many other civilizations also used shrooms during religious ceremonies, especially in Siberia. The tribes there used a type of shroom called Amanita Muscaria to help them endure the cold winters by altering their state of mind. When Russian migrants arrived and settled in the area, they also began using magic mushrooms.

The Ancient Greeks also used shrooms during the Eleusinian Psychedelic Rebirth Rites - rituals that took place in the dark ages. These rituals were meant to connect the people with Demeter, the agriculture goddess, and honor her. During these rituals, people from all walks of life would gather in Eleusis and drink a magic potion called kykeon which was believed to be a mix of psychedelic mushrooms. During these rituals, the participants would experience spiritual insights and healing. Famous philosophers like Aristotle and Plato were known to attend these ceremonies.

Magic mushrooms found their way to the Middle East as well, specifically Egypt. Many ancient Egyptian artworks showed illustrations of magic mushrooms which confirmed their popularity. The Ancient Egyptians believed that the god of agriculture and death, Osiris planted the mushrooms into the earth because they didn't grow from seeds. For this reason, the Ancient Egyptians considered magic mushrooms to be divine and referred to them as "food of the gods." However, not everyone was permitted to consume magic mushrooms, only upper-class citizens and priests.

American scientist Terence McKenna believed that shrooms played a huge role in human evolution. His theory stated that Homo erectus evolved into Homo sapiens due to consuming psychedelic compounds which heightened their consciousness by doubling the size of the human brain. This is a controversial theory, but we must admit that it is an interesting one.

From everything we have discussed so far, it seems that magic mushrooms were used in different civilizations worldwide. So how did they reach the western civilization and the new world?

The Modern History of Shrooms

The first documentation we have of shrooms in the west was an intoxication incident in 1799. A British family cooked a meal with Psilocybe Semilanceata, which is also referred to as Liberty Cap. However, after consuming the meal, the family members began showing hallucinatory symptoms like euphoria, hysteria, and pupil dilation. They had no idea what they had consumed, and we can assume they weren't so excited about the results. This incident introduced magic mushrooms to the western world, and in 1803, they were classified as new species and were named Agaricus

Semilanceatus. However, in 1877 they came to be named Psilocybe Semilanceata.

Shrooms in the New World

Now fast forward to the 20th century and the arrival of shrooms to the new world. Reko and Schultes, who were both ethnobotanists, discovered psilocybin mushrooms, but at that time, they weren't referred to as magic mushrooms or shrooms just yet. They found out that doctors in Mexico were using these mushrooms on their patients and that they caused depression in the nervous system. In 1939 the two published their findings. When ethnomycologist and American banker Gordon Wasson and his wife Valeria Wasson heard about Psilocybin mushrooms, they decided to travel to Central America to experience them for themselves and learn all about them. The Wassons, under the guidance of local shamans, tried the shrooms and were more than happy with the results. In fact, the Wassons were among the first people from the western world and the new world to participate in a mushroom ceremony.

In 1957, Gordon and Valeria Wasson published their findings in "Life" magazine in an article titled "Seeking the Magic Mushroom." This was the first time ever the term "magic mushrooms" was used. Gordon sent some of the magic mushroom samples he had collected to mycologist Roger Heim who, along with scientist Albert Hoffman the inventor of LSD, wanted to learn more about the mushrooms after reading about them in Wasson's article. In 1958 Hoffman also acquired samples and was the first to successfully isolate the compounds psilocin and psilocybin. He identified them as the active ingredients and synthesized them. Pharmaceuticals later sold them under a different name, Indocybin.

The impact of Wasson's article didn't stop here. Timothy Leary, a Harvard professor, was inspired by Wasson's work and curious. He decided to try them for himself and set off to follow in the steps of the Wassons. Leary traveled to Mexico to experience the magic of the shrooms and claimed that they made him a new man. He stated that what he learned during his five-hour trip was more profound than anything else he had learned in his lifetime.

With the help of his friend Richard Alpert, Leary created the infamous Harvard Psilocybin Project, a series of experiments to discover if psilocybin could help treat various emotional issues. Leary and Albert had noble intentions, and the experiments were legal then. However, they used their students and prison inmates as subjects. There were so many red flags around the project as students were pressured into participating in the experiment. After many concerns were raised, the project was shut down in 1963. However, this didn't stop Leary, who began distributing psychedelics nationwide. This was during the hippie movement, so you can imagine how popular the shrooms were then.

Magic mushrooms didn't only catch the attention of people in the science world. The news of these powerful mushrooms also reached the literary world, and many wanted to satisfy their curiosity. American poet Allen Ginsberg heard about the Harvard experiment (before it shut down) and tried them.t Ginsberg fell in love with them and brought along two of his famous friends, jazz musician

Charles Mingus and American novelist Jack Kerouac, to join in the fun.

Psilocybin's popularity wasn't slowing down, largely due to the hippie movement. This left the government no choice but to completely ban the use of psilocybin. In 1971 the law came into effect. It wasn't just psilocybin's popularity that prompted the government to take this action, but it was also fears over the lasting effects the drug could have on individuals. Former American president Richard Nixon believed at the time that this law was necessary as it was the start of what he referred to as the "War on Drugs."

It is important to note that only the psilocybin molecule was illegal, but the mycelium and spores were not because they don't contain the drug. In the mid-1970s, people all over the country began cultivating shrooms indoors, and a thriving underground industry delivered psilocybin spores through the mail. Anyone who wanted to make a profit from selling psilocybin spores simply had to learn to cultivate them indoors. Many people chose to cultivate psilocybe cubensis, first discovered in Cuba and used in many other regions like South and Central America. The reason behind Psilocybe cubensis's popularity is that they were somewhat potent, and people could grow them in controlled settings. However, this cultivation method has undergone dozens of changes over the years.

Amateur mycologists across the country began using guerilla-wild crafting of various species of psilocybin mushrooms, especially active ones. Later, professional mycologists began searching for active psilocybin mushrooms all over the country. They became very popular in the 1970s as more and more people began cultivating these mushrooms. Another type of psilocybin mushroom, psilocybe cyanescens, was considered more potent than psilocybe cubensis. Home growers found it difficult to cultivate these mushrooms indoors. Psilocybe cyanescens later became known as "weed mushrooms."

Jumping to the 1980s, mycologists began cultivating more native mushroom species. In 1983, mycologists Paul Stamets and Jeff Chilton wrote a manual for cultivating mushrooms called "The Mushroom Cultivator." In the book, they mentioned a method called "the natural culture," which is an outdoors cultivating method and doesn't require a controlled environment, unlike indoor cultivation.

The history of growing shrooms would be incomplete without mentioning Terence and Dennis McKenna. In 1975, Terence's brother Dennis was inspired by an article to grow mushrooms indoors. He decided to use simple household items like mason jars for the process. He used spores he got from Ecuador that he and his brother had used before and experienced their out-of-body experience. The indoor cultivation method worked, and both brothers published a guide in 1976 with instructions on cultivating magic mushrooms indoors. Their book was called "Psilocybin: Magic Mushroom Grower's Guide." The book stated that growing magic mushrooms indoors was a simple process. They even compared it to canning jelly at home. Naturally, they focused on psilocybe cubensis, which can only be grown indoors in a controlled environment. The book inspired many people; since then, it has become one of the most prominent cultivation guides.

Shrooms had a long journey from the old world to the new world. You have probably noticed how ancient civilizations and the new world treated magic mushrooms differently. Ancient civilizations embraced these mushrooms and treated them with the utmost respect. Many of these cultures considered shrooms to be divine and only nobility and religious figures were allowed to consume this gift from the gods. Many cultures used these mushrooms to either celebrate their gods or connect to a higher power. Shrooms were featured in various myths and artworks to highlight their importance. There is still so much that we don't know about how ancient civilizations used and cultivated shrooms, but we know that shrooms were accepted, respected, and divine. It took shrooms centuries to finally reach the new world. However, when they did, they weren't treated with the same respect as in ancient cultures.

Naturally, many people were curious about this type of mushroom. The more the word spread about shrooms, the more curious researchers and scientists were. We can safely assume that the arrival and spread of the magic mushrooms in the new world were the best things to happen to these shrooms. The new world was where scientists studied psilocybin mushrooms, isolated their compounds for the first time, used them for various experiments, and gave them the name "magic mushrooms." It was also the place cultivation methods came into being. Firstly, the indoor method that many cultivators made into a business, then the outdoor method that many growers turned to for other types of mushrooms

Although they were extremely popular, especially during the hippie era and many people felt changed by the trans experience they underwent, the American government wasn't so receptive. They fought, banned, and initiated a war on drugs and, in particular, on the magic mushroom.

Both the old and new worlds paved the road for shrooms and how we view and use them in the modern world.

Shrooms Today

Right up to today, magic mushrooms remain illegal in many places. However, this hasn't slowed down their popularity. Nowadays, as mental health issues are on the rise and become less stigmatized, more people are talking about magic mushrooms and how they can help people suffering from mental illness. Many people feel they can trust these mushrooms because of their long cultural history. More voices now than ever before call for the legalization of shrooms. Various studies have been conducted and have shown how psilocybin mushrooms can be an effective treatment for various mental health issues. In 2018, researchers at Johns Hopkins University discovered that magic mushrooms could be an effective treatment for PTSD, anxiety, and depression. They also discovered that they could help smokers quit this bad habit for good.

In the 1990s, cultivating magic mushrooms was no longer a secret. Cultivators worked on simplifying the cultivation method and adding a few tweaks. Thanks to the internet, many people would publish various cultivation instructions. In fact, the internet has changed the game, and new forums and websites each day offer various resources on psychedelics. Cultivators and mycologists no longer felt alone or shunned and could communicate with like-minded people and swap cultivation tips with one another. They became a community with their own language and debate. Suppose a cultivator makes a mistake or messes up something. In that case, they can easily turn to their online community, where they can find people who will happily offer helpful advice and feedback. As a result, indoor cultivation has become extremely popular, with more and more people practicing cultivating methods.

The popularity of these forums doesn't seem to be slowing down either, with cultivation becoming easier and more accessible than it used to be. Thanks to the use of technology, more people get the chance to experiment with different cultivation methods. However, the psilocybin mushrooms' biggest issue still remains - they are still illegal and considered a Schedule 1 drug. The government still refuses to accept that they have medical value, and there are still concerns that people may abuse the drug.

This hasn't stopped scientists from researching the mushroom to prove that its advantages outweigh its disadvantages. Their discoveries have greatly impacted the government's decision to reconsider, as we will find out in the next part.

Different Laws Surrounding Psilocybin Mushrooms

In 2019 and 2020, after the results of Johns Hopkins University's research were announced, Denver, Colorado, Santa Cruz, Washington DC, Somerville, and Cambridge have all decriminalized magic mushrooms. Although this is a huge step, it still doesn't make magic mushrooms legal. In 2020, Oregon became the first state that not only decriminalized psilocybin but made it legal for therapeutic use as well. In the same year, Canada followed Orgeon's footsteps and made the use of psilocybin legal for people suffering from depression and people in palliative care. However, it isn't legal for anything else other than its therapeutic use.

Jamaica has taken a different route from its American neighbors and legalized psilocybin mushrooms. People can cultivate, sell, and consume mushrooms all over the country. The Netherlands, which doesn't have a "War on Drugs" policy, has decriminalized psilocybin mushrooms as well. In fact, shrooms were legal and sold openly in the country. But in 2008, a tourist passed away after consuming various psychoactive substances, and psilocybin mushrooms became illegal. Brazil is another country that allows psilocybin psychedelic brew. However, the Brazilians differentiate - psilocybin is illegal, but psychedelic fungi aren't. That said, Brazil has no records of arrests for cultivating or consuming shrooms.

Psilocybin mushrooms are also legal in Peru, where various companies offer shroom retreats. In Portugal, all drugs are, in fact, decriminalized. Again, this still doesn't make them legal. However, it has been known that you can use psychedelics without any legal consequences.

Although shrooms seem to be legal in many places around the world, the U.S.A still has a long way to go. Will it ever become legal? Honestly, no one knows. Laws change daily, as do people's mentality, so all we can do is hope. Many people all over the country are pushing for this change, especially after the many discoveries showing the benefits of magic mushrooms on mental health. The mental health issue has been under the spotlight for a few years now, giving people, including patients, the chance to advocate the legalization of shrooms. Psilocybin mushrooms have expedited the evolution process. Although this is still controversial, shouldn't it inspire more governments to give a chance to the thing that helped us transform from apes to talking and thinking creatures?

Chapter 3

Species of Psilocybe

If you want to become a home grower of magic mushrooms, the more knowledge of different types of shrooms, the easier it will be to know how to cultivate them and which techniques you should use. You also need to know about the various compounds found in shrooms - and their effects. The effects depend on several factors, including the environment and equipment used in cultivation. The symptoms vary from sensory to emotional to physical - and in the correct doses, they can also be beneficial for treating medical conditions. Finally, the chapter will reveal the most common type of magic mushroom cultivated worldwide.

Compounds Found in Shrooms

Magic mushrooms contain many chemical compounds, some of which are known to cause psychedelic effects, as we have read. Magic mushrooms' most prevalent psychoactive compounds are psilocybin, psilocin, nor-psilocin, aeruginascin, baeocystin, and nor-baeocystin. From these, psilocybin and psilocin are the most well-studied compounds, as their effects on the human brain are known to be the greatest. Psilocin, in particular, is one of the most potent natural psychoactive substances. And since psilocybin is the precursor of psilocin, its effects are equally crucial to understand.

While scientists are still unsure of the connection between all these compounds, studies show a clear correlation between their amounts in individual shrooms. For example, shrooms with high levels of psilocybin also contain larger quantities of psilocin. The various compounds also interact with each other and the serotonin receptors of the human brain. For example, aeruginascin seems to modify the pharmacological effect of psilocin by increasing the number of serotonin receptors in the brain. Since psilocin is very similar in structure to serotonin, it binds to these additional receptors - resulting in an enhanced euphoric mood after consuming shrooms.

Like many other biochemical agents produced in mushrooms, psychoactive compounds are all the byproducts of the nutrients absorbed by the mycelium. Shrooms are subject to environmental changes, and their psychedelic content could drastically change with even the slightest shift in the environment. Any change in temperature, humidity, and soil condition could affect the growth of mushrooms and the number of psychoactive substances they contain. The appearance of competitors, predators, and diseases may also have a role in determining the levels of these agents. In addition, the various parts of a shroom possess different amounts of organic compounds. For example, mature caps are known to have the highest amount of psilocybin compared to the other parts of the fruiting body.

There is also a difference in the quantities of psychoactive compounds between wild magic mushrooms and farmed ones. Wild shrooms have high variability in their biochemical composition— or, in other words, they are an unreliable source of these compounds. Besides the expected variation between the different species, varieties, and strains, variations can occur between batches taken from the same strain. The largest difference seems to be in the psilocin content, which, in wild mushrooms, ranges from 0.21 to 2.02%. The size and the age of wild mushrooms also affect their content, with overly mature plants possessing the least amount of psilocybin and psilocin.

Cultivated shrooms also show a difference in psilocybin content, but the differences are only notable in the first flush (harvesting period of one generation). After several successive flushes, the quantity of psilocybin and psilocin can be increased to four times its initial level. Some shrooms don't contain psilocin at all in the first generation of fruiting bodies. However, after the fourth generation is raised in a controlled environment, they gain high levels of this compound. While the amount of psilocybin shows no variations in controlled harvests, the amount of this compound in farmed shrooms is nearly double that of psilocin.

Not only that, but the type of substrate used in shroom farming can also alter their psilocin and psilocybin content. Some growth mediums help increase the amount of these compounds in shrooms, while others will inhibit their production. Psilocybin is particularly sensitive to the levels of amino acid tryptamine in the growth medium.

The Psychoactive Effects of Psilocybin

Consuming magic mushrooms unleashes a cocktail of compounds with potentially psychoactive effects into the bloodstream. These compounds travel to the nervous system and brain, where they launch several biochemical processes. These processes result in the release of feel-good hormones and several other compounds responsible for the following psychological symptoms: One of the most well-known is the so-called "psychedelic trip," which is essentially a result of a change in one's mood, consciousness, sensory experience, and perception. These changes can last from two to six hours - depending on the number of shrooms consumed and their potency.

Another effect people may experience under the influence of Psilocybe has altered awareness. This is closely related to the heightened sensory experience, as it makes a person pay more attention to details. As a result of this, things one finds aesthetically pleasing normally become even more attractive under the influence. For example, if one is in a crowded place, the number of stimuli can become too much, and one gets overwhelmed. This happens because the mind gets stuck on a single stimulus for too long under the influence of psilocybin. Whereas normally, it would quickly process any stimuli and move on to the next one.

Sensory overload can be avoided if shrooms are consumed in a tranquil setting. This is where a person feels comfortable enough to relax and isn't subjected to too much sensory input. In this type of setting, people can experience new ideas and explore them. They can also process their emotions through the sensory experience, as their minds can focus more on their origins. Deep thoughts about values and revaluation of character are also fairly common results of this "trip."

Time distortion is another effect people report having after consuming magic mushrooms. These are related to visual and auditory hallucinations that distort one's perception.

At high doses, the mind becomes incapable of handling the amount of sensory input and the process of psilocybin, which leads to a phenomenon called ego death. The term "ego death" refers to a state in which a person experiences the complete loss of their subjective self. While it may seem frightening at first, in many cases, an ego death has a transformative effect on one's mind and soul.

When it comes to hallucinations, they may or may not happen - and can come through various sensory channels. Their intensity, length, and type depend on the strength and dosage of the shrooms consumed. The most common type of hallucinations is close-eyed visuals, open-eyed visuals, and auditory hallucinations. Close-eyed visuals manifest as recollecting memories, seeing vivid colors, or experiencing dream-like sequences. Open-eyed visuals involve having a changed perception of the environment, like seeing inanimate objects and surfaces ripple or patterns forming and moving before your eyes. At higher doses, these objects can seemingly morph into different ones as your mind tries to process things that aren't even there. Auditory hallucinations include experiencing sounds clearer and louder or more distorted. At higher doses, people reported experiences such as hearing how the words in music and speech have changed when, in fact, they haven't. Their minds were simply trying to find a deeper meaning behind the words under the influence of psilocybin.

Since there are still a lot of unknown issues surrounding several unknown factors surrounding psilocybin, predicting exactly how a psychedelic trip will go is nearly impossible. However, by ensuring an optimistic, relaxed mindset and using the correct dosage, you can have a positive experience.

How one behaves after consuming magic mushrooms usually depends on how many and how regularly a person takes shrooms. If a regular user takes a small dose of shrooms, you may not even notice that they're on a trip. On the other hand, if a newbie takes a large dose, their behavior can become erratic and unpredictable. Whatever mood they were in before taking psilocybin will be heightened. If they were happy beforehand, they'll probably laugh a lot under the influence-and if a person is sad, they'll become very emotional.

While the psychological outcome of shrooms is more widely known, it's important to note that they can also cause physical symptoms. Most of these symptoms directly result from psilocin's psychoactive effects on the brain.

Here are some of the physical effects that taking magic mushrooms can produce:

- Numbness, particularly in extremities and the face
- Dry mouth, and when taken in high doses, can be a precursor to nausea and vomiting
- Increased heart rate and elevated blood pressure
- Muscle weakness, involuntary movements like twitching or convulsions
- High body temperature, sweating, followed by chills and shivering
- Exaggerated reflexes
- Frequent urination and loss of urinary control

Because of shrooms' effect on elevating, raising self-awareness, and promoting deep thinking, Psilocybin mushrooms also have potential health benefits. They can be beneficial for treating chronic and acute mental illnesses, including depression, anxiety, PTSD, and even addictions. They also show promising results when used in conjunction with psychological counseling, particularly after traumatic events and grief. Small amounts of psilocybin can also help alleviate migraines, cluster headaches, and pain in other chronic conditions without the psychedelic effects. While the research on these and similar effects is ongoing, the promising results are clear enough to attract the public's attention. The stigma of consuming magic mushrooms has largely been broken, with many health workers accepting their benefits as an alternative form of treatment.

Types of Magic Mushrooms

Since the name "Psilocybin" is commonly used for all magic mushrooms, people don't know that there are different types of shrooms. In fact, scientists have so far identified over 180 Psilocybe mushroom species—and this is not even counting all the strains and varieties! If you add all of these to the equation, the different psilocybin types are virtually limitless. And every different mushroom holds different potency levels, even if grown under the same environmental conditions. The following guide will take a closer look at the most common magic mushroom varieties and provide a detailed description.

Psilocybe Semilanceata

Also called Liberty Caps, Psilocybe semilanceata is considered one of the most potent magic mushrooms you can grow. In fact, they are ranked as the third most potent Psilocybin mushrooms worldwide. They thrive in a rich, acidic substrate, preferably one that contains organic manure as a fertilizer in controlled farming conditions. This is because, in the wild, they use decomposing organic material of animal nature.

Psilocybe semilanceata is usually found growing in the wild, as it thrives on many different substrates. It was the first native species to be discovered and officially recognized in Europe. Since then, it has grown naturally throughout the Northern Hemisphere. However, cultivating it can be challenging due to the high level of moisture its growth requires. It is typically farmed only outdoors.

While these shrooms are small, they have large leather-like caps compared to their size. These caps are brown, bell-shaped, and attached to stems that curve. The caps themselves taste like flour. Under them, you will find 15-27 narrow gills containing spores. When the shroom stem or cap is removed or damaged, the gills start to turn blue, indicating decay, so extracting spores should be done as quickly as possible.

Psilocybe Cubensis

Psilocybe cubensisis the most common type of magic mushroom consumed and grown globally. They can be found in the US, Central America, the northern parts of South America, and Southeast Asia. They can be just as quickly grown indoors as they are cultivated outdoors. For this reason, they have reached the status of a true "classic."

When they grow indoors, Psilocybe cubensis can be more potent than most shrooms grown in controlled conditions. However, this is dependent on whether they are grown correctly.

There are more than 60 identified strains of Psilocybe cubensis, and all of them grow large, with caps reaching up to 3 inches in diameter. Due to their size, the caps are often weighed down by gravity, so they tend to flatten out when they reach maturity. Under the caps, you'll find tightly packed gills that turn brown to black when the spores mature enough to be released. If the cap or the stem is removed or damaged, the mushroom becomes bluish-purplish and will soon start to decay. Some of the most commonly known strains of Psilocybe cubensis are Penis Envy, Florida White, and Golden Teacher.

Psilocybe Mexicana

Psilocybe mexicana grows in Central and South America, where it has been used for centuries by indigenous people for treating common ailments or as a tool for rituals. It can be grown indoors and outdoors, though it requires considerable attention. Its appearance is similar to that of Psilocybe semilanceata, as it also has a bell-shaped or conical cap. The size of the cap ranges in diameter between 0.4 and 0.8 inches and hides dark-colored gills with spores in them. The color of the fruiting part of Psilocybe mexicana is beige, with an occasional green or blue undertone, which is only visible in the sunlight. When the cap or the stem is damaged or broken, they turn a darker shade of blue.

Psilocybe Cyanescens

Psilocybe cyanescens, or Wavy Caps, are characterized by their curvaceous caps - which can reach up to 2 inches in diameter. When it matures, the unusually shaped cap is a caramel brown color, and as it starts to dry out, this color slowly fades to light beige. The gills containing mature spores are similar in color to the caps. If they are removed or damaged, the caps, the gills, and the stems all turn blue due to rapid oxidation.

First identified in England, Psilocybe cyanescens is commonly grown in North America, Central & Western Europe, the Middle East, and New Zealand. Their preferred growth substrates are mulch beds and woodchips. Cultivating these mushrooms is relatively easy since they are readily available and inexpensive. In fact, it's suspected that their spread was accidental. It's said to have happened when they were unwittingly being transported from one territory to another in lumber and other raw wood products. They've become one of the most prevalent types of magic mushrooms used around the globe. Psilocybe cyanescens are highly potent, even if cultivated outdoors - which is the most common way of growing them due to their large amount of space. Despite this, there has been a steady increase in their growing areas in recent years.

Psilocybe Azurescens

Psilocybe azurescens is another common variety of magic mushrooms. In the wild, it grows in North America but can be cultivated anywhere in the Northern Hemisphere. Its nickname, "the flying saucer," comes from the large caps shaped very similarly to a saucer. When mature, the caps are flat and have a caramel brown color that shines in black and blue hues. The gills are dark brown or black but turn blue when damaged, similar to the rest of the mushroom.

Its intense potency is another reason for many of the nicknames of this variety. Besides the Flying Saucer moniker, Psilocybe azurescens also goes by the name of Blue Runner, Azzie's, and Blue Angel. While this has never been officially confirmed, many users claim that this is probably the most efficient Psylocybe variety on the planet. In nature, they thrive in extremely high humidity, such as on loose stones and decaying wood near large bodies of water. Unlike other shroom varieties that prefer warm temperatures, Psilocybe azurescens has no trouble withstanding cold temperatures.

Psilocybe Baeocystis

Psilocybe baeocystis is a common inhabitant of the Pacific Northwest, where it also thrives in controlled conditions. This variety has a thin, rippled, conical-shaped cap. Depending on the amount of energy these shrooms can get from the substrate, their caps can grow from 0.5 to 2 inches in diameter. The mature caps are dark brown with a greenish hue, while the gills have an unusual electric blue coloring. The chalk-white color of the stems adds another contrast to the appearance of this variety, but when it dries, it darkens. Depending on the size of the cap, the stem can be curved or straight—the larger the cap is, the more curved the stem will be.

Psilocybe Caerulescens

Thanks to its fame in the culinary world, Psilocybe caerulescens has recently become one of the most cultivated magic mushrooms. Apart from North America, these shrooms also grow naturally in Central America, where they've been used for native ceremonies for centuries. They thrive in areas where landslides have occurred and buried organic material, which the shrooms can use as the source of nutrients., Psilocybe caerulescens is also called the Landslide Mushroom. However, they can be cultivated in a controlled environment as long as it's done outdoors, at a high altitude, and at low temperatures. This variety has low to moderate potency, and its effect passes within 3-5 hours.

Psilocybe Caerulipes

Psilocybe caerulipes, or Blue Foot, is a rare variety occasionally found in North America. However, they can grow in a relatively common type of substrate—making their cultivation relatively easy. They thrive on decaying wood in forests and near rivers, which can be replicated with moist wood chips. The cap of Psilocybe caerulipes is medium-sized, and has an unusually blue hue, hence the nickname. The caps turn slightly darker when the fruit matures. The gills underneath the caps have a similar color. This variety is highly potent - and even more so when cultivated in a controlled environment.

Psilocybe Tampanensis

Going by the names of Magic Truffles and Philosopher's Stones, Psilocybe Tampanensis is widely known for its characteristic sclerotia, which contains high amounts of psilocybin. The structure grows underground, which makes accumulating highly potent compounds much easier. However, the intensity of these compounds isn't as overwhelming as is the case with other, similarly powerful varieties. While Psilocybe Tampanensis is a rare find in the wild, it thrives in shrooms and farms all over the Northern Hemisphere. Its caps, stem, and gills all have a light beige color that darkens when the mushroom drops its spores or is damaged.

Chapter 4

Sterilization

From the previous chapter, you've learned how many factors can influence the psychoactive substance content of shrooms. You now have the perfect foundation for learning more about growing conditions. One of the first lessons to learn is how to maintain optimal growing conditions and the importance of keeping things sterile during the entire process.

While sterilizing growth media and the area you are working on is a tedious task, there is a reason behind it. All your hard work—transferring cultures on the growth medium, inoculating jars, and making fruiting chambers - can be ruined by a single colony of bacteria or a few mold spores. This chapter is dedicated to the process of minimizing the risk of pesky contaminants destroying your growth. It will explain how you can create a sterile environment, growth media, and secure handling processes to ensure success. You will also be given a few tips on figuring out whether an area is sterile enough so that it isn't harmful to anyone who comes in contact with it. You'll learn to keep track of the sterility of all surfaces and how to keep yourself clean, too. Knowing where contamination might come from gives you the advantage of taking a proactive approach and doing everything necessary to reduce the risk and mitigate damages.

The Importance of Sterilization

Shrooms require a moist environment and an acceptable growth medium. In addition, when growing magic mushrooms at home, specific care must be taken to avoid contamination that could destroy the shrooms or make anyone sick. One way to prevent contamination is by sterilizing everything you use, including equipment and growth medium.

You may wonder if sterilization is necessary for mushrooms that grow in the wild. Well, for one, wild shrooms grow in an environment that's not perfectly balanced, and the only reason magic mushrooms survive in the wild is because they find a way to beat their competition. While fighting over resources, they lose some of their nutrient and psychoactive content. In addition, the energy they could've spent on growing becomes wasted on trying to beat their competitors. To cultivate magic mushrooms at home, you must create an environment you can control. This way, you'll eliminate any competitors that could potentially prevent your shrooms from growing. This will force the mycelium and the fruiting bodies to grow much faster and allow them to take in more nutrients - leading to a higher concentration of psychoactive substances.

However, there is much more to sterilization than preventing magic mushrooms from having to compete against mold and other pathogens. Shrooms aren't the only organisms that will lose out if there is competition; you also have a lot to lose during the process—and not just in time and resources. Regularly inhaling shroom spores can be dangerous, even if they don't contain psilocybin or psilocin or aren't contaminated with mold. Spores can cause respiratory infection and neurological symptoms, which are far from pleasant. If you're not careful enough, you can also transfer the spores onto someone else and make them ill from inhaling. People suffering from respiratory conditions or autoimmune disorders are often sensitive to any type of air pollution. For them, inhaling shroom spores can have dire consequences.

Sterilizing the substrate and the work area kills most of the potential biological and chemical pollutants before your mushrooms begin to grow. There are several different sterilization methods you can use. Which ones you choose depends on your preferences, the amount of material you need to sterilize, the strains you want to grow, and the type of growth medium you use. You can eliminate contaminants from the growth medium or surfaces using rubbing alcohol, peroxide, or a pressure cooker. Cooking them at the right temperature or using a professional sterilizer are also viable solutions.

Sources of Contamination and How to Avoid Them

How clean your environment needs to be, depends on which process you are currently doing and what you hope to achieve, and the end of it. It's also important to note that creating a 100% sterile environment is virtually impossible. That said, it's always better to go a step further and try to get as close to a perfectly sanitized environment as possible than to do nothing and leave it all to chance. The only way to do this is by knowing the different sources of contamination. After all, it's not just molded spores in the air you need to worry about. Your hands, breath, tools, and even your clothes can be a source of pollution. Contaminating the mushroom cultures or substrates and cross-contamination of several different Psilocybe strains are all issues you should worry about. Below, you will see all possible sources and several practical ways to increase your chances of eliminating them.

The Substrate

The most common reason for contamination in a substrate is inadequate sterilization. This usually happens if you either process items in bulk or don't pay enough attention to each individual object. Failing to complete sterilization or pasteurization could mean losing the whole batch. The substrates and grains you buy in bulk often contain millions of microorganisms, not to mention dormant spores—ready to compete and overpower the shroom spores. These will need to be eliminated or, at least, have their numbers reduced to a minimum. Otherwise, the shroom spores and mycelium won't have a chance of fighting against them.

Any grain spawn and sawdust fruiting blocks should be sterilized before inoculation. Sterilization means subjecting them to high temperatures and pressure for a prescribed period of time. For grain spawns, the ideal sterilization period is 90 minutes at 15 PSI. Whereas for fruiting blocks, complete sterilization takes 2.5 hours at the same pressure setting. This is done using a stovetop pressure canner big enough to accommodate all the material and can reach the required pressure.

Pasteurization is another way to sterilize your substrate, and it's particularly effective if your substrate is straw. Straw should be pasteurized at approximately 150–180 degrees Fahrenheit for at least 90 minutes. A great way to do this is to use a propane burner placed under a large water-filled metal container. This creates a water bath that can be heated to the correct temperature and kept at it for the required time.

Working Area

When it comes to your working area, the most likely source of contamination for mushroom growers is the air. Mold spores and other microscopic contaminants are everywhere around you. The most efficient way to reduce air pollution is to use a laminar flow hood. This device constantly channels a clean stream of air into your working surface, allowing you to do safe mycological work. If properly used, it can also eliminate airborne contaminants. While flow hoods are a significant investment, they can definitely make inoculation work much more safely.

Another option for reducing airborne contaminants is by using a still air box. This is a large, clear box with arm holes cut into its sides so that it can be cleaned from the inside. This can come in handy if you consider that the air isn't the only source of pollutants in the working area. With a still box, you can have clean air and a working surface you are only touching with a sterilized object and gloved hands. Since the size of the box only allows you to slide your hands in, doing work with grain spawns and fruiting blocks can be challenging. On the other hand, it can be perfect for doing an initial inoculation and working on small-scale projects.

The Cultivator

Dirty hands, skin, clothes, and even the breath of the cultivator are often a huge source of contamination. Your skin and clothes contain an obscene amount of contaminants that could easily out-rival your inoculant. Showering, washing your hair, and getting into clean clothes before doing any work is highly recommended. Another option would be to wear scrubs over your clothes and shoes as foot protection to avoid allowing contaminants to get through.

It is also imperative to wash your hands thoroughly before the procedure and wear surgical gloves whenever possible. Keep in mind that washing your hands means scrubbing under the fingernails too! Use generous amounts of hand sanitizer or wash your hands immediately after you are done, even if you were wearing gloves the entire time.

Wearing a medical-grade face mask is also highly recommended. This will prevent you from breathing in spores or introducing contaminants onto the substrate and work surface. If you can't or don't want to wear a mask, you should avoid opening your mouth as much as possible until you finish your work.

As a cultivator, following the proper sterile techniques at every stage of the growth process is crucial. These are the ones that enable you to keep up the sterile condition in your substrate and working area. While this may take a little practice, you will learn how to work effectively while keeping things sterile with your mind focused. Apart from learning the appropriate techniques, you must also be aware of how these may be the source of pollution if done incorrectly. For example, when working with a laminar flow hood, you should always hold any materials vulnerable to contamination, such as spores, substrates, and mycelia, upstream of the flow. Open dishes should always be placed closest to the hood's filter.

You must be careful with what you touch, too. Substrate dishes must be opened by holding their lids at the back end of the container and downstream of the flow at all times. You must also work as quickly and effectively as possible. Sterile material should be exposed for the barest minimum amount of time required to finish the work.

The Tools

If not sterilized regularly or incorrectly handled after sterilization, your tools can also become a source of contamination. One little mistake, like not sanitizing your scalpel or blade between culture transfers, can introduce competitors into your substrate and poor-quality shrooms.

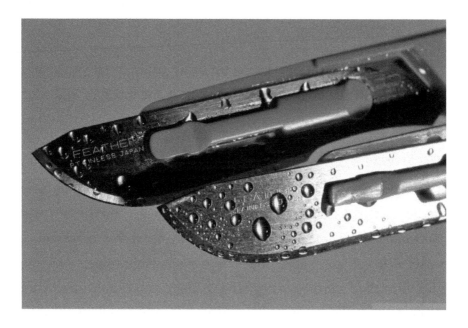

Here are some ways to sterilize your tools before and in between uses:

- **Flaming:** Scalpels and other tools can be sterilized by being heated up in a flame until they become red. Most metal tools designed for lab work are thin, so all you need to do is hold them in the flame of an alcohol lamp or lighter for 20-30 seconds. Place it at the edge of your substrate to cool it down when you are done.

- **Rubbing Alcohol:** Wiping down your tools and major surfaces with alcohol is a must before working with shrooms. You can also use this technique to clean the outside of grain jars, agar plates, and grow bags before and after handling them. Use a lab-style bottle to eliminate any contaminants that could get into the inoculum or fruiting body chamber without you having to pour the alcohol from a regular bottle.

- **Dry Sterilization:** There are many commercially available dry sterilization for sterilizing your tools before and after using them.

The Spores

You can take all the necessary precautions to keep your surfaces sterile and your work adequate—but it won't matter if your inoculum is contaminated. If you are buying spores or shrooms, verify that you are getting them from a reputable source who can guarantee their sterility. After buying them, you should store your product, so it doesn't get contaminated. Avoid handling them as much as possible until you are ready to start the inoculation process. When using spores or mycelium you've grown on your own, you should handle them with sterile tools, surfaces, and body from harvest to inoculation.

How to Know if the Area Is Sterile Enough

Shrooms can be cultivated in different types of growing mediums— all of which are equally suitable for other organisms, including pathogens. As easy as it is to inoculate the growth medium with mushroom spores or spawn, it is equally easy to transfer contaminants. And as fast as the mycelium grows, so will the unwanted microorganisms. This is both good and bad. On a positive note, you will know soon if you've transferred any unwanted pathogens to the substrate. There are several ways to figure it out:

- You notice the foreign microorganisms are growing-often faster than the mycelium or fruiting bodies.

- You notice that your mycelium isn't growing - something is preventing it from accessing nutrients.

- You notice that the fruiting bodies appear distorted or of a different color than you expected.

Unfortunately, all these signs mean you'll have to start the process again from scratch. So, to prevent this, the obvious solution is to figure out whether the area you are working on is sterile enough. Being super careful will also help you eliminate the possibility of spreading shroom spores through the air and making yourself or anyone else ill.

Of course, there are many other ways to check if an area is sterile enough before you begin to notice contamination. Here are some of the ways to keep track of the sterility of your shroom cultivation process:

- **Keeping Moisture Away:** Use dry sterilization techniques as much as possible to keep away humidity and prevent mold and other pathogens from growing.

- **Keep Everything in Sight:** Never lose track of your tools after sterilizing them. If you misplace an item and find it later on, there is a good chance you didn't handle it properly.

- **Avoid Unnecessary Handling:** Picking things up when you don't need them increases the risk of contamination—both for the areas you are working with and yourself.

- **Don't Drop Anything:** If a sterile item drops, it may get damaged—in which case, you shouldn't use it. If an object you used to handle spores falls, you instantly contaminate the area. If you use this tool again, you could contaminate the shrooms.

- **Use the Right Tools:** Non-serrated kitchen knives can be used; however, their blades are made from a more compact material than the blade of the scalpel, making them harder to sterilize by flame. Not heating them up properly between processes can result in incomplete sterilization and contamination. Rather use a scalpel - it will help you to work faster—which further reduces the risks of contamination.

Staying Clean

Although achieving perfect sterility for working with shroom spores is nearly impossible, every step you take in the sterilization process will increase your chances of success. With the right tools and techniques and by taking a proactive approach, you will have a good chance of beating contaminants. Staying clean means constantly working on maintaining the spores where they belong and not allowing any competitor to hinder their growth.

The best way to achieve this is to have a sterilization schedule that covers all the possible sources of contamination. That said, the most attention should always be paid to the area you're working in. After all, this is where the contaminants come from and where you can inadvertently release shroom spores into your environment. Keep a log of your sterilization processes. Each time you sterilize, disinfect, or pasteurize any surface the spores come in contact with. After each time, note how effective you were in eliminating contamination. If a foreign microorganism begins to grow in your inoculated substrate or someone gets sick from inhaling shroom spores, you will know that your space wasn't sterile enough. Next time, you will have to pay more attention.

Using parafilm is another way to keep the surfaces that spores and mycelium come into contact with clean and contaminant free. Its porous material with a high stretching capacity that's perfect for sealing dishes after inoculation. It lets air through but filters out anything else, including mold spores and other pathogens. An alternative for this would be to use masking tape - although this is a bit more challenging and may not allow for proper air circulation.

Use an alcohol lamp instead of a lighter. An alcohol lamp is nothing more than a jar full of alcohol with a submerged wick that's attached to the bottom of the container. You are supplying a constant flame to your lab area by lighting the wick. Unlike using a lighter or any other heat source to keep relighting, an alcohol lamp gives you better control over the flame and will help keep contamination at bay.

Being extra vigilant about the dangers of contamination and knowing what contaminants can be is crucial. The most common contaminants are mold, bacteria, and yeast cultures - although other chemical or biological pollutants may just as easily affect the growth of magic mushrooms. Even if the shrooms contain the appropriate level of psilocybin, this doesn't mean they will be good for you if contaminated. Bacterial growth and mold spores can make you sick if you consume a mushroom grown in a contaminated growth medium.

Sterilization reduces the likelihood of growth issues for your shrooms and illnesses caused by possible contamination. However, some mushrooms do not grow well in sterilized growth media and must be grown outdoors. Using nutrient-rich environments that don't require sterilization or are impossible to keep perfectly sanitized can be a suitable option for cultivating these. However, these strains will require even more attention due to the lack of a sterile environment. Magic mushrooms growing in unsterilized growth media need to be supervised. Any discoloration or decay can indicate contamination that should be remedied immediately.

Chapter 5

What You Need to Grow Shrooms

Now that you've understood what shrooms are, the history of their cultivation, and the psilocybe species (and their respective effects), the next step is to understand how to grow them.

As discussed in the previous chapter, sterilizing everything around you is essential to growing shrooms safely. However, sterilization is simply the first step of growing your shrooms; cultivating spores can take some work.

To ensure that your cultivated shrooms grow properly and you don't have to worry about making a mistake and ruining them, it's essential to have the correct equipment. So, before you start the actual growing process, here's what you should have on hand.

Magic Mushroom Spores and Spore Syringes

Spores are the basic ingredient for growing shrooms at home. They're the equivalent of seeds for plants, and without them, you won't be able to grow any magic mushrooms.

Numerous varieties are available, which can make choosing which one to grow a bit challenging. While you likely have your preferred variety of magic mushrooms, choosing the strain to grow at home is not simply a matter of preference – there are other factors to consider, including the availability of spores and if it's easy to cultivate your chosen type at home.

Psilocybe cubensis is generally the most popular mushroom species for home growing and consumption. If this is the first time you're cultivating shrooms at home, the best Psilocybe cubensis strains for you to consider are B+ and Golden Teacher.

While strains such as Penis Envy are significantly more popular for consumption, B+ and Golden Teacher are more receptive to and forgiving of changing growth conditions and ideal for beginners. It's best to work up to growing your preferred strain of Psilocybe cubensis instead of letting weeks of hard work go to ruin.

It's also essential to remember that Psilocybe cubensis and its strains are not the only types of magic mushrooms available for home growing – they're simply the most popular. Other species of mushrooms you can consider include:

- Psilocybe semilanceata
- Psilocybe cyanescens
- Psilocybe mexicana
- Panaeolus cyanescens
- Psilocybe tampanensis
- Psilocybe azurescens

If you're worried about the potency of non-Psilocybe cubensis mushrooms, don't be. It's certainly not the most potent species available to you – Psilocybe azurescens, for example, is significantly more potent than Psilocybe cubensis.

Aside from choosing the strain in question, the other important consideration regarding magic mushroom spores is sourcing them. Some growers report consistent issues with sourcing spores and have faced numerous challenges when doing so, including cross-contamination, wrongly identified strains, and empty syringes that contain only water and no spores.

To avoid these issues, it's essential to choose a reputed buyer.

Magic mushroom spores are, in themselves, legal to own in numerous countries, including:

- The United States (barring the states of California, Idaho, and Georgia)

- Canada

- France

- The Netherlands

- Italy

- Mexico

- The United Kingdom

This loophole in the law makes it relatively easy to find companies selling spores online. Some options for you to consider include:

- Ralphsters

- Mushroom Prints

- The Magic Mushrooms Shop

- Viking Spores

- Spores Lab

Once you've chosen a strain and a supplier, all that's left for you to do is to order the spores. Spores will reach you in "spore syringes" of 10-12 cc each. You can then use these syringes to "sow" the spores (like you would with seeds) in a substrate to ensure their growth.

Substrate

The substrate is essentially the medium in which the mushrooms will grow, similar to how soil acts for plants.

However, it's not simply a growth medium – it's also a food source. If you want your shrooms to grow properly, getting the substrate right is essential.

You can make your own substrate instead of buying some. You'll need organic brown rice flour, vermiculite, and filtered/distilled water. The basic recipe is 2 parts vermiculite, 2 parts organic brown rice flour, and 1-part water, all mixed together in a large bowl.

To make the substrate, you should:

- Add the vermiculite first. You'll need 500 ml of vermiculite for five half-pints jars of spores.

- Next, add water to the vermiculite. You should add about half as much water as you used for vermiculite.

- Finally, add as much of the organic brown rice flour as you did vermiculite. Mix the three ingredients thoroughly until you see them form an even coat of flour over damp vermiculite

Once you've prepared the substrate, fill it in the mason jars you'll use when growing the shrooms. Make sure to leave about 3 cm from the top empty, and fill this section with dry vermiculite. Then, seal the jars with their rubber seals and wrap some tinfoil over them.

After you've prepared your mason jars, the next step is to sterilize them.

You've already understood the importance of sterilization in the last chapter. The substrate mixture needs to be sterilized as doing so will kill off any competing mold and bacteria that may be present in it. If these competing microorganisms are allowed to grow, they will severely inhibit the growth of your shrooms.

To sterilize the jars:

- Fill them in a pressure cooker or Instant Pot.

- Fill the pot with water and bring the cooker up to boil.

- Let it run for at least 30 minutes before turning off the heat and removing the jars from the cooker/pot.

- Allow the jars to cool down and dry out before starting with the growing process.

One of the major problems when growing shrooms is contaminated substrate. No matter how careful you are, it's relatively easy for the substrate to become contaminated with mold spores from the air. As mentioned, this can severely inhibit the growth of your shrooms.

To solve this issue, you should either build a sealed glovebox (covered further down in this chapter) or buy a laminar flow hood. This will help keep the substrate free of mold spores. Another option is to use plenty of alcohol to continue sterilization, but this will also require you to spend significantly more time monitoring your shroom growth than you would otherwise.

Another option is to create self-sealing injection ports in the lid of your jars after you've finished sterilizing the substrate. This will allow you to inject the spores without needing to open them and expose them to the outside air.

To create these ports, you'll need to:

- Poke holes in the lid of your jar with a nail

- Cover the hole with some gasket sealer. You can find these high-temperature sealers at an automotive shop or store that sells automotive equipment.

- Allow the sealer to dry fully.

- When you're ready to add your spores, inject them directly through the sealer. The holes will self-seal when you pull the syringe back out, reducing its exposure to outside air and the chance of contamination from spores naturally present in that air.

Other Equipment

Other things you'll need for growing shrooms include:

- Mason jars. Ideally, they should be wide-mouthed to ensure good airflow and translucent so that you can keep an eye on the mushroom growth happening inside.

- Perlite

- A spray bottle

- 70% Isopropyl alcohol cleaning solution: This will help ensure your growing area remains sterile

- A lighter

- Nitrile or latex gloves

- A measuring cup

- Mixing bowl

- Small towel

- Micropore tape

- Strainer

- Surface disinfectant

- Surgical mask

- Air sanitizer

- A hygrometer for monitoring the temperature and the humidity of the fruiting chamber

- Food dehydrator. This is technically required right after you finish growing your shrooms – magic mushrooms don't stay fresh for long, and dehydrating them allows you to store them for longer. If you're only growing enough to use immediately after the mushrooms are ready, you probably won't need this – but if you plan on storing your shrooms, it's a must.

You will also need an incubator and a fruiting chamber.

Incubators and fruiting chambers can both be purchased from a store. However, if you're looking to keep things as budget-friendly as possible, it's also possible to make your own.

Incubator

An incubator is a relatively uncomplicated piece of equipment and is often not needed in the first place. If there's a dark, warm, and dry spot in your home where you can place your inoculated jars, you likely won't need an incubator.

However, if finding such a spot is a challenge, an incubator can be a lifesaver. To make one at home, you'll need:

- Two identical, opaque containers

- An aquarium heater

Here's what you'll need to do to make the incubator:

- Fill one container about 30% of the way with water
- Place the aquarium heater in the container and turn it on
- Stack the second container inside the one you filled with water
- Place your jars inside the second container, and then seal the container

Your jars will spend 1-2 weeks in these containers until they are colonized with mycelium, and you can continue on to the next step. Make sure to keep an eye on them while they undergo incubation – by day three or four, you should see white thread-like structures forming near where you inoculated them.

You should also keep an eye out for contamination. Some common visible signs include:

- Green/blue growths
- White fuzzy growths
- Oily look

If a jar has been contaminated, it must instantly be removed from your incubator. Contamination is infectious; leaving it unattended will also infect the rest of your jars.

Fruiting Chamber

The fruiting chamber is where you place your jars after they have been colonized with mycelium to finally see your shrooms grow.

Like incubators, they can be easily purchased from a retail store or made at home.

To make a DIY fruiting chamber, you'll need:

- A clear container that can hold all your jars
- 70% Isopropyl alcohol cleaning solution
- A drill
- Perlite
- Filtered water

Here's what you'll need to do:

- Drill holes in the top and the side of your clear container. This will let in enough airflow to ensure proper fruiting of your shrooms.
- Wipe the container with the isopropyl alcohol cleaning solution
- Wait for a few minutes until the alcohol evaporates completely from the surface of the container.
- Cover the container's bottom with about 3 cm (1 inch) of perlite
- Moisten the perlite with filtered (or distilled) water. Stop adding water before the perlite becomes too wet. If you do accidentally add too much, allow it to drain off before continuing with constructing your fruiting chamber.

- Place the jars inside the container with their lids. Alternatively, if you can't find a container tall enough to hold the jars, remove the mycelium cake from the jars and place it on a jar lid before placing the lids inside the container.

And that's all you need to do – your fruiting chamber is now good to go.

You'll need to check on the shroom growth daily and should ideally take the lid off the container and let in some fresh air from a fan for a couple of minutes each day. Additionally, you will also need to use the spray bottle (filled with distilled water) to spray the perlite and prevent it from drying out.

When using the spray bottle, ensure you don't spray the mycelium accidentally, as doing so can cause it to be contaminated with bacteria. Within a few days, you should start to see small mushroom "pinheads" forming on the sides of the mycelium cake.

When you use your fruiting chamber, you'll need to choose its placement carefully. Make sure you don't place it in a spot in your house that naturally has a lot of mold growth so that your mycelium doesn't become contaminated. Additionally, adding a filtration material like polyfill over the vent holes you created can also lower the risk of contamination by an outside agent.

Other Techniques

Remember that these are only the basic ingredients required for growing shrooms using the PF Tek technique, which will be covered in-depth in the next chapter. Other growing methods will require different ingredients, including:

- **Sterilized Rye Grain**: This is required for the grain spawn technique, which will be covered in Chapter 8. This technique involves creating a liquid culture from your mushroom spores. This liquid culture is then injected into a bag of rye grain, which is where your mushrooms will grow.

- **Agar Powder:** Also known as agar-agar, this is used as part of the agar technique for growing shrooms. This helps you grow your shrooms with a significantly reduced risk of contamination. However, growing mushrooms with agar are significantly more complex than the PF Tek technique, which is why first-time growers rarely use it. You can learn more about this technique in Chapter 7.

Numerous other ingredients will be required if you're using the agar growth technique. The ingredients will depend on the agar recipe you're using. However, in general, you will need to have some form of sugar and nutrients to promote shroom growth. Some options include:

- Malt extract

- Malt powder

- Molasses

- Malt-based drinks

You can also make your own sugar-nutrient solution by boiling potatoes. Once they've boiled, remove them from the water and use the cloudy broth left behind in your agar recipe.

Other ingredients you'll need for this technique include:

- Cling film
- Petri dish substitutes. You can use clean, sterilized, unused take-away sauce containers for this
- A beaker or Erlenmeyer flask. If you can't access either, a glass jar will do
- Concentrated yeast extract. If you can't find any, you can use Vegemite or Marmite as substitutes
- A scalpel
- A thin glass rod
- Pressure cooker
- Glass jars
- Thermometer
- 70% isopropyl alcohol cleaning solution
- Hydrogen peroxide, 3% concentration

You'll also need a still air box or glovebox, which you can make at home.

To make this, you will need:

- Large plastic storage container. Preferably, choose one that has an airtight or near airtight lid.

- An 800g-1kg tomato tin. Alternatively, you can use a tuna can. You just need the can portion, so if you've got an old, empty tin, that will do just fine.

- Oven mitts

Here's what you'll need to do:

- Heat the tin until it's hot.

- Use the heated base to cut two holes in the box. They should be situated so that you can comfortably insert both your arms into the hole at once. Wear your gloves while completing this step, as the hot tin can burn you otherwise.

- Once the holes have been made, file down the edges so there are no sharp edges that might injure you or tear your gloves.

- Wipe down the box with 70% isopropyl alcohol cleaning solution to ensure it's sterile

If you're using the grain spawn technique, here's a list of all the equipment you'll need to make your grain spawn:

- Mason jars and modified lids

- Sterilized rye grain, as mentioned above. If rye is not available, you can use oats, wheat, or sorghum instead

- A bucket

- Aluminum foil

- Hot distilled water

- A pressure cooker

- Mycelium for growing mushrooms

- 70% isopropyl alcohol cleaning solution

- Gloves and disposable wipes

Alternatively, you can buy readymade spawn jars with pre-made grain spawn ready-to-grow shrooms.

Grow Kits

As mentioned above, shroom spores are technically legal to sell. Due to this, shroom grows kits are also legal because (barring California, Idaho, and Georgia) there are no laws preventing you from possessing or, more importantly, selling shroom spores.

Grow kits are a good alternative if you're interested in growing your own shrooms but find gathering all the equipment challenging. These kits come complete with pre-inoculated substrate and other ingredients you'll need to grow the mushrooms and the mushroom spores themselves.

Some kits come with everything but the spores, depending on where the company producing them is based and the local laws. Once again, this saves you the trouble of finding or making the ingredients you need to grow your shrooms.

The material that comes with grow kits depends on the seller and the price. More expensive kits contain everything from heaters and air filters to substrate jars and latex gloves. However, more budget-friendly options may only include the substrate (and the spores).

If you already have the spores or know where you're buying them from, you can also use grow kits designed to grow non-psychedelic mushrooms. However, if you're going this route, make sure to check the kit and ensure it doesn't also include the mushroom mycelium – while those kits are great for growing the mushroom species they're intended for, they're pretty much useless for shroom cultivation.

As with buying spores, if you're buying a magic mushroom grow kit, make sure to buy from a trusted seller. Non-spore-containing kits are easier to source and experiment with, as you have legal recourse if you're sold a faulty product. However, if you're buying a kit with spores, you may not have a legal solution if an untrustworthy supplier cheats you unless you live in an area where shroom cultivation is legal. So, doing your research and looking at reviews before making a purchase is essential.

Now that you know what equipment you need to grow your shrooms, the next step is to understand the growing process. The next few chapters will cover various techniques you can use to grow shrooms, including:

- PF Tek

- Agar

- Grain spawns

- Outdoor cultivation

As mentioned above, PF Tek is the easiest option for first-time growers. However, depending on the strain, you want to grow and your experience with growing non-psychedelic mushrooms, you may choose to opt for one of the other techniques.

This book will also cover fruiting containers in further detail, giving you other options when building your own and explaining how and why you should also build a humidity tent along with the container. We'll explain how to monitor and adjust humidity levels and lighting to ensure your mushrooms grow properly and explore how you'll use and manage casing soil. Finally, we'll also cover the harvesting of your fully grown magic mushrooms and how to store them properly.

So, if you're itching to get started with growing your own shrooms, the only thing left for you to do is turn the page and keep reading!

Chapter 6

Psilocybe Fanaticus Technique

Now that you know the basics of mushroom cultivation, it's time to delve into some of the more advanced methods used to grow these mushrooms. In this chapter, we will be discussing the Psilocybe Fanaticus technique. This popular method among amateur growers is relatively simple and doesn't require expensive equipment.

With the information in this chapter, you can decide for yourself if the Psilocybe Fanaticus technique is suitable for you. We will cover everything from the sterilization and inoculation process to contamination prevention. By the end of this chapter, you will know how to make a spore syringe, which is necessary for this technique.

PF Tek

Psilocybe Fanaticus is a technique that mycologist Robert McPherson developed in the early 1990s. It is a method of growing psychedelic mushrooms using wood chips as a substrate. The main advantage of this method is that it gives you a greater yield of mushrooms in a shorter period of time. The Quality of the mushrooms is also often higher when grown using this method. With a little practice, anyone can learn how to grow high-quality mushrooms using this method.

Another advantage of this method is that it is easy and doesn't require sterile conditions. In nature, psychedelic mushrooms grow on dung or decomposing wood. The Psilocybe Fanaticus technique imitates these natural conditions by using wood chips as a substrate. The Psilocybe Fanaticus technique is an easy way to grow psychedelic mushrooms, and it can produce excellent results if done correctly.

The Process

The first step in the Psilocybe Fanaticus technique is to find a suitable location for your mushroom patch. The patch should be in an area that receives partial sun and is well-drained. Once you have found a suitable location, the next step is to prepare the substrate. To prepare the substrate, straw or sawdust is soaked in water and then inoculated with mushroom spores. The substrate is then placed in a plastic bag and left to incubate for several weeks.

Once the substrate has colonized, it can be fruited in various ways, including outdoors on a log or indoors in a terrarium. Fruiting occurs when the mushroom mycelium slowly breaks down the wood chips, releasing nutrients that the fungi use to fruit. When the conditions are right, the mushrooms will begin to fruit. Once the mushrooms have begun to be fruit, they can be harvested and consumed.

Pros

The Psilocybe Fanaticus technique is considered to be one of the most efficient ways to grow mushrooms and has several advantages over other methods. Here are some of the pros of this technique:

1. **Much Higher Yield**

    It gives you a much higher yield of mushrooms than other methods. This is because the roots of the mushrooms can access more nutrients in the soil. It is not uncommon for a single patch to yield several ounces of mushrooms. The average yield is about 1/2 ounce per square foot.

2. **Higher Quality Mushrooms**

    In addition to a higher yield, the Psilocybe Fanaticus technique also produces higher-quality mushrooms. The mushrooms grown using this method are larger and have a higher concentration of psychoactive compounds. Mushrooms grown using this method can contain twice as much psilocybin and psilocin as those grown using other methods.

3. Less Likely to Contaminate

This method is less likely to contaminate the mushroom crop with bacteria or fungi. This means you can avoid losing your crop to mold, which is a common problem with other methods. It's also relatively easy to do and doesn't require sterile conditions, making it a good choice for beginners.

Cons

However, the Psilocybe Fanaticus technique is not without its drawbacks. Here are some of the cons of this method:

1. Limited to Wood Chips

This method is limited to growing on wood chips. This means that you will need to find a good source of wood chips, which can be challenging. In addition, the wood chips must be of a certain quality for the mushrooms to mature. This can make it difficult to find a suitable substrate.

2. Time-Consuming

This method can be time-consuming, as the substrate must be prepared and then left to incubate for several weeks. Once the substrate has colonized, it can take several more weeks for the shrooms to fruit. This means that you will need to be patient to see results.

3. Requires Some Skill

This method requires some skill and knowledge to be successful. Unlike some other methods, there is no room for error. If the substrate is not prepared correctly, the shrooms will not mature. This means you need to have a thorough understanding of the process before you start.

However, the Psilocybe Fanaticus technique is still considered to be one of the best ways to grow shrooms because it yields a higher quantity and quality. If you are looking for a way to cultivate, this is definitely a method you should consider.

Better Tek

Do you think there is a better technique for growing Psilocybes? While the Psilocybe Fanaticus technique is considered to be one of the best ways to grow mushrooms, there are always ways to improve. There is no one-size-fits-all answer to this question. It depends on your specific needs and preferences. Ultimately, it is up to you to decide which method is best for you.

One way to improve on the Psilocybe Fanaticus technique is to use a different substrate. Instead of wood chips, you can use straw or manure. This will give the shrooms more nutrients, yielding even more. Another way to improve the Psilocybe Fanaticus technique is to use a different mushroom species. Some, such as Psilocybe Cubensis, are more resistant to contamination. This means you can avoid losing your crop to mold or bacteria.

You can also use a different method of inoculation. Instead of spores, you can use a piece of the mushroom. This is called a "mycelium transfer," and it can be done by taking a piece of the mushroom and placing it in the substrate. This will introduce the mycelium to the substrate and help it colonize faster.

While there are ways to improve the Psilocybe Fanaticus technique, it is up to you to decide which method is best for you and what facilities you have available to you.

Sterilization Process

The Psilocybe Fanaticus technique requires a stringent sterilization process. This is necessary to kill any bacteria or fungi that could contaminate the substrate. There are a few different ways to sterilize, and we've detailed below the most common methods and their step-by-step instructions:

1. Boiling

The easiest way to sterilize the substrate is to boil it. This will kill any bacteria or fungi that are present. While boiling is the easiest method, it is also the least effective. This is because some microorganisms can survive at high temperatures. The advantage of boiling is that it is quick and easy.

To boil the substrate, you will need:

- A pot

- Water

- Substrate

- A strainer

- A container

Instructions:

Step 1: First, fill the pot with water. The amount of water you need will depend on the size of the pot and the amount of substrate you are sterilizing.

Step 2: Next, add the substrate to the pot.

Step 3: Then place the pot on the stove and bring the water to a boil.

Step 4: Once the water is boiling, let it simmer for 30 minutes.

Step 5: After 30 minutes, remove the pot from the heat and let it cool.

Step 6: Once the pot is cool, strain the substrate.

Step 7: Finally, transfer the substrate to a container.

2. Pressure Cooking

Another way to sterilize the substrate is to pressure cook it. This method is more effective than boiling but is also more time-consuming. The advantage of pressure cooking is that it will kill all bacteria and fungi. To pressure cook the substrate, you will need:

- A pressure cooker
- Water
- Substrate

Instructions:

Step 1: Add around two cups of water to the pressure cooker.

Step 2: Then, add the substrate.

Step 3: Place the lid on the pressure cooker and seal it.

Step 4: Next, turn on the pressure cooker and set it to 15 PSI.

Step 5: Once the pressure cooker reaches 15 PSI, let it cook for 30 minutes.

Step 6: After 30 minutes, turn off the pressure cooker and let it cool.

Step 7: Once the pressure cooker is cooled down, open it, and remove the substrate.

3. Baking

Baking is another option for sterilizing the substrate. This method is less effective than boiling or pressure cooking but is quick and easy. The advantage of baking is that it is less likely to damage the substrate. To bake the substrate, you will need:

- An oven
- Substrate

Instructions:

Step 1: Preheat the oven to 200 degrees Fahrenheit.

Step 2: Then, add the substrate to an oven-safe container.

Step 3: Next, place the container in the oven and bake for 30 minutes.

Step 4: After 30 minutes, remove the substrate from the oven and let it cool.

4. Microwaving

Microwaving is the quickest and easiest way to sterilize the substrate. However, it is also the least effective method. To sterilize the substrate in the microwave, you will need:

- A microwave
- Substrate

Instructions:

Step 1: First, add the substrate to a microwave-safe container.

Step 2: Then, microwave the substrate for 30 seconds.

Step 3: Remove the substrate from the microwave and let it cool.

Inoculation Process

Once the substrate has been sterilized, it is time to inoculate it. This is the process of adding the spores to the substrate. This can be done by mixing spores with water and injecting them into the substrate, such as vermiculite or brown rice flour. Once the spores have been injected into the substrate, they will need to be incubated to encourage germination.

The incubation period can vary depending on the type of substrate and the temperature, but it typically takes between two and four weeks for the spores to germinate. After that, the newly formed mycelium can be transferred to a fruiting chamber, where it will continue to grow and produce mushrooms.

The most common method of inoculation is with a spore syringe. A spore syringe is a syringe that is filled with water and spores. To make it, you will need:

- A spore print
- A sterile syringe
- Distilled water

Instructions:

1. First, sterilize the syringe by boiling it in water for 10 minutes. This will kill any bacteria that may be on or in the syringe.

2. Take it out of the boiling water and let it cool.

3. Once the syringe is cool, add the spores to the syringe. To do this, hold the spore print over the opening of the syringe and gently tap it until the spores fall into the syringe.

4. Then, add distilled water to the syringe. The amount of water you add will depend on the size of the spore print. For a small spore print, add around 1ml of water. For a large spore print, add around 5ml of water.

5. Once the spore print is wet, gently swirl the syringe to mix the spores and water.

6. Finally, inject the spores into the substrate. To do this, insert the syringe needle into the substrate and slowly depress the plunger.

Growth Process

Once the spores have germinated, the mycelium will begin to grow. The mycelium is the white, thread-like structure that makes up the body of the mushroom. The mycelium will continue to grow and spread through the substrate until it reaches the sides of the container. This process can take anywhere from two weeks to two months, depending on the type of mushroom and its growing conditions.

Once the mycelium has reached the sides of the container, it is time to fruit the mushrooms. This is done by increasing the humidity and temperature of the growing environment. The shrooms will begin to form within a week or two and will be ready to harvest in another couple of weeks. When they mature, they will have brown or black spores on the underside of their caps. These spores can be used to make a new batch of the substrate.

Preventing Contamination

One of the most common problems with growing mushrooms is contamination. Contamination can occur at any stage of the process, from sterilizing the substrate to harvesting the mushrooms. The most common cause of contamination is bacteria and other fungi. These can enter the growing environment in many ways, such as on your hands, in the air, or in the syringe.

When bacteria, fungi, or mold spores find their way into the substrate, they can quickly multiply and contaminate the entire batch. Contamination can also occur if the growing environment is not sterile. To prevent contamination, it is important to sterilize all of the equipment that will be used. This includes the container, the substrate, and the syringe. Here are some tips for sterilizing your equipment:

1. Use Distilled Water

One of the most common ways contamination can creep into your cultivation is using tap water to water the crops. Tap water contains various dissolved minerals and other impurities that can encourage the growth of bacteria and fungi. So, it's vital to use distilled water whenever possible. Distilled water is completely free of impurities, making it an ideal choice for watering shrooms. In addition, distilled water can also be used for cleaning your tools and equipment.

2. Use a Pressure Cooker

One way to reduce the risk of contamination is to use a pressure cooker. A pressure cooker is an essential tool for sterilizing equipment. Pressure cookers work by heating water to a boiling point and then trapping the steam inside. This creates a sterile environment that is free of bacteria and other contaminants. They are also a great way to sterilize tools and equipment.

3. Use Bleach

Bleach is a powerful disinfectant that will kill any mold or bacteria it comes into contact with. Simply mix one cup of bleach with nine cups of water to use it. Then, soak your containers, tools, and work area in the solution for at least five minutes. Once everything has been soaked, rinse it off with clean water and allow it to air dry.

This method may seem a bit extreme, but it is the best way to ensure that your growth area is sterile and free of contaminants.

4. Use Gloves

The spores of Psilocybe Fanaticus are very fragile and easily destroyed by careless handling. One way to protect the spores is to wear gloves when you are potting them or moving them around. This will keep the spores from being crushed or damaged. In addition, it is crucial to avoid cross-contamination between your gloves and other surfaces. Be sure to wash your hands thoroughly after removing your gloves and avoid touching any surfaces that might be contaminated.

5. Use a Face Mask

A simple way to protect yourself from spores is to wear a face mask. This will stop spores from being inhaled and will also protect your eyes from being exposed to the spores. In addition, remember to avoid touching your face while you are working with spores. If you do happen to touch your face, be sure to wash your hands thoroughly afterward.

6. Use a Laminar Flow Hood

A laminar flow hood is a device that creates a sterile environment by using a stream of filtered air. Laminar flow hoods are often used in hospitals and laboratories but can also be used in the home. Laminar flow hoods can be used to sterilize equipment and can also be used to protect against cross-contamination. These devices are relatively expensive, but they are worth the investment if you are serious about growing mushrooms.

7. Use Alcohol

Rubbing alcohol can be used to sterilize equipment and surfaces. Simply apply the alcohol to a clean cloth and wipe down the desired area. Allow the alcohol to air dry, and then you will be ready to start growing. Alcohol is a powerful disinfectant that will kill any bacteria or mold it comes into contact with.

8. Use Hydrogen Peroxide

Hydrogen peroxide is yet another effective disinfectant that can be used to sterilize equipment and surfaces. To use it, simply mix one cup of hydrogen peroxide with nine cups of water. Then, soak your containers, tools, and work area in the solution for at least five minutes. Once everything has been soaked, rinse it off with clean water and allow it to air dry. This method is effective but should be used cautiously as hydrogen peroxide can be harmful if inhaled or ingested.

9. Use Vinegar

Vinegar is a weak acid used to disinfect surfaces and equipment. Mix one cup of vinegar with nine cups of water. Then, soak your containers, tools, and work area in the solution for at least five minutes. Once everything has been soaked, rinse it off with clean water and allow it to air dry. Vinegar is not as effective as some of the other methods on this list, but it is a good option if you are looking for a natural disinfectant.

The Psilocybe Fanaticus Technique is a great way to grow mushrooms. It is simple and easy to follow and very effective once you get the hang of it. However, there are a few things that you need to be aware of before you start growing. First, this method is very susceptible to contamination. If you are not careful, your shrooms will be contaminated, and you will not be able to harvest them.

Second, this method requires a lot of patience. The shrooms will not grow overnight, and it may take several weeks for them to mature. Finally, this method is not foolproof. There is always a chance that your mushrooms will not grow or that they will be contaminated. If you are willing to take the risk, then the Psilocybe Fanaticus Technique is a great way to grow shrooms.

Chapter 7

Agar Technique

This chapter will explain the agar technique and how it is used for growing psilocybe shrooms. We also explain different processes related to growing shrooms, including incubation, cloning, subculture, and dealing with contamination. Finally, we discuss the various ways to store your strains and how to inoculate tubes.

What Is the Agar Technique?

Agar is made from red algae and is commonly used as a setting agent in desserts to preserve fruit and as a thickener for soups. On top of its culinary uses, agar is also a critical ingredient in microbiology worldwide. Petri dishes containing agar create an excellent environment for growing different types of bacteria or fungi, such as mushrooms. In short, agar is a "culture media" or a substrate containing different types of nutrients and vitamins required to grow various microorganisms.

Agar diffusion is a technique that describes molecular movement through the matrix created by the gelling of agar. The molecular movement is determined by its concentration when the technique is used in a controlled environment. This phenomenon creates the foundation for agar diffusion, which is used to determine the resistance or susceptibility of a bacterial strain to a particular antibacterial agent like antibiotics.

For instance, if an antibiotic is added to agar, it tends to move from a region consisting of high concentration to other regions with lower antibiotic concentration. The technique can also be performed by placing disks consisting of an absorbent material soaked with the selected antibiotic onto the agar surface. The antibiotic will diffuse from the disk into the agar. The diffusion technique makes screening bacteria and detecting any form of resistance easier.

How Is Agar Technique Used for Growing Psilocybe Mushrooms?

Using agar, you can grow cultures of different microbes, and you use different recipes to grow specific species. To grow spores, you should know that they come as spore solution in a syringe, prints, or collected on swabs. You can also collect spores by gently scraping the gills of mushrooms, but there is a big likelihood of contamination this way which is why it's not recommended. The best method to grow your spores is to add a small number of spores to the agar. Carefully spread them across the surface in a way so you can easily watch germination. Don't spread the spores across the entire surface of the agar because it will be difficult to track germination. Use your spore syringe to squeeze a few drops onto the agar and spread them evenly across the surface. When you use the swab, gently skim it across the surface. You can also scrape some print spores and apply them to the agar.

How to Use Agar to Grow Shrooms

When you grow shrooms using agar, ensure you work closely and in a sterile environment to prevent contamination. The spores usually take 7 to 14 days to germinate, Contaminants could also be present, so if you notice it, you should cut and move your mycelium.

The mycelium for shroom-growing species has a white thread-like texture and often grows in a powdery form. You can also see the growth of long thick mycelium known as "rhizomorphic." The growth of mycelium can vary even if the species are on the same plate. During the early stages of growth, it can be difficult to differentiate mycelium from contaminants.

The mycelium should start as what is called a clear hype, and when it reaches the stage where it appears as white tufts, it will begin to expand. These tufts must appear consistently together with the streaks, which will help you notice the difference if any other form of mycelium appears. Contaminants are easy to spot in time to get rid of them because they germinate quicker than the spores. They also mature and change color and texture quickly as your spores grow. So, once you notice these changes, you should be ready to transfer the mycelium.

If you realize that your spore solutions constantly contaminate the agar, you can use the Dilution Tek. Add 1ml of Dilution Tek to 9 ml of sterile water, then spread the mixture across the surface. You can have several dilutions, which will help promote spores' growth without contaminants. You can also use the colored agar method or put a backlight on the agar plate to be able to observe the fine hyphae.

You must have enough spores to achieve the fungi's full life cycle. Single spores cannot create shrooms; they must combine with compatible hyphae to create and reproduce. Be sure to keep a close eye on the healthy mycelium developing and move them to new plates to prevent the spread of contaminants.

Quickly cut the leading edge away from the mycelium if you notice any contaminants. You must be cautious and know that it may be difficult to determine the species until you fruit your mycelium. Always check for contamination carefully, and all spore prints must be labeled to avoid confusion. If you suspect your spores have been contaminated, starting the growth process with fresh mycelium is also a good idea. Once the process is messed up in the beginning, you will likely have a poor output.

Tissue Cultures

Mushrooms consist of specialized hyphae, which can return to their exploratory form of negotiating their environment and seeking nutrients once they are given the opportunity. You must take a small sample to get the cleanest hyphae in the shroom and place it on agar. It will start growing - this process is known as tissue culture - using mycelium from fresh mushrooms to form new viable cultures.

The overall quality of the mushroom, including its freshness, will determine your success. It is straightforward to work with a specimen created in a clean environment, which can result in minimal or no contamination. If you are using foraged specimens, you need to be creative with your agar technique.

To germinate your spores, you can add hydrogen peroxide (H2O2). Hydrogen peroxide is a powerful oxidizing agent that can be used as a bleach or to clean wounds or cuts, as well as in the process of growing your own shrooms. You add it to agar to slow down bacteria and kill contaminant spores. It becomes functionally sterile as it cools when you add it to your agar. Mycelium adapts itself to larger concentrations of hydrogen peroxide. It is mainly produced within cells as a result of their metabolism. However, the mycelium will be shocked when it is moved to peroxide agar, which can take some days to recover, so don't be alarmed, be patient.

To make the water sterile, you can use an agar recipe consisting of a 3% H2O2 solution and add 1% of the contents to make sterile water. Add 2 ml of hydrogen peroxide if you want to create a 200ml recipe. Remember that heat can destroy hydrogen peroxide, so use a thermometer. When the agar cools and reaches between 45 and 55 degrees Celsius (113 to 131 degrees Fahrenheit), add your H2O2 and mix well. You should monitor every step to ensure you get the best results.

When dissecting the shroom, sterilize your knife using a jet flame lighter. Divide it in half and get a small sample from the place where the cap and stem join. Put your sample into peroxide agar and wait to see the changes. You will begin to see the tissue sample changing and becoming hairy.

Take out the hairy sample and put it on the agar's surface to begin the growing process. Always check for contaminants on your sample. If you observe undesired particles, you can resample or start over the process. Try to make several tissue samples if you observe any problems. Creating a tissue culture takes time, so try to have many samples since the chances of survival will be slim. Contaminated stains will produce poor-quality mushrooms.

Taking Care of the Cultures

It is important to keep the agar clean and sterile to take good care of your culture. When you add tissue culture or spores to the surface of the agar, seal the petri dish tightly using cling wrap. While laboratories can use Parafilm, a cling film is sufficient for household uses and is also less expensive. The main goal of sealing the culture is to keep mites, dust, and insects at bay since they can cause contamination. Storage in sealed bags provides an extra layer of protection.

Store your plates at room temperature of about 64 to 78 degrees Fahrenheit. Keep them in a container you can place on top of your fridge, or you can consider using a hot water cylinder. Lower temperatures are not ideal because they slow down the mycelium. On the other hand, warmer temperatures promote contamination. Trichoderma favors temperatures that are above104 degrees Fahrenheit, so you can use a reptile heating mat. As long as room temperature is maintained, you need not worry about getting a special gadget to protect your culture.

Make sure you label each petri dish with a name, date, media used, and any other relevant notes. If you have an extensive culture collection, it can be difficult to remember all the details, so labeling is vital. The labels also help warn your housemates that the cultures in the fridge are not for consumption.

How to Inoculate Tubes

The metal tool used to transfer cultures must be sterilized before each transfer. The tip must be heated to red-hot using a burner or alcohol lamp flame. Wearing gloves is a good precaution to take while doing the inoculation inside a transfer hood. To inoculate a 400-450g substrate, you need to use clean and healthy growing cultures that fill about a quarter of a large 100mm plate diameter. The size of substrate you want to inoculate should determine the tool you can use for the exercise.

The mother culture or inoculum must be healthy, actively growing, and uncontaminated, and it should be actively growing strain on agar. Cut the agar culture using a large, sterilized blade. Cut the mycelium and agar into small squares and transfer them to the sterilized seeds inside your spawn container. You must shake the inoculated spawn container to distribute the culture pieces inside the substrate. This helps establish growth centers inside the spawn container and promotes the colonization of the substrate.

Incubate your inoculated spawn container at 23 degrees Celsius and 73 degrees Fahrenheit and keep it in darkness. You can also use a clean cardboard box as an incubation container, but keep it at a room temperature of about 73 to 77 Degrees Fahrenheit. Wrap your spawn containers with aluminum foil to protect them from light. The incubation process lasts between 10 and 20 days after the complete colonization of the substrate. Store your mature spawn in the fridge at 4 degrees Celsius (39 degrees Fahrenheit) in darkness until you need to use it. The spawn stored in the fridge can last several months unless it gets contaminated or dries out.

Incubation

Incubation comes after inoculation, and this is the period when the fungus has not yet fully established its hold on the substrate. The nutritious substrate will be prone to contamination during this stage. In most cases, colonization of the nutritional spawn substrates must be performed in a sterile and enclosed environment to keep bacteria and other contaminants at bay.

Growing mycelium produces a considerable amount of heat, which can be damaged if placed in an area with a very high temperature. You should maintain an ideal temperature range of about 75-80degrees Fahrenheit where you keep your growing mycelium. Higher temperatures are likely to encourage the growth of contaminants, and they may kill the mycelium. On the other hand, temperatures that are lower than the range above can slow down the colonization process. So, it is a delicate balancing act to get the right temperature to work in.

If you use a jar to grow the mycelium, it must be kept at room temperature because the growing contents inside the jar will be warmer. Different incubation techniques like the incubator, heat bomb, and tub-in-tub incubator were specifically developed for this purpose. However, an incubator is not necessary unless the temperature in the room with incubating jars is below 22 degrees Celsius (72°F).

Many people believe that mycelium grows faster in total darkness, but there is no scientific data to support this notion. However, direct exposure to sunlight can be detrimental. Artificial light is enough for the incubation period. There should also be enough gas exchange during the incubation process. Mycelium produces carbon dioxide, which should be exchanged with external air.

Cloning

When you choose to grow shrooms, you should know that the forest is the source of all stains used for commercial purposes. Collecting spores from wild mushrooms can be tricky if you don't know the genetics. However, you can use cloning to make strains to grow shrooms in the lab.

You can also use cloning to copy shrooms that have outstanding characteristics and unique genetics like faster colonization times, larger fruits, and other valuable traits. The process of cloning mushrooms is simple and similar to those used for cloning cultivated species, wild plants, or fruits bought from the store.

You only need to harvest a piece of tissue from a specific mushroom fruit body and then place it on agar. When you transfer the tissue to a nutrient-rich agar medium, the cells will spring into action. This method works even on harvested mushrooms since their fruitbody will still be living, and the cells are still capable of reproducing.

Subculture

Subculture refers to transferring a shroom culture to a substrate or fresh culture media. If you intend to develop another strain, use the subculture method. This helps to increase the quantity of shroom culture that will be used for rejuvenation or propagation. However, the subculture will weaken over time.

Dealing with Contamination

Besides selecting and moving mycelium, you should know the tricks involved, especially when dealing with bacteria. It can be challenging to deal with unwanted fungal contaminants. The best way to work with agar is to pour warm agar over the tissue culture. You should know that mycelium also grows through the agar and not only on the agar's surface.

When doing tissue samples, don't use the peroxide agar tek. Instead, place your tissue samples on the standard agar under sterile conditions, just like you would with spores on agar. As long as you keep things clean, you can handle your tissue cultures outside the commonly used Still Air Box (SAB). If the spores land on peroxide, they will be killed. If the mushroom is contaminated, you are likely to have different problems. For instance, fungi like cobweb mold can spread quickly.

If you are dealing with wood-loving shrooms or psilocybe azurescens, you need to begin the process on cardboard. Boil the cardboard for about 20 minutes, take a small sample, and place it on the board. While contaminants don't grow on the cardboard, they can grow in the mycelium and take a while to be visible.

Different Ways to Store Your Strains

When you check your mycelium, you'll see it covers the surface of the agar. To keep your fungi cultures alive, take sections of the leading part of the mycelium and move them to new agar plates. The cultures on the leading edge are the strongest and healthiest, so cut squares from the edges. When there are no signs of contaminants, you can store your strains in the fridge.

Whenever you make a transfer, you can identify the purity of the mycelium. If there are contaminants, you'll see them quickly. Using a different media like MEA to PDA for each transfer is critical. Repeat the process to keep the mycelium active, which will also help it adapt to various nutrients and substrates.

You can also make liquid cultures from agar cultures. Constant transfers will lead to the weakening of the mycelium. Therefore, keeping a pure master culture in cold storage makes sense. You can then take small samples from this culture for inoculating other liquid cultures.

By now, you should be getting an idea of what is needed to grow your own shrooms successfully. In this chapter, we have explained different concepts you should know about the agar technique. We covered various aspects such as incubation, cloning, subculture, dealing with contamination, and storage of your strains. The following chapter focuses on creating grain spawns.

Chapter 8

Grain Spawns

In this chapter, we start by explaining what grain spawn is and how to prepare it. Then, we will discuss the process involved in the transfer from agar to grain spawn. Following that, we discuss the steps involved in inoculating grain spawn into syringes, explain how to incubate the jars, and outline how to prevent contamination and boost growth. Finally, we highlight the measures you can take to transfer grain to grain and how to use grain spawns on a larger scale.

What Is a Grain Spawn?

Grain spawn is a technique used to grow mushrooms, but little is known in this sector. It consists of sterilized grains that are inoculated with mycelium culture. A mass of growing mycelium will consume the inoculated grains. The fully colonized grain spawn is used as the starter culture when you want to grow mushrooms.

Due to their application and appearance, the grains are often referred to as mushroom seeds and is. Added to the substrate, which is then colonized by the mycelium culture. Various growing media can be used as substrates, including straw, mulch, paper, hardwood sawdust, coffee grounds, and more.

How Do You Prepare a Grain Spawn?

If you want to prepare your grain spawn, you first need to choose the appropriate type of grain. Hydrate the grains overnight and sterilize them in a pressure cooker. Inoculate your sterilized grains with mycelium culture, which was grown on agar, or - you can buy it in the form of a liquid culture syringe.

The grain spawn can take about 10 days to three weeks before it becomes fully colonized and ready for use. Alternatively, you can buy readymade spawn jars with sterilized, nutritious, and whole oats that are perfect for producing grain spawn for mushroom growing. To make your own grain spawn, you will need mason jars, 1 kg grain (wheat, oats, rye, sorghum, etc.), a bucket, hot water, a pressure cooker, gloves, and others. Follow the steps below to prepare your grain spawn.

- Hydrate the grain - boil water, turn off the heat, then add the grain. Allow it to soak for about an hour.

- Drain the grains and spread them evenly to dry slightly.

- Pack your slightly damp grain into a reusable culture jar. It should be 2/3 full, and cover the jar with aluminum foil.

- Sterilize your jar for about 90 minutes. You can use a pressure cooker to sterilize your grain.

- Inoculate your grain with agar or liquid culture once it cools. Use a space with little airflow to prevent contamination.

- Shake your jars once mycelium has colonized about 50 to 70% of the grain. This helps to distribute mycelium evenly and increases the colonization speed. Keep the jars in darkness and at room temperature. Your grain spawn must be ready for use between 14 and 21 days.

How to Transfer from Agar to Grain Spawn

Different types of agar can be used to create fungal mycelium; the common ones are Malt Dextrose Agar (MDA) and Potato Dextrose Agar (PDA). Alternatively, you can consider premixed commercial agar, but it is relatively expensive. The agar tube with mushroom mycelium is the master culture. You can transfer the culture from one tube to another under sterile conditions if you want to share it with other cultivators.

To increase the amount of your culture, you can grow it on grain, which is known as grain spawn. You can easily transfer the shroom cultures that grow on grain by pouring the contents from one jar to the other. For instance, you can use one jar of grain spawn to inoculate several gallons of substrate used to grow mushrooms.

How to Inoculate the Grain Spawn to Syringes

When you've created your shroom culture, you can add it to sterilized grain. The shroom mycelium will work through the grain to colonize it. When your grain is fully colonized, you can make more grain spawn.

Sterilized grain can be inoculated from either a spore syringe or liquid culture. To do this, you should first sterilize the tip of the syringe using a flame until it is red hot. Lift the lid of the grain jar and quickly inject the syringe, which the liquid will cool. It is also possible to inoculate your grain jar by injecting the liquid culture through the filter without opening the lid.

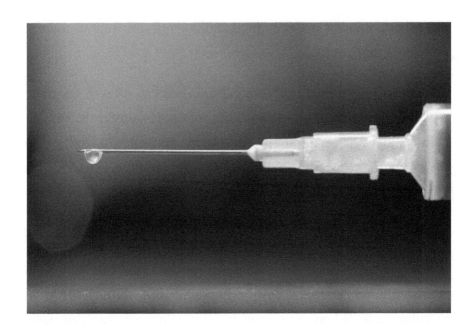

How to Incubate the Jars

When you inoculate your jars, you should keep them at a temperature of 80 degrees Fahrenheit to boost faster development. This temperature is ideal since the jars are generally warmer than the surroundings, given that mycelium emits heat. Don't forget to label and date all your jars and put them in a place that is room temperature, away from direct sunlight. As long as your jars are inside a room, there is no need to buy an incubator.

During colonization, be sure to shake your jars to spread the grain. It can take between one to three weeks for the jar to be fully colonized. You can consider grain-to-grain transfer during this time to make more spawn. Regarding incubation, remember that your jars must be kept in a safe place.

How to Prevent Contamination of Spawns and Boost Growth

When you grow mushrooms from scratch, you must have a sterile environment and always use clean tools to handle your spawns. The process of transferring cultures, inoculating grain jars, and creating fruiting blocks can be spoiled by a single mold spore. Various sources of contamination can affect your spawns, as we've discussed previously - mold spores, contaminated tools, your hands, clothes, your breath, substrates, or even shroom cultures can harbor contamination. The following are some of the measures to take to reduce contamination.

Airborne Contaminants

The air around you is a major source of contamination since it carries mold spores and other invisible contaminants that can ruin your project. To reduce airborne contamination, you need to use a laminar flow hood. If used properly, it's a great investment because it makes your life far easier by eliminating a significant amount of contaminants.

A still air box is another effective option that can play a pivotal role in reducing airborne contaminants. This big clear tote has holes on the sides that are designed to help you clean the interior. SAB is another effective option for small-scale agar growers.

Contamination from Substrates

Badly or incomplete pasteurization or sterilization of substrate can cause a lot of hard work going down the drain. The grains and bulk substrates often contain dormant spores and organisms that need to be eliminated to prevent a situation where they will end up competing with your shrooms.

The substrate should always be sterilized before inoculation. This is done by putting the grain through high temperatures and pressure for a long time. You can use a stovetop pressure canner large enough for your material. Grain spawn should be sterilized for about 90 minutes, whereas sawdust usually requires about two and a half hours to be sterilized.

Pasteurization is another option you can consider reducing contamination if you use straw as your bulk substrate. You can pasteurize your straw at between 149 to 180 degrees Fahrenheit for about 90 minutes. One way to do this is to use a large drum of water and a burner to create a hot water bath.

Contamination Caused by the Cultivator

Things like dirty clothes, dirty hands, breath, hair, and cultivators can be a huge source of contamination. Your hands and clothes can attract several contaminants. Before doing any lab work, ensure you thoroughly wash your hands and clean your clothes. Cut your fingernails since they can trap bacteria, and use hand sanitizer. When conducting mycological work, you also need to use latex gloves. A face mask is also appropriate since it prevents you from breathing in your mycological work, which can introduce contaminants. Try not to open your mouth or speak while handling lab work.

Use appropriate techniques.

Use proper sterile techniques when doing lab work. You should be aware of the potential sources of contamination and know the measures to take to mitigate them. For instance, when you are dealing with a laminar flow hood, you might have susceptible materials upstream. An open agar dish must be placed closer to the filter.

You must also pay attention to what you touch and how you handle open agar dishes. It is vital to work quickly to keep contaminants at bay. Do not keep your jars open for a long time.

Contaminants from the Tools

Contaminants can also be introduced by unsterilized lab tools, especially when you are working with agar. To avoid this, you need to flame your scalpel or any other tool you use to sterilize them. For example, hold the scalpel in a flame for about 30 seconds until it glows red. When you place it into a jar, it will cool instantly. You can also use a lighter to heat your scalpel.

Alcohol is another effective sterilizer you can use to wipe your tools and all the surfaces before starting your mycological work. Use it to wipe other instruments like grain jars, grow bags, and agar plates. Use the right alcohol, which is designed for lab work. There are different lab supplies; you can also consider creating an environment free from contaminants when you perform your lab work.

Getting the right tools for the job can make your life easier. Some things are not complicated. For example, you can use a simple alcohol lamp to supply flame in the lab, and you can use it for sterilizing your culture syringes or scalpel. When sealing your agar jars, you can use a parafilm consisting of porous material. It works to transfer air while at the same time filtering unwanted particles to keep the contents inside clean. You can also use masking tape, which is cheaper and easier than other options.

When choosing a scalpel, make sure it is one you are comfortable using when you transfer culture, clones, or perform different forms of agar work. They come with various blade sizes and are used for cutting and scraping different types of materials. If you use a kitchen knife, make sure it is sterilized.

Staying clean when you perform different tasks related to mushroom growing can go a long way in preventing issues like contamination. While perfect sterility might not be possible in mycological work, you need to do everything possible to increase your chances of success. You stand a better chance of beating the contaminants with the right technique and tools. More importantly, you must have a positive mindset.

Transferring from Grain to Grain

When you use grain as your primary substrate for the spawn to grow shrooms, you should know the different ways of transferring it. Follow the steps below to transfer from grain to grain.

1. Use fresh and sterile grain substrates like barley, oats, brown rice, wheat, corn, popcorn, rye, sorghum, millet, or bird seeds to prepare your jars. Fill the jars with grain

up to about 60 % level and leave some space for grain spawn, which you should add on top.

2. Before doing anything - you should think about sterility. Use a face mask, gloves, gown, cap, and raincoat.

3. Choose a spawn jar consisting of white mycelium. Check it for issues like sourness, mold, and metabolites. You should only use healthy mycelium for inoculation. Wipe the jar down using alcohol.

4. Shake the jar to break the spawn inside without opening it. Use your hands to tap all the sides of the jar. All the clumps of grain mycelium must be broken down into independent grains.

5. Before the grain to grain transfer, make sure you clean the table with alcohol, removing bacteria and contaminants from the surface. You can also use a quartz lamp to disinfect your room for at least 30 minutes before carrying out any work. You may require SAB, a laminar flow hood, and a glove box. If you don't have these tools, you can use a clean room that has been disinfected.

6. Wipe all your jars with alcohol, and focus on where the lids connect with the jar. Get rid of any suspicious compounds that could contaminate the contents inside the jars.

7. Open a spawn jar with mycelium and another jar containing uncolonized contents. Inoculate the grain mycelium into the jar with a sterile grain substrate. Then close the jar you have inoculated with a lid consisting of an air filter and set it aside. You don't need an inoculation port on the jar, only a breathing filter that promotes gas exchange.

10. Repeat the process of manipulating each jar you have prepared from grain to grain. Make sure you do this quickly and do not leave any jars open for too long. Share the spawn between similar jars. Mycelium from one jar can be shared among 10 jars with the same volume.

11. The grain spawn transferred to each jar stands a higher chance of fast and successful colonization. If your grain spawn is very dense and difficult to break inside the jar, you can use an inoculation needle or sterile spoon to transfer it. However, you must remember to sterilize your tools with alcohol first to prevent contamination.

8. When you finish your grain-to-grain transfer, make sure you thoroughly shake your jars to spread the grains mixed with mycelium evenly. When the contents are evenly spread inside the jar, you can easily achieve 100% colonization.

9. Keep your jars in a dry, warm, and dark place with an average temperature range of between 81° F84°F for effective colonization. Room temperature is enough for colonization, and you may not need an incubator. Depending on the mushroom species you intend to grow, it can take between one and two weeks for your jars to fully colonize.

What Is the Best Choice for Grain-to-Grain Transfer?

Smaller grains such as millet can quickly colonize the grain substrate after the process of grain-to-grain transfer. These smaller grains usually have several mycelial development points, which will enhance the colonization process. Spawn on small grains can also be used for grain-to-grain inoculation. However, purified grain without husk is not ideal for G2G inoculation. Whole grains are perfect for the purpose.

Once you have got a fully colonized grain spawn after your grain-to-grain transfer, you can store it in the fridge for up to three months at a temperature between 42° F and 57°F.

How to Use Grain Spawns on a Larger Scale

You can grow shrooms in buckets if you want to use grain spawns on a larger scale. You can also use bags and other containers, but buckets are the simplest and most inexpensive. Regardless of the size of the storage space you have, using buckets is a great option as you can stack them. When you choose this option, you don't need additional support. However, you should know that buckets require thorough cleaning to prevent contamination. You also need to handle them carefully when they are full.

You can use different substrate forms depending on the type of shroom you want to grow. You will need an inexpensive 20-liter bucket. Be sure the bucket is free of chemicals or other contaminants. For a 20-liter bucket, you will need about 1 to 2.3 kg of grain spawn. A 10 % spawn rate means you can quickly increase your odds. Get appropriate substrate mixes like wood chips or straw. Make holes in your bucket, and when everything is ready, you can start the process of growing mushrooms.

This chapter covered everything you want to know about grain spawn - how to prepare it, transfer it from ager to the grain spawn, and how to inoculate it. We also explained the incubation process of jars and the measures you can take to prevent contamination and boost growth when using this method of growing mushrooms.

Chapter 9

Fruiting Containers and Casing Soil

This chapter starts by explaining what fruiting containers are and how to make them. We move on to explain how to make a humidity tent, how to explain its humidity level, and lighting should be adjusted to create the right conditions for growth. In the next section, we will discuss the concept of soil casing and how to prevent contamination when you make it. Finally, we explain the process involved when you harvest your mushrooms.

What Are Fruiting Containers?

Farmers use a fruiting container with limited space to grow different plants. In this case, we focus on a mushroom fruiting chamber, which is known as an enclosed place designed to mimic the natural conditions where different mushroom species would normally grow. A fruiting container provides certain conditions for the fungi to be able to produce shrooms from mycelium. However, different types of mushrooms have different requirements. Therefore, the design of your fruiting container depends on the kind of mushroom you want to grow.

If you are a small-scale grower, a monotub is the most common type of fruiting shroom container. This is a large container with holes drilled in the sides for proper ventilation, and it is filled with substrate. This is a simple chamber and is easy to use. The fruiting shotgun chamber is similar to the monotub, but it is ideal for mushrooms that grow from a bag. A Martha grows tent is another option and consists of plastic sheeting shelves. The hydroponics tent is a larger version of the monotub and a Martha fruiting chamber. Do your research to get something that suits your needs.

How to Make a Fruiting Container?

The simplest fruiting container comprises a clear plastic bin with a lid. All you need to do is drill about four to five holes in the container's sides and ensure you wash and dry it thoroughly before use. Pour about 4.4 to 8.8 liters of perlite into the container, then add some water until it is absorbed. The perlite must not be sodden, and it should create a layer of about two to three inches at the bottom of the container. Choose a place where your container gets the appropriate humidity, CO_2, temperature, and lighting conditions.

The next step is to transfer your colonized mushrooms. Before handling your mushroom culture, wash your hands with sanitizer first, and wear sterile gloves. Gently remove the mushroom culture cake and place it on top of the damp perlite in your container. You should space the cakes a few inches apart on the chamber floor. Use distilled water to mist the inoculated cakes at least twice a day and use the plastic lid to fan them.

Be careful not to let your cakes get too wet because this can cause mold. You should also mist the lid using a fine misting bottle. Maintain constant levels of temperature and humidity. Other mushrooms require hot conditions, while others perform well in a cool atmosphere. Check the requirements of your shroom before growing it. You can also use a fan, humidifier, or heater to create appropriate conditions. Remember, you can grow mushrooms in almost any container you can imagine if it has consistent CO_2, light, and humidity.

How to Make a Humidity Tent

To grow your mushroom, you need the following items to make a humidity tent.

- An empty room to put your hydroponics tent

- A hydroponics tent

- LED light strips

- Wire or plastic shelving to hold your bags of spawn

- Fans

Then choose your tent according to what you want to do with your crops. Are you going into business or For commercial operations, a space of 25 feet by 15 feet is big enough to give you a yield of about 150 to 200 pounds of mushrooms weekly. You must know how you intend to lay your shelves inside the tent. Remember to leave sufficient space so you can move around the room easily when you harvest.

The next step is to prepare the basic structure of the hydroponic tent. Make sure the floor is clean, and there are no sharp objects that can damage the tent. Install shelving once you erect the tent, which can vary depending on the size of your tent. Plastic shelving is ideal since it is lighter and easier to move. However, wire shelves are appropriate for more weight. You should be careful when you choose wire as it is susceptible to rusting. Wooden material is not ideal since it can rot or warp due to excessive humidity.

The next step is to install lighting - LED is more appropriate. This kind of lighting is energy efficient and gives sufficient light to allow you to carry out your business. You also need to install ventilation, which can include fans and vents on the tent to allow free air circulation. You will need to connect running water to your fruiting chamber. A mister or humidifier would be ideal, and you must have a source of energy to run your fan's mister and any other equipment that requires power.

The last step is to install automation equipment to monitor humidity, CO_2, temperature, and lighting levels in your fruiting chamber. You need items like a thermostat, CO_2, and humidity controllers that can turn off water and fans when certain conditions have been met. However, you still need to inspect your humidity tent to ensure everything is okay.

How to Maintain its Humidity Level

Shrooms grow well in a wet environment, allowing you to enjoy all-year-round cropping. Mushrooms contain 92% water, so you need to create a perfect environment for them to grow. To prevent your mushrooms from drying, you should keep the humidity level above 80% in the fruiting tent. The following steps will guide you through this.

Adjust Lighting and Ventilation Systems

Your grow tent's lighting and ventilation system are critical to maintaining the right humidity and temperature levels. You can either increase or decrease airflow to adjust the airflow in your tent, which affects humidity. It is also a good idea to install an adjustable ventilation fan. Ensure your tent has enough vents to increase airflow, which also helps reduce temperature and humidity. Ventilation in the tent directly affects the temperature in the tent. If you increase humidity by decreasing airflow in the tent, it means you also increase the temperature.

Adjust Temperature

You can also adjust the humidity level in the tent by controlling your temperature levels. If you decrease the temperature in the grow tent, you will reduce humidity generation, which will drop. You can open windows to allow a cool breeze to come in, lowering the temperature. In warm weather, you can also use a fan or air conditioning system to lower the temperature and humidity level.

Use a Dehumidifier

A dehumidifier is an effective solution to help you maintain the humidity in your grow tent at desired levels. However, you must have a budget to install this system. This device is designed to reduce excess humidity in the grow tent and maintain it to a certain level. It reduces humidity and has a tent to collect water that accumulates inside your tent. Other dehumidifiers have built-in automatic features to shut them down when humidity reaches the desired level. You can also use it to generate heat if it is required.

Adjust Your Air Conditioner

An adjustable external air conditioning unit is also very useful. For a small tent, you can use a portable air conditioner. It helps remove heat from the air. Condensation occurs when the heat is eliminated, which also lowers the moisture level in the air. If you don't have an air conditioner, make sure there is no massive temperature gap that can affect your shrooms. More importantly, you must insulate your tent.

How to Adjust Lighting in the Humidity Tent

Mushrooms require some light during their growth stage. The mushrooms grow towards the sun in a natural environment, although they do not use photosynthesis like other plants. Your shrooms just require a little light, but make sure it is not too harsh. Excessive light can cause stunted growth or dry your mushrooms.

Light also produces heat, which causes evaporation, which can increase the atmosphere's humidity. As we have highlighted, humidity must be kept at the right level in the grow tent for optimum growth. You need a proper ventilation system to control the humidity in your tent.

When you set up lights in your grow tent, attach a pulley system to the ratchets. This helps you adjust the height of the light. If you want to increase humidity and temperature, you can lower your lights so they are close to the plants.

Create the Right Conditions

At the beginning of your grown journeys, you'll find that you'll have to tweak the conditions in your tent until you are familiar with what works. Once you are happy that you've learned what needs to be done, you'll be able to control the growing condition relatively easily

All you need to do is to ensure that you check your mushroom fruiting chamber regularly. If something stops working, you should quickly attend to it because it can affect your shrooms. Monitor your mushrooms as they grow and pick them when they are ripe. Clean your tent regularly, especially when you remove old spawn bags. Do not add anything new to your grow house before cleaning everything. Mold, mildew, spores, and other contaminants can build up in your tent over time, so a deep clean will be needed.

It is also recommended that you grow your harvest in batches and then harvest all at once. When all the bags are ready for harvesting, you can pull them out and give your chamber a perfect clean. Use a diluted bleach solution to scrub the walls and shelving, which will help to kill bacteria or natural fungi.

What Is Casing Soil

Casing soil consists of peat, which has several small and larger pores that affect the flow of water. Very tiny pores absorb water at a slow rate, but they can hold it for a long time. In contrast, large pores absorb water at a faster rate and release it just as quickly. All these conditions are required for the growth of mushrooms at some point. The rapid absorption of water is ideal during the mycelium growth stage, while the slow release is required during the formation of the pinhead.

How to Make Casing Soil and Prevent Contamination

To make a casing layer for your mushrooms, you must have a 50-50 mixture of vermiculite and peat moss that has been moistened. These are pasteurized for about 30 to 40 minutes. The mixture must have the right amount of water; not be soggy or too dry. You need the following items to make your casing soil.

- A large container

- Polypropylene bag

- Pressure cooker or a large pot

- Peat moss

- Vermiculite

- Temperature probe (optional)

The first step is to mix peat moss and vermiculite in a large container such as a 5-gallon pail. Try to maintain a ratio of 1:1, although it might not be perfect. Add water to the mixture until your casing layer reaches field capacity. You can test the field capacity by taking a handful of the mixture and squeezing it. If you can't squeeze any water out, it means it is too dry, or if water comes from a light squeeze, it is too wet. When you squeeze the mixture, only a few drops should come out.

The next step is to pasteurize before adding the contents since the casing is prone to contamination. However, you should know that a 50-50 mixture of vermiculite and peat moss does not produce much nutrition, so sterilization might not be necessary. To pasteurize the soil, you should keep it in a mushroom grow bag and simmer the contents in a pot for about 45 to 60 minutes. The case tends to float, so put a heavy item on top of the bag. You can use a probe thermometer to get the correct temperature. This helps eliminate guesswork. The mixture should reach a temperature of about 145°F to 176 °F and stay there for around 30 minutes.

When you are satisfied that your mixture has pasteurized, remove it from the pot and leave it to cool until it reaches room temperature. Adding hot casing to the block can kill the mycelium and prevent it from fruiting. It's a good idea to wash your hands and wear nitrile gloves to eliminate any chance of contamination of the mixture.

The last step is to place your casing soil in the fruiting chamber and then wait. While the humidity must not be very high, make sure your casing layer does not dry completely. After about four to seven days, you should start seeing pins protruding through the casing.

How to Harvest the Shrooms

Before harvesting your shrooms, you should know the signs that indicate they are ready. The harvesting times for mushrooms differ depending on the type of each species. When the pinning process begins, you'll get an idea about when to harvest your shrooms.

The pinning process means you have created a perfect environment and that the pins emerging will quickly develop into mushrooms. You should harvest the mushrooms before the pin becomes a fully fruiting body, which can take place in a few days. When the pin begins to form, it will take about 72 hours or three days to develop into a fruiting body.

Depending on the type of mushroom you are growing, you can pick early if you want. However, it's a good idea to wait until the proper shape of the mushroom forms. You also need to understand that if you wait for the veil to break, it will distribute spores on the surface, and shrooms will grow in the casing. As a general rule, you need to start picking your mushrooms once you realize that the cap is open. And be sure to do it before the veil is broken. Many growers prefer to use a mushroom knife to cut the stem closer to the surface. A small stump is left behind when you use the cutting method. When dealing with small-scale production, you don't need to use a knife to harvest your shrooms.

If you have large-scale production, you need to harvest quickly to prevent the spores from spilling onto the bed. If you don't have a cutting tool, you can use your hand to harvest the mushroom and follow the steps below.

1. Wear sterile rubber gloves to prevent the chances of contamination by mold or bacteria. First, wash your hands with soap and water, then put on the gloves. All the containers and tools used during the harvesting process must be sterilized before they come into contact with fresh mushrooms.

2. Hold the base of the mushroom with two fingers and gently twist and pull the stem. Break the strands holding the stump and ensure you don't damage the mycelium network in the stem. Handle the cap carefully to prevent damage. Some people consume the stems, so you should also pull them out gently.

3. You can use tweezers to pull out the ones that are shorter and hard to reach. Pick them carefully since they will be soft.

4. When there is any remaining peat moss or substrate on the stem, use a brush to clean it. Once you have harvested your shrooms, it's time to preserve them.

In this chapter, we have explained different concepts related to fruiting containers and casing soil. There are various methods you can use to make your fruit containers. We also covered several aspects related to humidity levels and how you control it in your grow tent. There is a section dedicated to explaining soil casing and how you can make it before you grow your shrooms. Finally, we explained how you could harvest your crop.

Chapter 10

Outdoor Cultivation

The first thing you should keep in mind is which mushroom strain will give you the best quality. Not all strains are the same. They usually differ in the ratios of psilocin, psilocybin, and other alkaloids as well. The main thing you should focus on when choosing a strain is strength. This is because strength is the one quality that can help you differentiate between various shroom strains. Additionally, consider how strong you want your shrooming experience to be. Some people prefer a strong trip, while others prefer a gentler one.

Not all psilocybin mushrooms have the same potency. So, consider how you plan to use the shrooms. For instance, if you plan to macro-dose, we suggest you opt for strong strains. With stronger strains, you will get the high you hope for with fewer pieces. As a result, you will avoid feeling the nausea that usually accompanies eating too much. There are shroom users who have mentioned that different strains offer different trips. For instance, some people have said that the B+ shrooms provide less visual effect but a stronger body load. While others have said that the African Transkei shrooms provide a very unique spiritual experience.

That said, some shroom users believe that all psilocybe cubensis mushrooms have a similar effect. Whether you choose weak or strong, you will be able to micro-dose and macro-dose. We recommend that you use weak strains if you are going to microdose because that will protect you from overdosing. Keep two things in mind: the strength of the strain and the trip you hope to experience. Generally, choosing the right strain is pretty easy once you figure out your needs.

These are some of the best options for strong trips:

- Psilocybe Mexicana
- Blue Meanies
- Amazonian Cubensis
- Golden Teachers
- Penis Envy 6

- African Transkei

These are some of the best options for gentle trips:

- B+

- Cambodian Cubensis

- Brazilian Cubensis

Outdoor Mushroom Cultivation Method

Although mushrooms usually grow indoors, you can still cultivate them outdoors. There are several cultivation methods that you can try.

Soil

If you have a lawn, you can easily grow magic mushrooms beneath it in the soil. Just make sure that it contains organic matter.

Instructions:

- Cut out a square 4cm deep and 25cm across

- Using a fork, loosen the soil

- Spread the magic mushroom's spawn over the surface

- Rake about 1 cm deep

- Replace the turf square

Make sure that the soil remains moist. We can't determine exactly how long it will take your shrooms to grow because it usually depends on the humidity of the weather.

Straw

Although straw is considered a waste product in American agriculture and much of the produce isn't organic and sprayed with pesticides and herbicides, it can still be a great cultivation method for mushrooms. Unlike plants and vegetables, many mushroom species are able to convert pesticides and herbicides into non-toxic compounds. As a result, your shroom will be toxic-free, and the straws will be even cleaner than when you started the cultivation process. Straw mushrooms usually grow a lot faster than others. This method is also perfect if you hope to grow your mushrooms on a large scale.

Instructions:

- Chop the straw to about 5cm lengths
- Put it in a plastic bag, fill it with water, and leave to soak for a few hours
- Drain thoroughly

- Put the straw in a filter bag and sterilize the bag at 15 psi for 3 hours

- Next, evenly divide the spawn over the sterilized bag of straw

- Gently shake the jar of spawn for a few seconds

- Then, inoculate the straw with the spawn

- Open the straw filter bag and pour in the mycelium, then seal the bag

- Leave the bag in a damp spot (68 to 77°F) for two to six weeks to give the spawns the chance to colonize

- Then move the bag to a moist and warm spot

- Cut slits into the bag to allow the mushrooms to grow through

- Leave the bag for two weeks

Logs

Generally, mushrooms grow on every part of a tree, whether it is alive or dead. If you walk in the woods, you often see mushrooms growing on a tree's roots or leaf litter. Mushrooms are connected to trees and usually prefer to grow around them. Allow your shrooms to grow in their own environment by cultivating them on logs. In fact, this method will keep the medicinal effect of the shroom intact. It's also very easy and won't take much preparation or maintenance, which makes it perfect if you are a beginner or have a busy schedule. You must use fresh cut logs for this process. You should also make sure that the logs don't contain any other types of fungi.

To cultivate the magic mushrooms, make a hole in the log, seal the spawns into it, then leave them in a moist and shady spot. The speed of growth will depend on the species and the type of wood you are using. However, expect to see results in 6 to 12 months. It is important to note that this method isn't suitable for all types of shrooms and will take a much longer time than the other methods.

Wood Chips

Cultivating mushrooms with wood chips is very simple. Preparations for this method are easy, won't take much time, and requires little to no maintenance. Just make sure to follow these instructions to ensure the process runs smoothly.

Instructions:

- Clear your space from debris

- Fill ⅔ of a 1-liter plastic container with wood chips, then fill it with boiling water

- Let it sit for 12 hours or overnight, then drain the water

- Wash your hands thoroughly, then open the grow kit

- Using a fork, gently break the mycelium

- Place the contents of the grow kit in the wood chips container

- Distribute the wood chips and the mycelium using a clean fork

- Next, cover it with a layer of wet cardboard, preferably the brown kind

- Loosely place the container's lid to let it breathe

- Leave the container for a month at room temperature in a dust-free and clean environment

- Once the container's content turns white, then it is fully inoculated

- Put the rest of the wood chips into a large bucket and let them soak in boiling water overnight. Then drain the water

- Wash your hands, fill the cardboard box with the moist wood chips, and add the wood chips colonized by mycelium

- Mix everything evenly using a clean fork

- Leave the cardboard box open and bury it in a shady spot (under a tree), then cover it with a 1 cm layer of moist soil with grass seeds

Make sure that the wood chip bed remains undisturbed and away from children or pets that may step on it. You will see results in six months.

Choosing a cultivation method is mainly a personal preference. We recommend that you either use the straw, soil, or wood chip methods because they aren't only simple, but you will also see results fast. The log method takes much longer and works with only selected types of magic mushrooms.

Shroom Substrate

Unlike plants, shrooms don't need photosynthesis to survive and grow. Psilocybin mushrooms grow by feeding on decomposed material found in nature. The mycelium uses the substrate to get nutrition and energy. The most popular and effective mushroom substrate is hardwood sawdust with a mixture of vermiculite and coconut. Sawdust is extremely cheap, and you can find it easily as well. That said, we don't recommend using sawdust alone; it is better if you mix it with wood chips. Wood chips greatly improve the magic mushroom's structure and the spores' colonization speed.

However, you should use the right sawdust type because some types don't work with shrooms. For instance, we don't recommend using soft woods as they simply don't work as a substrate. If you are looking for an alternative to hardwood sawdust, then look no further than wood pellets.

Location and Depth

Location, location, location. We can't stress enough the importance of choosing the right location for cultivating your shrooms. When choosing a location, the one thing to remember is the lighting. Magic mushrooms love the sun and usually require indirect sunlight. So, it is best to make sure your shrooms get plenty of light. However, don't leave the patch of mushrooms in direct sunlight for a long time. The best outdoor place to grow your shrooms is your backyard since it is near you and will be easy for you to maintain and care for. However, if you don't have a backyard or your backyard isn't an option, choose a place that is nearby and within walking distance so you can check on them daily and avoid missing the harvest.

Do you live near a forest? Grasses and shrubs will make an ideal place for cultivating shrooms. Forests are also easily accessible and provide the perfect environment for them to grow. Water is another vital consideration. Sealed slopes or any subsurface water flow will provide the perfect location for the mushrooms to thrive. In some cases, all these options may not be available to you. Don't fret; there is a solution. Simply opt for any location that is accessible and provides sunlight and moisture.

When it comes to the depth of the substrate for your magic mushrooms, it should be about 3 to 5 inches.

Preventing Contamination

The last thing you want is to do everything right and then realize that your magic mushroom batch is covered with mold. Contamination can happen whether you are a beginner or have been cultivating mushrooms for years. So, keep these things in mind to avoid any contamination issues with your shrooms.

Keep Everything Clean

It goes without saying that sanitizing everything will prevent contamination. The tools that you use, like jars, containers, and syringes, must be sterilized. Air currents and pests can also cause contamination. For this reason, you should take your time with the preparation process. Treat the process like it is a scientific experiment in a lab, with everything being cleaned and sterilized using alcohol. In addition to sterilizing all your tools, wash your hands thoroughly before each step and clean and flame your tools between each use as well. You can also wear a mask and food-safe gloves if you forget to wash your hands and ensure you don't spread your germs.

Make sure to clean the area where you are working. Before you start, we recommend you list all the contamination sources and also write down potential mistakes or anything that can go wrong and contaminate the shrooms.

Keep an Eye on the Shrooms

We mentioned that you should cultivate the shrooms in your backyard or a nearby area to keep an eye on progress. By observing the shrooms, you'll notice any changes immediately and be able to take the necessary action before your crop gets ruined. For instance, you may notice odors, discoloration, dusty textures, or slime as the result of bacteria. There are various contaminants for each stage of the growth process, so keep your eyes open.

The growing conditions can also cause contamination. For instance, too much carbon dioxide or moisture isn't good for the shrooms. So, make sure you take your time with each step and don't skip or take shortcuts with any instructions. For instance, drain the substrate like the straw properly and let it take all the time it needs. In some cases, you may do everything right, but you notice your jars still getting contaminated. Unfortunately, there is nothing you can do here to salvage the shrooms. However, if your bulk gets contaminated, just cut the infected parts. The earlier you catch the contamination, the better.

Discoloration

Discoloration doesn't necessarily mean the shrooms have gone bad. Sometimes, the discoloration can be normal, so you need to be able to tell the difference. For instance, psilocybe mycelium may turn blue, and that's normal. Other types of mushrooms may turn brown as they grow. Familiarize yourself with the growth behavior of different species of magic mushrooms so you can recognize if the discoloration is concerning. Some types develop colored liquids as they mature. Again, this is normal. You should only be concerned if the production of the colored liquid is excessive because this can indicate that the shrooms are contaminated.

Mold

Watch out for mold. It is the number one contaminant danger to home-growing. There are various types of mold, and each has a different color. You may notice your shrooms are covered with cottony mycelium. The mold will cause discoloration at first, which you may not be able to spot right away since it is a little darker than the mycelium. Usually, high humidity can increase mold and contamination, so if you lower it, you may be able to fix the problem.

Green mold can also infect and contaminate the shroom. It usually appears in the form of white mycelium that will cover the whole mushroom and produce green spores. Sanitizing the tools and surfaces can help prevent the appearance of green mold. If you notice red and pink mold, destroy the shrooms immediately because this fungus is fast growing.

The fungus gnat is an insect that can feed on the mushroom and cause bacteria and rotting. Again, sanitization is your best option here to ensure this insect doesn't get to the shroom.

The Different Stages of Shrooms Growth

To know which stage of its life cycle the mushroom is at, you should learn what happens during each stage.

- A mature mushroom usually drops spores
- The spores that fall on the ground are usually referred to as spore germination
- They then meet other compatible spores
- Mycelium originates, pinheads originate
- Primordia formation, growth mushroom, mature, then drop spores
- End of life cycle

During each stage, there are a few things that you should do:

- Obtain the spores
- Make the substrate
- Inoculate
- Incubate

- Place the mushrooms in fruiting conditions

- Pinhead formation

- Mushroom growing

- Make a spore print

How to Replenish the Beds after They're Dormant

If your shroom's bed goes dormant, there are a few things that you can do to bring it back to life.

Bury the Block

Burying the shrooms' bed can be a great solution to encourage their growth. You will begin to see results in a couple of weeks.

- Dig an appropriate size hole in a shady spot

- Take the mushroom block out of the box

- Place it in the soil

- Cover it with 1 inch of soil

- Water the soil just like how you water your garden

- Make sure to check the block frequently

Inoculate the Mulch

You can start with new beds or inoculate the ones you already have.

- Evenly spread a layer of mulch around a shady area

- Prepare for inoculation

- Gently and evenly spread the crumbled block on top of the mulch

- Alternate between the layers of the mulch and the mushroom block

- You can either leave the top layer as mulch or mix the block and the mulch with your hands, then cover the surface with a top layer of mulch

- Hydrate the batch

- Make sure to keep it hydrated; it shouldn't dry out

Outdoor cultivation is an effective method for growing mushrooms. Indoor cultivation may not always be an option for some people. If you have a garden or a backyard, you should take advantage of them and use one of the cultivation methods we have discussed to give outdoor cultivation a chance. Again - location is key. Make sure that the shrooms have enough light, but don't leave them for a long time in the sun. The second thing that you should keep in mind is contamination. One mistake can ruin the whole process. Several things can cause bacteria, which can result in mold and rotting. Therefore, you should stay focused while cultivating. Sanitization is vital before and during the preparation process. Make sure that everything is clean and wipe surfaces between steps. Washing your hands and wearing a mask can also guarantee that the shrooms remain clean.

Cultivating mushrooms outdoors is a lot easier than you may think. Just keep everything mentioned here in mind and make sure to frequently check on your shrooms to guarantee that nothing has changed or gone wrong.

Conclusion

Growing psilocybin mushrooms can be a demanding task. While cultivating the shrooms themselves isn't an issue, ensuring their quality and proper active substance content can represent a challenge. Before you start growing your shrooms, you first need to arm yourself with patience, as this is crucial for ensuring your safety.

The different species of psilocybe contain different types of active substances. So, it stands to reason that the first step is to choose why and which species you want to cultivate. Having chosen the species, you can move on to getting together all the equipment and material necessary for growing that specific type of shroom. This will also depend on the specific cultivation technique you choose to use.

The Psilocybe Fanaticus Technique or Agar Technique are just two of the cultivation methods you can choose - and both have their advantages and disadvantages. For example, the former isn't a bit more complicated, although it allows for tailoring so you can make the process easier for you. The latter is a more straightforward method and doesn't allow for any deviations. Whether you opt for either of these methods depends on what you want preferences and the equipment you can obtain and handle.

When it comes to preparing the equipment, there is one fundamental rule to follow - keeping everything sterile. Everything the spores come in contact with from pressure cookers to filter discs to mason jars and Petri dishes will need to be sterilized for several reasons. For one, you will need to ensure that the spores you use won't leave the area they are growing on and won't cause harm to anyone who may come in contact with it. Second, sterilization will allow you to avoid contamination that can cause magic mushrooms to develop chemical compounds unsafe for consumption.

Another aspect of shroom cultivation you'll need to pay particular attention to is handling grain spawns. Inoculating the grain spawn into syringes and incubating them in the jars without contaminating anything takes a lot of concentration. Make sure to do this with a clear head and away from distractions. Fruiting containers are popular ways to incubate magic mushrooms - provided you also build a proper humidity tend to keep the soil moist and ready for the spores to germinate. Casing soil is the perfect type of soil for cultivating mushrooms - but once again, you must learn how to prepare it by avoiding any possibility of contamination.

Certain shroom species thrive in an outdoor environment, so if you have room for them in your garden or backyard, feel free to transfer them outside. If you choose to do that, you will need to prepare the soil - in a way that benefits the strain you will be using. This may involve mixing wood chips and sawdust into the ground and choosing the proper depth and location to avoid contamination. An added advantage of this method is that it allows you to replenish empty beds as soon as you remove the full-grown shroom you grew in them beforehand.

Thank you for buying and reading/listening to our book. If you found this book useful/helpful please take a few minutes and leave a review on Amazon.com or Audible.com (if you bought the audio version).

References

Psycom.net - Mental Health Treatment Resource Since 1996. (n.d.). Psycom.Net - Mental Health Treatment Resource Since 1996. https://www.psycom.net/psilocybin-magic-mushrooms

Woolfe, S. (2022, May 17). Growing Magic Mushrooms. Healing Maps. https://healingmaps.com/growing-magic-mushrooms/

The life cycle of the mushroom. (n.d.). Mushplanet. https://mushplanet.com/basic-cultivation/the-life-cycle-of-the-mushroom/

What are Magic Mushrooms? (n.d.). Alberta.Ca. https://myhealth.alberta.ca/Alberta/Pages/What-are-magic-mushrooms.aspx

Psycom.net - Mental Health Treatment Resource Since 1996. (n.d.). Psycom.Net - Mental Health Treatment Resource Since 1996 https://www.psycom.net/psilocybin-magic-mushrooms

Hedley, E. (2021, August 2). The Life Cycle of a Mushroom. Teelixir. https://teelixir.com/blogs/news/mushroom-life-cycle

Wetzel, C. (2020, November 2). Watch an Amazing Time-Lapse of Growing Mushrooms. Smithsonian Magazine. https://www.smithsonianmag.com/science-nature/watch-amazing-time-lapse-growing-mushrooms-180976118/

Woolfe, S. (2021, June 25). Why Has Growing Magic Mushrooms At Home Suddenly Started To Boom? Healing Maps. https://healingmaps.com/growing-magic-mushrooms-at-home-popularity/

AllTheRooms, W. by. (2019, March 5). Legal psychedelics: Countries with the most relaxed laws. AllTheRooms - The Vacation Rental Experts. https://www.alltherooms.com/blog/legal-psychedelics-countries-relaxed-laws/

Dorr, A. (2021, December 2). The history of psilocybin: Magic mushroom use through the ages. Mushroom Revival. https://www.mushroomrevival.com/blogs/blog/the-history-of-psilocybin-magic-mushroom-use-through-the-ages

Dy, K. (2021, August 11). A brief history of magic mushrooms across ancient civilizations. Psychedelic Spotlight. https://psychedelicspotlight.com/history-of-magic-mushrooms-across-ancient-civilizations/

Elkins, J. (2021, May 30). Psilocybin mushrooms then and now. Mushroom Revival. https://www.mushroomrevival.com/blogs/blog/psilocybin-mushrooms-then-and-now

Hartman, S. (2021a, July 24). The definitive history of psilocybin and magic mushrooms. DoubleBlind Mag. https://doubleblindmag.com/mushrooms/about-magic-mushrooms/history-of-psilocybin/

Hartman, S. (2021b, July 24). The definitive history of psilocybin and magic mushrooms. DoubleBlind Mag. https://doubleblindmag.com/mushrooms/about-magic-mushrooms/history-of-psilocybin/

Hitt, C. (2020, August 26). The long history of magic mushrooms. Thrillist. https://www.thrillist.com/news/nation/history-of-magic-mushrooms-origin-story-facts

Lewis-Healey, E. (2021, September 10). The legal status of psychedelics around the world. Psychedelic Spotlight. https://psychedelicspotlight.com/legal-status-of-psychedelics-around-the-world/

Vayne, J., & Stone, R. (2018, March 4). The eleusinian psychedelic rebirth rites of ancient Greece are making a comeback. Ancient Origins. https://www.ancient-origins.net/history/eleusinian-psychedelic-rebirth-rites-ancient-greece-making-comeback-009693

What is the history of psychoactive mushrooms? (n.d.). Drug Policy Alliance. https://drugpolicy.org/drug-facts/history-psychoactive-mushrooms

Dorr, A. (2021, April 1). Psilocybin Mushrooms of the World: Seven Different Species. Mushroom Revival. https://www.mushroomrevival.com/blogs/blog/psilocybin-mushrooms-of-the-world-7-different-magic-mushroom-species

Discover the Many Types of Psilocybin Magic Mushrooms. (2022, January 6). Cannabis Central. https://www.veriheal.com/blog/discover-the-many-types-of-psilocybin-magic-mushrooms/

Barbara E. Bauer, M. S. (2019, March 4). Chemical Composition Variability in Magic Mushrooms. Psychedelic Science Review. https://psychedelicreview.com/chemical-composition-variability-in-magic-mushrooms/

Psilocybin (Magic Mushrooms). (2019, March 27). Drugscience.Org.Uk. https://www.drugscience.org.uk/drug-information/psilocybin/

Health Canada. (2012, January 12). Psilocybin and psilocin (Magic mushrooms). Canada.Ca. https://www.canada.ca/en/health-canada/services/substance-use/controlled-illegal-drugs/magic-mushrooms.html

Shields, T. (2017, April 30). A Mushroom Growers Guide To Preventing Contamination. FreshCap Mushrooms. https://learn.freshcap.com/growing/preventing-contamination-when-growing-mushrooms/

Does Mushroom Growing Medium Need to Be Sterilized? (2012, December 6). Home Guides | SF Gate. https://homeguides.sfgate.com/mushroom-growing-medium-need-sterilized-55957.html

Basics of sterile working. (n.d.). Mushplanet. https://mushplanet.com/basic-cultivation/basics-of-sterile-working/

Why are hygienic precautions important when growing your Magic mushrooms? (2018, May 9). Magic Mushrooms Shop Blog. https://www.magic-mushrooms-shop.com/en/blog/grow-mushroomswork-clean

The Sterilization and disinfection of Magic Mushroom cultivation materials. (2012, November 7). Magic Mushrooms Shop Blog. https://www.magic-mushrooms-shop.com/en/blog/how-to-sterilize-cultivation-materials

Cooke, J. (2021a, April 30). How to grow magic mushrooms: The easy way. Tripsitter. https://tripsitter.com/magic-mushrooms/cultivation/

Cooke, J. (2021b, May 31). Where to buy magic mushroom spores (Canada, USA, Europe). Tripsitter. https://tripsitter.com/magic-mushrooms/spores/

Dawson, B. (2022, May 1). How to shop for magic mushroom grow kits on Amazon. MEL Magazine. https://melmagazine.com/en-us/story/psychedelic-mushroom-growing-kit-amazon

Hartman, S. (2021a, July 15). Mushroom grow kits: The 5 best mushroom grow kits - DoubleBlind mag.

Hartman, S. (2021b, August 9). How to use Agar in Mushroom Cultivation. DoubleBlind Mag. https://doubleblindmag.com/mushrooms/how-to-grow-mushrooms/how-to-use-agar/

How to make A Still Air Box. (2020, September 21). EZMushroom | Grow Mushrooms the EZ Way; EZMushroom. https://ezmushroom.com/recommended-equipment/how-to-make-a-still-air-box/

How To Make Mushroom Grain Spawn - the complete guide to
growing mushrooms. (2019, May 18). Urban Spore
Mushrooms; Urban Spore. https://urbanspore.com.au/how-
to-grow-mushrooms/how-to-make-grain-spawn/

Magic mushrooms: How to grow Psilocybin Mushrooms at home.
(2020, July 16). Third Wave.
https://thethirdwave.co/psychedelics/shrooms/grow-
psilocybin-mushrooms/

Maravelias, P. (2022, March 21). How to grow shrooms for you
and your buddies for under $200. High Times; High Times
Magazine. https://hightimes.com/culture/how-to-grow-
shrooms-for-you-and-your-buddies-for-under-200/

Steinhardt, J. (2021, February 12). Hackers, Mason jars, and the
psychedelic science of DIY shrooms. Wired.
https://www.wired.com/story/hackers-mason-jars-
psychedelic-science-diy-shrooms/

The Mushroom Guy. (2020, April 21). Best mushroom growing kits
for beginners and experts. Healing-mushrooms.net.
https://healing-mushrooms.net/best-mushroom-growing-kits

The Mushroom Guy. (2021, July 9). How to grow Magic
Mushrooms (Psychedelic Psilocybin Shrooms). Healing-
mushrooms.net. https://healing-mushrooms.net/grow-magic-
mushrooms

Woolfe, S. (2021, November 2). How to grow psilocybin
mushrooms in your own home. Healing Maps.
https://healingmaps.com/how-to-grow-psilocybin-
mushrooms-home/

Biology:PF tek. (n.d.). Handwiki.org.
https://handwiki.org/wiki/Biology:PF_Tek

Gandia, A. (n.d.). PF tek. Mediamatic.
https://www.mediamatic.net/en/page/225455/pf-tek

Mcpherson, R., & Fanaticus, P. (n.d.). Psilocybe Fanaticus TEK.
Psilosophy.Info.
http://www.en.psilosophy.info/pdf/psilocybe_fanaticus_tek_
(psilosophy.info).pdf

PF Tek - easy to follow guide for growing mushrooms. (2020,
February 1). Urban Spore Mushrooms; Urban Spore.
https://urbanspore.com.au/how-to-grow-mushrooms/pf-tek/

PF TEK - Psilocybe Fanaticus. (n.d.). Com.Br.
https://xdocs.com.br/doc/pf-tek-psilocybe-fanaticus-
6nw19m496281

PF_tek. (n.d.). Bionity.com.
https://www.bionity.com/en/encyclopedia/PF_Tek.html

PSYLOCYBE FANATICUS. (n.d.). Preterhuman.net.
https://cdn.preterhuman.net/texts/drugs/nansnook3c/tek/psyl
ocybe_fanaticus_tek.htm

(N.d.). Archive.org. http://classic-
web.archive.org/web/20020929011135/www.fanaticus.com/

Aseptic techniques and preparing bacterial plates. (n.d.).
https://www.bbc.co.uk/bitesize/guides/z2kvw6f/revision/7

Hartman, S. (2021, August 9). How to use Agar in Mushroom
Cultivation. DoubleBlind Mag.
https://doubleblindmag.com/mushrooms/how-to-grow-
mushrooms/how-to-use-agar/

Growing magic mushrooms at home. (n.d.). Streetdirectory.Com. https://www.streetdirectory.com/etoday/growing-magic-mushrooms-at-home-cpwjja.html

Addgene: Protocol - how to inoculate a bacterial culture. (n.d.). Addgene.Org. https://www.addgene.org/protocols/inoculate-bacterial-culture/

Tovell, J. (2021, September 11). Growing mushrooms indoors: Incubation and grow rooms. JCBGourmetMushrooms. https://jcbgourmetmushrooms.com/blogs/johns-thoughts/growing-mushrooms-indoors-incubation-and-grow-rooms

Shields, T. (2018, September 25). How to clone mushrooms. FreshCap Mushrooms. https://learn.freshcap.com/growing/how-to-clone-mushrooms/

What is grain spawn? (2020, July 15). Urban Spore Mushrooms; Urban Spore. https://urbanspore.com.au/what-is-grain-spawn/

Shields, T. (2017, May 31). How to inoculate grain jars and make any grain spawn you want. FreshCap Mushrooms. https://learn.freshcap.com/growing/how-to-inoculate-grain/

Wood, M. (n.d.). Getting started with mushroom cultivation. Mykoweb.com. https://www.mykoweb.com/articles/cultivation.html

Shields, T. (2017a, April 30). A mushroom grower's guide to preventing contamination. FreshCap Mushrooms. https://learn.freshcap.com/growing/preventing-contamination-when-growing-mushrooms/

Grain to grain transfer (G2G). (n.d.). Shroomok.com. https://shroomok.com/en/wiki/Grain_to_Grain_Transfer_(G2G)

Farm-It, U. (2022, April 10). How to grow mushrooms in buckets. Urban Farm-It. https://urban-farm-it.com/how-to-grow-mushrooms-in-buckets/

Grant, A. (2019, September 21). DIY mushroom house ideas – tips for setting up A mushroom fruiting chamber. Gardening Know-How. https://www.gardeningknowhow.com/edible/vegetables/mushrooms/making-a-mushroom-fruiting-chamber.htm

How to control humidity in grow tent? Step-by-step guide. (n.d.). GardenSynthesis. https://gardensynthesis.com/how-to-control-humidity-in-grow-tent/

Sayner, A. (2020, December 10). How to build a mushroom fruiting chamber: 7 steps. Gocycle. https://grocycle.com/how-to-build-a-mushroom-fruiting-chamber/

den Ouden, M. (2018, March 1). Mushroom casing soil. Mushroom Office. https://www.mushroomoffice.com/mushroom-casing-soil-3/

Shields, T. (2018, March 5). Growing mushrooms using a casing layer. FreshCap Mushrooms. https://learn.freshcap.com/growing/growing-mushrooms-using-a-casing-layer/

24High. (n.d.-a). Different types of substrates for mushroom cultivation! 24High. 24high.com. https://www.24high.com/en/blog/76/WHAT-TYPES-OF-SUBSTRATE-ARE-THERE-FOR-GROWING-MAGIC-MUSHROOMS

24High. (n.d.-b). Growing magic mushrooms outdoors. 24high.com. https://www.24high.com/en/blog/125/HOW-DO-I-GROW-PSILOCYBIN-MUSHROOMS-OUTDOORS

Crombie, L. (2020, November 9). How to grow mushrooms: top tips for growing outdoors and in. Gardeningetc.com; Gardeningetc. https://www.gardeningetc.com/au/advice/how-to-grow-mushrooms

Hartman, S. (2021, July 15). Mold on mushrooms: Contamination tips for shroom growers. DoubleBlind Mag. https://doubleblindmag.com/mushrooms/how-to-grow-mushrooms/mold-on-mushrooms/

Houghton, K. (2022, March 16). Outdoor mushroom cultivation methods: An overview. The Forest Farmacy. https://www.theforestfarmacy.com/blog/outdoor-mushroom-cultivation-methods-an-overview

How to get more life from your "Spray & grow" mushroom kit. (n.d.). North Spore. https://northspore.com/blogs/the-black-trumpet/what-to-do-with-your-mushroom-grow-kit-when-its-done

Monotub tek mushroom cultivation method walk-through. (n.d.).
North Spore. https://northspore.com/pages/mono-tub-
cultivation-method-walkthrough

Parsons, A. (2021a, January 4). Everything you need to know about
magic mushroom substrates. Zamnesia.com.
https://www.zamnesia.com/blog-everything-magic-
mushroom-substrates-n2151

Parsons, A. (2021b, August 26). Creating A magic mushroom
outdoor patch. Zamnesia.com.
https://www.zamnesia.com/blog-creating-a-magic-
mushroom-outdoor-patch-n374

Psilocybe cubensis on straw. (n.d.). Mushplanet.
https://mushplanet.com/cultivation-techniques/psilocybe-
cubensis-on-straw/

Sumpter, L. (2022, March 28). How to identify A contaminated
magic mushroom culture. Zamnesia.com; Zamnesia.
https://www.zamnesia.com/content/546-how-to-identify-a-
contaminated-mushroom-culture

The life cycle of the mushroom. (n.d.). Mushplanet.
https://mushplanet.com/basic-cultivation/the-life-cycle-of-
the-mushroom/

(N.d.). Getmysupply.Co. https://www.getmysupply.co/journal/how-
to-choose-a-mushroom-strain/

Sobers, M. (2020, September 24). How to Grow Magic Mushrooms [All You Need to Know]. WayofLeaf. https://wayofleaf.com/psychedelics/how-to-grow-magic-mushrooms

Woolfe, S. (2022, May 17). Growing Magic Mushrooms. Healing Maps. https://healingmaps.com/growing-magic-mushrooms

Milton Keynes UK
Ingram Content Group UK Ltd.
UKHW020819110823
426718UK00014B/542